This book belonged to Dad, ~~[illegible]~~.
He loved the story on page 46 about the
family who holidayed in Dovercourt.

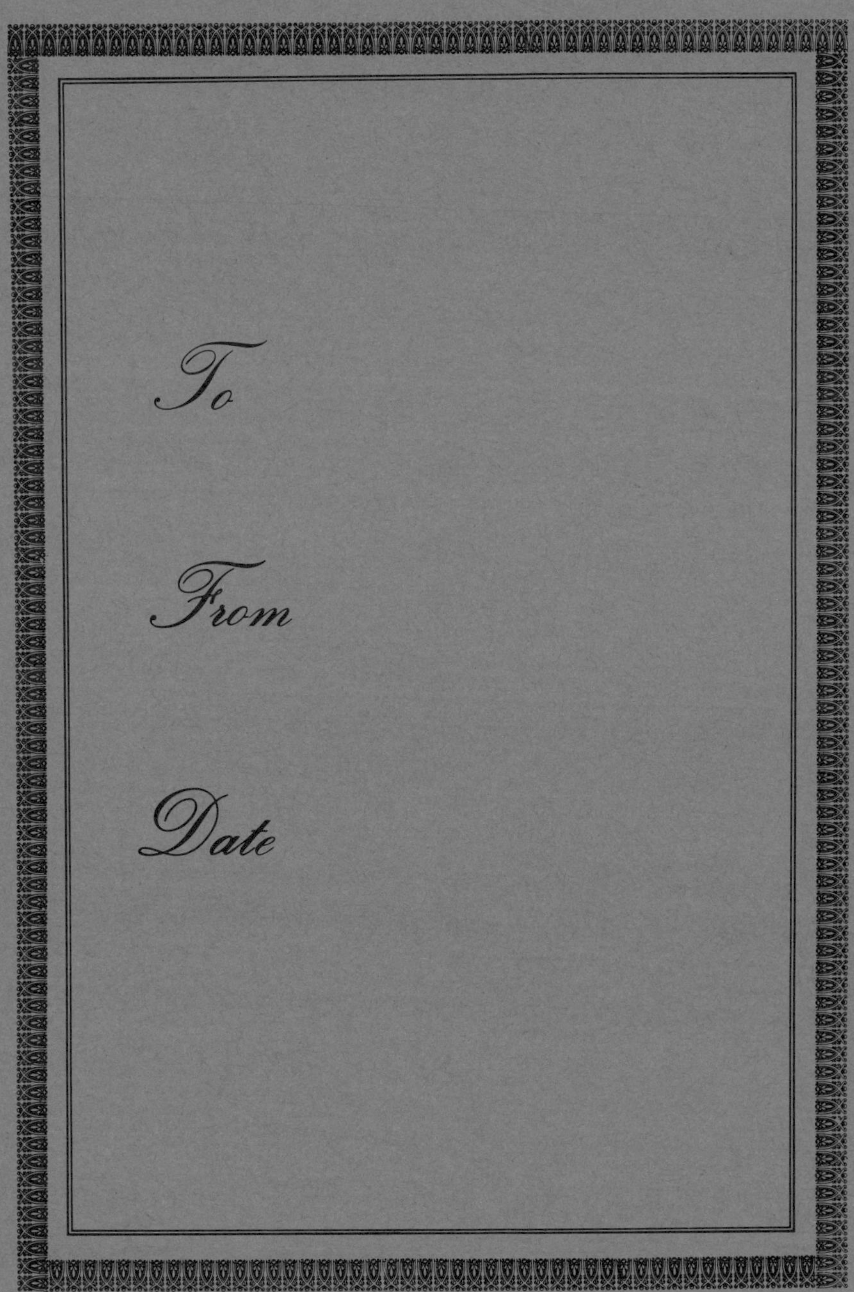

EAST ANGLIAN GOLDEN BOOK

Compiled by
Michael Watkins

EAST ANGLIAN MAGAZINE LIMITED IPSWICH SUFFOLK

To all those who love
East Anglia

Printed and published in England by
East Anglian Magazine Ltd,
6 Gt. Colman Street,
Ipswich, Suffolk.
I.S.B.N. 0. 900227 72 9

Cover painting after John Constable
by Robert Burrows ©T. & J. Baker

CONTENTS

For reasons of verisimilitude the contents of this anthology are reproduced exactly as they first appeared in the East Anglian Magazine. To add to the confusion, they have been assembled to give geographical variety rather than in chronological order! M.W.

INTRODUCTION

by Michael Watkins

Historically, 1935 was unmemorable. It marked the Saar plebiscite for return to Germany, Baldwin succeeding MacDonald as Prime Minister, hostilities between Italy and Abyssinia – little else of cosmic significance. The previous year had been evilly notable for Herr Hitler's emergence as Dictator; while Edward VIII's abdication after a reign of 325 days, touched that year with melancholy. Yet it would be improper to dismiss 1935 as entirely inauspicious. If the rest of Europe was having a dull time, Suffolk struck a seam of pure gold. For it was in 1935, fifty years ago, that the *East Anglian Magazine* first appeared.

I have before me Vol. 1, price two shillings and sixpence. The editor was Charles Rigby and his inaugural issue contained articles on the Sugar Beet Subsidy by the Earl of Denbigh, Changing Village Life by the Dowager Lady Suffield, Norfolk Church Organs by the Reverend Gordon Paget, and notes on bird migration by 'Gyrfalcon'. Initial subscribers included the Marquess of Lothian, Viscount Rothermere, Lord Fairhaven, the Hon. Roger Coke and many more grand folk to whom Mr Rigby vowed to 'satisfy every taste and whet every reasonable appetite'. Sugar beet subsidies were perhaps a lavish offering of good intent.

The frontispiece was a picture of King George V, bearded and grave, broadcasting into a 'wireless' microphone. The implication being maybe that His Majesty was personally enjoining his East Anglian subjects to order-their-copies-today. In my mind's eye, I see those devoted subjects tuning into their crystal sets to catch their sovereign's sales-pitch, slicing nutritious Hovis as they did so, sipping Ovaltine.

I like to think that Lords Lothian, Rothermere, *et al*, did not typify readership of the *East Anglian Magazine*. Indeed, I have friends – 'Granny' Spall of Stonham Aspal; William Gibbons, retired horseman of Barking; Edith Esling, 105 years old as I write, of Barham – who followed the magazine through good times and bad. For the magazine never pretended to be anything it wasn't. It was a parish magazine, the parish boundaries extending from The Wash to the Isle of Ely, from Cambridge to Colchester, Aldeburgh to Acle. It was for country-lovers, not social climbers.

All of which would have been above my head. A recent graduate from the perambulator, my literary attainments were marginal; and had you told me that one day I would be closely associated with the magazine, I would have continued playing with my bricks with seraphic indifference. But it is said that we cannot escape our destinies, and part of mine – from 1962 until 1983 – was to be willingly manacled to the EAM. For 21 years my friend Julian Spence and I jointly edited the magazine. They were good years.

Meanwhile, back in 1935, there seems to have been what is known in City boardrooms as a 'dawn-raid'. By the second issue Mr Rigby had been replaced by R.A.N. Dixon who immediately and magnanimously reduced the cover price to one shilling. He was obviously a man to go far. As he did, celebrating the 100th issue in June 1950 and a 'take-over' of the *Norfolk Magazine* in 1956. There was, of course, the temporary inconvenience of World War II during which, in his September 1940 editorial, Mr Dixon apprised Reichsmarshal Hermann Goering of the 'strong concentrations of naval craft on the model yacht pond at Felixstowe', and that Bury St. Edmund's Moyses Hall – 'Moyses being a corruption of Moses' – was non-Aryan.

Shortly after, the EAM shut down for the duration, those bitter years. Then, in 1946, Mr Dixon announced that the magazine was back, to reflect the 'quiet simplicity of the enchanted kingdom of East Anglia'. His first post-war number included articles on Sutton Hoo's burial ship, Cromwell's head, how to cure toothache and why not to keep goats: so that readers were instantly reminded of the eternal verities.

In latter years rival magazines came and went. Largely, their contents were of a 'social' nature, which meant that they featured pictures of persons called Mrs Digby-Vane-Trumpington, General de Bility, Lady Daisy Chayne, drinking champagne and 'sharing a joke' at local hunt balls. So many jokes were shared that life must have been one of unrelieved hilarity. One by one these periodicals failed – possibly the champagne and the jokes simultaneously went flat – leaving the EAM to plod on.

'Plod on' was precisely what it did. In a modern world where to be 'with it' was the ultimate, the EAM was conspicuously without-it. It accepted that it was more bourgeois than princely, favoured conservatism to radicalism, that it was slow to change and uncharacteristically quick to condemn ephemera. In its time it published distinguished authors — Adrian Bell, Rider Haggard, Alfred Munnings, Norah Lofts, James Wentworth Day, Hammond Innes — but in the main its contributors included more mute inglorious Miltons than R.H. Mottrams. Its politics were of the parish pump variety; and when it ventured opinions, it did so thoughtfully and without vehemence. It was not particularly literate, neither was it hugely vocal. Having no axe to grind, it didn't do a great deal of good and, so far as I know, it did no harm whatever. Curiously, despite such a multiplicity of negatives, it was trusted — even loved.

Then, because it had more than a touch of the dodo in its genes, it couldn't keep going any more. In the same manner in which it had behaved all its life, shyly and without much fuss, it went into hibernation.

If you were to ask which single item, in the years of my stewardship, lodges ineradicably in my mind, I feel that I should come up with something responsible: like Jane Wight's essay on Medieval Illuminated Manuscripts. I suppose you'll put it down to my frivolous turn of mind if, in fact, I tell you that I best remember a story from the East Anglian and His Humour columns . . . about the old boy who, boasting in the pub one evening, announced: 'I have a bath regular, once a year — whether I need it or not.'

So you will know what to expect from this anthology, this golden book: a self-indulgent selection, my desert island choice, picked for no better reason than because they would keep me company. To me, they represent not so much the best, as the most companionable of those fifty not inglorious years.

The magazine's title and publishing house behind it are now in other hands — Terry and Juanita Baker's hands; and I believe, and fervently hope, that they are waiting patiently to get the old bird on the move again. The future contains so many imponderables — Russian tanks may grind over the Orwell's brave new bridge, the Almighty Hamburger may drown at sea — but I like to think that we still have a little sense left, that we are not wholely bent on destruction. For if we destroy all the dodos, we shall in a way be witnessing the spectacle of our own extinction.

Tarston Hall
Needham Market

To Suffolk

—by CECIL LAY

I

When mavises began to build,
And lilac-twigs again were filled;
When buds had thickened in the glen,
And ducks in couples sought the fen;
When sticklebacks were rosy-gilled,
And blackthorn blanchèd petals spilled;
When frogs were stirring in the mud,
And chestnuts sticky in the bud;
Said I, when night shall equal day,
From winter-quarters I'll away.

II

When robins fed their spotted young,
And catkins from the hazels hung;
When warbler flaunting warbler sung,
And squirrels in the pine-trees hung;
When days were bright, and skies were blue,
And yokels 'gan again to woo;
When thrush and blackbird early woke,
And leaves had bronzed upon the oak;
Said I, now cheerless days are done,
My pilgrimage shall be begun.

III

When swallows hawked in golden air,
And flowers were blooming everywhere;
When shores were gay with bathers bright,
And glowworms greenly shone at night;
When hay was mown, and cuckoos flown,
And Summer held her golden throne;
When cherries shone amidst their green,
And apples on the boughs were seen;
Said I, the time has come to start!
This home and I will shortly part.

IV

When martlets left the cobwebbed eaves,
And russet corn was bound in sheaves;
When sunflowers bent their aureoled heads,
And spiders spun their migrant threads;
When skies were poems ready writ,
And morning mists were infinite;
When berries dazed the insect throng,
And leaves fell through the robin's song;
Said I, the season passeth by,
My luck upon the road I'll try.

V

When winds were wild, and roofs untiled,
And coloured leaves in corners pilèd;
When bat and dormouse went to sleep,
And bough and sky did frequent weep;
When nuts were plucked, and medlars sucked,
And pheasants shot, and furrows mucked;
When suns were dim and days were brief,
And winds re-howled their ancient grief;
Said I, the road now calleth me,
A pilgrim once again I'll be.

VI

When pool and stream were frozen hard,
And cattle stayed within the yard;
When elms were red, and ash-trees black,
And sparrows robbed the farmer's stack;
When tilth and fallow changed to stone,
And hoodies fought around a bone;
When hands were numb and minds depressed,
When snow the naked trees had dressed;
Said I, I will away from here
In this hard season of the year.

Yet here I stay and years go by,
And Suffolk knows the reason why.

Memories of Edward FitzGerald

by ELEANORE FITZGERALD KERRICH.

Miss Kerrich is the great-niece of FitzGerald, whom she assisted as amanuensis in his work. Geldeston Hall, to which she refers, was the home of the Kerrich family for many centuries. In this article she puts forward an explanation of FitzGerald's marriage. She writes: "I know no other solution than the one I have given. It is so characteristic of him that I do not suppose there is any other."

ON the 4th November, 1856, in All Saints' Church, Chichester, were married Edward FitzGerald and Lucy Barton. It was a marriage as conscientiously entered into and as ill-assorted as any it is possible to imagine. Why it took place has proved an insoluble enigma to FitzGerald's biographers, to whom the thought that the key might lie in the hands of his nearest relations has never occurred. Let it at once be said that there is nothing in the explanation that reflects in the slightest degree on the honour either of the Bartons or of FitzGerald.

This marriage took place before I was born. It was by that time an accepted fact, neither shunned nor dwelt upon. It had ceased to exercise any influence in FitzGerald's life. Benson wrote at the time: "FitzGerald was obstinate with the obstinacy of a weak and sensitive nature." But Benson was not in possession of all the facts. I cannot remember the time when I did not know them, nor have I ever heard them challenged by the few who did.

The uneventful tale of FitzGerald's life has been so often told, that it is only needful here to remember that he came down from Trinity, Cambridge, in 1830, the richer for a Pass Degree and for some remarkable and life-long friendships. He appears to have gone almost immediately to Geldeston Hall, the home of his sister, Mrs Kerrich. In 1837, tired perhaps of moving from one relation's house to another, FitzGerald set up a little home of his own, connected with his name ever since as "FitzGerald's Cottage at Boulge." Churchyard's picture of it, embowered in roses and with far-reaching thatched eaves – the picture that FitzGerald gave to Cowell, and that accompanied the latter to Calcutta – is in my possession.

About 1837 FitzGerald became acquainted with Bernard Barton, and the friendship grew apace. In the earlier half of the nineteenth century, when railways were hardly established and newspapers were few and expensive, each little provincial town liked to boast its literary circle, whose members would while away long winter evenings in the discussion, perhaps of their own, perhaps of greater authors' works. Woodbridge appears not to have lagged behind, and to have discovered in Bernard Barton a sufficiently imposing and not too overwhelming figure-head. FitzGerald must have been thinking of this Society when, in June, 1847, he wrote from Geldeston Hall to S. Lawrence, the portrait painter, concerning Barton's portrait:

> "He is now sixty-three; and it won't do, you know, for grand climacterical people to procrastinate, nay, to *proannuate* – which is a new, and, for all I see, a very bad word.
> . . . Barton pretends he dreads having his portrait done; which is 'my eye.' So come and do it. He is a generous, worthy, simple-hearted fellow; worth ten thousand better wits. Then you shall see all the faded tapestry of country town life; London jokes worn threadbare; third-rate accomplishments infinitely prized; scandal removed from Dukes and Duchesses to the Parson, the Banker, the Commissioner of Excise, and the Attorney."

And again to Lawrence from Boulge, 30th January, 1848:

> "Barton is well . . . His portrait has been hung (under my directions) over the mantelpiece in his sitting-room, with a broad margin of some red stuff behind it, to set it off. You may turn up your nose at all this; but let me tell you it is considered one of the happiest contrivances ever adopted in Woodbridge. Nineteen people out of twenty like the portrait much; the twentieth, you may be sure, is a man of no taste at all."

For the sake of the portrait, which his daughter desired should "be done," it was as well that Barton did not "proannuate." In the Memoirs of Bernard Barton, prefixed to his "Collected Letters and Poems," FitzGerald writes:

> "On February 19th (1849) he was unable to get to the bank, having passed a very unquiet night – the first night of distress, he thankfully said, that his illness has caused him . . . In the evening, at half-past eight, as he was yet conversing cheerfully with a friend, he rose up, went to his bedroom, and suddenly rang the bell. He was found by his daughter – dying. Assistance was sent for; but all assistance was in vain. In a few minutes more, all distress was over on *his* part, and that warm, kind heart was still for ever."

What FitzGerald did not, indeed could not, write, was that in his agony, as he was passing, Bernard Barton joined his daughter's and FitzGerald's hands and gave the momentarily associated pair his blessing.

Had FitzGerald, at that supreme and last moment of his old friend's life, withdrawn his hand, had he immediately and positively disclaimed all share in an implied promise, the marriage, it is safe to say, would never have taken place. A man of the world (but such

Sketch by B. Granville Baker) WOODBRIDGE FROM THE DEBEN

FitzGerald was not) would have acted at once, and would have refused to understand anything more than a subconscious expression by an affectionate father of a wish unformulated until then. For I know of nothing pointing to an antecedent apprehension of the matter. There is certainly nothing of the kind in the "Memoir" from which I have just quoted. In this document, with a simplicity, a pathos, and a sense of humour amounting to delicate irony, FitzGerald's sure hand draws the Quaker Bank clerk's portrait, showing us his innocent vanity, his insatiable desire to see himself in print, and his social qualities, so kind, so facile, so entertaining. It is a piece of exquisite prose. FitzGerald himself calls it "dapper" writing, and speaks of the book as "of incredibly small value," and of his work on it as "a little good job done to further Miss Barton's pecuniary interests." It is not thus that one writes of one's affianced wife or of her father.

It is safe, therefore, to suppose (I have no data to go upon) that FitzGerald was not immediately conscious of any obligation such as he felt later. He was not then master of his entailed fortune; of personal vanity he was absolutely devoid, and he certainly was not in love with Lucy Barton.

When or how they came to an understanding I do not know. It is unlikely that anyone will ever know. After the death of both, and not long before her own, his "little Annie" (a niece) – undoubtedly the person in the world who best understood him – told me that into her keeping FitzGerald and Mrs Edward FitzGerald had entrusted the letters each had written to the other. She added that she meant to take the most effectual measures against their falling into any hands other than her own. This she certainly did, for I feel sure that they were destroyed unread.

FitzGerald's temperament refused the weight of obligation in any form. He paid servants, only to bid them not to work. He would refuse the repayment of a debt, lest he, by any means, should prove indebted. He gave, and gave generously, but let no one, however *proche parent*, presume to offer a return. When FitzGerald grasped Miss Barton's belief that her father expected he would marry her, his relatives – knowing his idiosyncrasies – must have known the marriage to have been a foregone conclusion. I have no reason to think that they offered either advice or opposition. Both bride and bridegroom were uncompromisingly middle-aged, the bride being several years the elder of the two.

The marriage did not take place until after the death of both of FitzGerald's parents, after which he came into possession of his considerable fortune. Mrs. Edward FitzGerald was received with all honour by her husband's relations, who never suspected her of any worse design than the impossible one of "mothering" him. To the younger members of the family she was "Aunt Lucy", and they were on Sundays instructed by her particularly dull presentment of Bible stories.

I cannot recollect ever having seen her. But during the eight years of my childhood that I passed, first at Grundisburgh and then at Woodbridge, in the constant presence (I do not call it "companionship") of FitzGerald, I frequently heard her spoken of – often as "My Elder." When she made an occasional visit to Woodbridge to the house of her friend, the well-known physician Dr. Jones, FitzGerald, if he knew the hour of her arrival, would proceed to the railway station to be the first to greet her. I have a confused recollection of his once abruptly breaking up a pleasant morning gathering in his garden, in order not to be behindhand with this ceremony which he thought her due.

The marriage lasted but a few broken months. I should suppose that Mrs. Edward FitzGerald was, eventually at least, as happy in regaining her freedom as was her husband his. It must have been difficult to live with a person who never laughed, who invested those in whom he was interested with qualities of head and heart ruled to a "counsel of perfection," and who was perpetually disillusioned by ordinary and everyday human nature taking its revenge. The two must have been a perpetual astonishment one to the other, and it was well that the strong commonsense dominant at the back of all FitzGerald's peculiarities came to the rescue. She was "born to rule," he said, and said also that he could have broken her will had he wished. But to him that alternative was impossible. They parted, she to outlive him for some years in the enjoyment of the generous income he settled on her, and he to return to that life of enduring friendships and ceaseless though undemonstrative mental activity, which was perhaps the only life possible to one of his complex and highly strung nature.

Others besides myself are of opinion that had there been no marriage there might have been no "Rubaiyat," or none at least as the world now knows it. The friction caused by his wife's endeavours to mould him to the pattern of that complacent, biddable, conventional *bourgeois* which would have been her *beau ideal* of a husband, produced, not that result, but such an eruption of mental discomfort as aroused his genius to its flashing point.

It is as little my intention, as it is within my capacity, to offer any opinion as to Omar the Tentmaker's hidden meaning – if he had any, which, I am told, good judges are inclined to doubt. On the other hand I am certain that FitzGerald, the most reticent of men, did not intentionally and of set purpose set forth in his Quatrains that which the world has been pleased to read into them – a reasoned description of his religious difficulties and a bid for sympathy.

He made his Translation (working rather quickly for him) and sent it early in 1858 to the Editor of "Fraser's Magazine." He writes to Cowell in September of that year:

> "As to my Omar: I gave it to Parker in January, I think, he saying Fraser was agreeable to take it. Since then I have heard no more; so I suppose they don't care about it; and may be quite right . . . My Go (such as it was) is gone, and it becomes Work, and the Upshot is not worth working for. It was very well when it was a pleasure."

The immediate stimulus, extreme mental depression and discomfort, was gone. In January, 1859, he is again writing to Cowell and again concerning the Persian:

> "I have no one now to prick the Sides of my Intent" (referring probably to Cowell), and further on, "I took my Omar from Fraser as I saw he didn't care for it."

From his published and dated letters and from other inferences, I have strong reason to suppose that some at least of the Rubaiyat was translated during visits paid to what was the home of his affections, Geldeston Hall. In its atmosphere of cheerful and practical goodness and unostentatious comfort, his natural melancholy found its natural antidote. One who was of the Geldeston house party between 1857-9 has told me of his sudden appearances; of his stepping into the drawing-room through the long garden window, and making known his presence there by the music his fingers could draw from his sister's stiff and reluctant Broadwood; of the room kept ever ready for him; of his writing-table with his papers in confusion – undusted, untouched, but lightly covered, lest when he returned to work upon them, a breath of air should have disarranged their sequence; of his quiet spacious bedroom above the library – looking out over park, meadow and marsh, then drained by busy though vacillating windmills – and giving without further let or hindrance on the running water that he loved. This was the sinuous Waveney, on whose placid bosom great wherries then made leisurely journeys between Beccles and Bungay.

To return to the Rubaiyat. So far as I have any evidence to the contrary, none of his family knew of its existence until after his death. No copy of the little quarto pamphlet in brown wrapper (I have lately been offered £600 for such a one could I produce it) have I ever seen or heard of at Geldeston, and my acquaintance with the books belonging to that house has been exhaustive. Copies of some of his other works were there, but of the Rubaiyat none.

It is from Geldeston Hall, however, that he writes in 1859 to Bernard Quaritch, having by that time got back his MS. from Parker:

> "I have been so harried about in Mind and Body by the Fatal Illness of a Friend, I have not had opportunity to see or write to you. Not that I had much to say: only I wished to ask you to Advertise Omar Khayyam in the Athenaeum . . . The Title outside the Pamphlet will of course do for the Advt. . . I will shortly let you know where to send me *my* Copies of Omar."

About a week later, April, 1859, he writes again to Bernard Quaritch from Geldeston Hall:

> "Dear Sir, – I enclose an Order to pay you for advts. in the Saturday Review, Athenaeum, and any other Weekly Paper you like (Spectator?), as also for any other incidental Expenses regarding Omar. I wish him to do you as little harm as possible, if he does no good. I shall be obliged to you to send me forty copies directed here by Eastern Rail, and then I hope I shall give you no more Trouble in this Matter.
>
> Yours truly,
>
> "EDWARD FITZGERALD."

And then we may suppose that the copies duly arrived at the not long-opened Beccles station, and were brought out to the Hall, an unostentatious parcel from a London bookseller. That would excite no comment, for FitzGerald was always buying books. And he would open it, perhaps in the privacy of his own room, perhaps in the kitchen when he paid his nightly visit there "after ten o'clock" (kitchens in those Victorian days being the recognised smoking-rooms in country houses).

Bernard Quaritch must undoubtedly be called the sponsor of this first edition, for had he not, with a discrimination in itself amounting to genius, perceived the quality of FitzGerald's work, and placed the copies given him where, amongst his stock, seekers after something unusual would find them, English Literature would have been the poorer for the loss of these Quatrains that Tennyson proclaimed "most divinely done."

To Westminster Hall

WHAT went ye out to see?

Not the pageant of six months ago with all the pomp of majesty and serried ranks of cheering crowds.

True, the same crowds are here to-day, but all are dumb, with tears their only language.

Then a muffled tramp is heard, like the dull thud of dying waves on a distant reef.

What went ye out to see?

A simple English funeral, a few out-riders, a gun carriage, an oak coffin, fitting sheath and shroud, for one who yesterday was the Lord of all England's embattled fleets, an empty crown (the weary head that wore it is at rest), a solitary Cross of fading flowers, tribute and device of one who is left to bear the double yoke of life alone.

A simple English funeral, befitting one who, though King and Emperor, was in a peculiar sense the Chief Commoner of the Realm. For what sovereign ever knew and loved the common folk so well?

And behind pace a handful of mourners, his sons, and in the midst his successor, half-staggering under the double load of to-day's loss and to-morrow's burden. The hearts of all bleed to see him thus.

And then the members of the household, perhaps in all a score of mourners.

But in this supreme crisis of the final act in life's drama, when monarch and peasant are one, these mourners are but the symbolic representatives of the vast mourning crowds around, and these again the symbolic representatives of the many millions of England and the Empire, the Empire which was in his thoughts to the last, and again not of these alone but of the whole globe which is in mourning to-day. We are weeping for a king, but they are mourning for a MAN, embodiment of all the best in humanity, the like of whom they may never see again. Such a concourse of visible and invisible witnesses the world has never known. Neither the hordes of Xerxes nor the hosts of Alexander nor the far-flung Empire of Caesar can compare with these. Only the last trump will mobilise a yet vaster multitude.

He has left forever the Norfolk home he loved so dearly, but now before the last final stage of his long journey, he must go to Westminster—not to Westminster Abbey, to lie awhile with his peers, but to Westminster Hall to lie among his own people. They cannot part with him yet.

What went ye out to see?

A dry reed shaken by the wind?

Yes, but a reed which was a conscious reed, a thinking reed, to use Pascal's immortal words, a reed which ever bent to the will of his people, yet which no tempests could uproot; a reed whose loving thought embraced all peoples and not his own alone and roused their love and respect in return. To-day their grief is sweeping like a tidal wave round the world.

A reed whose root lay deep in the heart of England, whose stem reached to the stars, and, because it reached to the stars, has found an everlasting root in that other Garden, the Garden of fadeless flowers, the Garth of God.

Cloudesley Brereton.

The Nightriders of Nacton

By Lt.-Colonel B. G. BAKER, D.S.O., F.R.G.S., F.R.S. Hist.

THIS is the time of year, when with the advent of Spring and the blooming of "those stinking violets" (I quote from recognised high authority on 'unting, and am not expressing my own feelings), the hunting season fades away into pleasantly stirring memories. Point to Point Meetings mark the official close of the season; they generally take place in April, some in May, when they risk getting mixed up with cowslips. They also become memories, some even legends.

Of such is the story of a sporting event that took place well over a century ago and is known as the "Moonlight Steeple Chase" or the "Nightriders of Nacton." Both titles are sufficiently accurate; the ride was certainly a steeple chase in the original meaning of the term as applied to the first recorded race of its kind. There may be, there probably were, other similar matches before 1752, when Mr. O'Callaghan and Mr. Edmund Blake agreed to race over a four and a half mile course starting at Buttervant, with the steeple of St. Leger Church as winning post. This race had much in common with the Point to Point of to-day, as had also the famous exploit of the "Nightriders." The fact that the course was run by moonlight sets the race as something apart, something entitled to a special niche in sporting history. And again, the fact of its being a nightride suggests that it was one of those impromptu affairs that are generally so much better fun than highly organised entertainments. The country over which the course was laid is clearly defined in the title "Nightriders of Nacton," and the starting point was Ipswich – then still the hospitable if temporary home of horse soldiers. The horse-trough in the old cavalry barracks is generally given as the actual starting point. The inspiration came from the officer's mess whence

1. Ipswich. Watering Place behind the Barracks. Preparing to start—All sorts of odds—the Gray for choice.

2. The Large Fields near Biles's Corner. Whoop and away!—The Major in trouble. Subden's linen suffers.

3. The Last Fence near Nacton Heath. Accomplished smashers—and a run upon the Bank.

4. Nacton Church and Village. The finish—and a good five still alive. Grand chorus—the Lads of the Village.

emerged those figures gleaming white in the moonlight, suitably disguised in night-gown and tasselled night cap. You may be able to visualize the cavalcade leaving the barrack somewhere down by Commercial Road, rattling over the cobbles of College Street out into the open and rising ground by Holywells, and then for a clear run over heath and plough to Nacton. You can arrive at the same goal to-day, and with less exertion, by bus, but not if you take the cross-country line of the "Nightriders", chiefly because a 'bus is not built for cross-country work. If your 'bus arrived at all it would probably be festooned with the washing of many families; the face of the countryside has altered vastly since Ipswich contained, or tried to contain, mounted troops.

There are with us always people who are not content with general knowledge but must go into details; these are called experts, other terms of abuse having already been overworked in all directions. When two or three experts are gathered together you may, with luck, collect four or five divergent opinions. Several opinions are possible on the subject of those who achieved this famous feat; were they dragoons, hussars or lancers? Here the expert insists on coming in with argument on sumptuary regulations of long ago, regarding braid and buttons and such like distinctive marks of the King's livery uniform. There are such fine distinctions, one broad band of braid favoured by heavy dragoons, two bands by light cavalry, on some occasions coloured red, on others gold. The artist, H. Alken, got over this by the use of nightgowns that cloaked any departure from strict accuracy, for what does your true artist care about braid and buttons? For braid he has no personal use whatever, a button here and there at emergency points in his clothing, suffice his simple needs; as a matter of fact, high authority in the County states that according to tradition, backed by sufficient proof, the nightriders were not dragoons, hussars or lancers, but the gay lads of a smart battery of Royal Horse Artillery stationed at Ipswich when all the world was young and could tell one end of a horse from another.

Everyone surely knows H. Alken's prints depicting this historic ride. They are obviously the work of an enthusiast and one who knows his job, but for a curious error to which reference will be made later. We have seen that the artist has "camouflaged" the regimental distinguishing marks under nightgowns. In this he was surely justified not merely on grounds of artistic expediency, but also of historic fact. There is perhaps some cause for complaint in his treatment of the landscape which all art lovers should excuse on account of artistic licence; "quod licet Jovi no licet bovi", which sounds less rude in Latin than it does in translation, and warns the ordinary individual that he may not do as the artist did and move Nacton Church from its dignified position at Broke Hall to the middle of the village.

Harking back to the curious error in the prints mentioned above. Those who own a set should look again at the print showing the riders taking the wattle fence and gate, the latter being smashed by one of the horses. Moonlight throws a strongly marked shadow of the broken gate, but the shadow itself shows no break. In later reprints this error is corrected with the quaint result that the value of the first print becomes considerably enhanced; but not, alas, to the extent which some who own prints of that edition fondly imagine.

The Black Death

and other plagues in East Anglia

by R.P. Mander

Owing to the insanitary conditions prevailing in the Middle Ages, and to the narrowness of the streets, which prevented the flow of fresh, pure air, it is considered that at no time was the whole country immune from an epidemic of some kind. There were, however, peak periods when the outbreaks were so violent and wide-spread as to be looked upon as separate epidemics instead of as the result of previous visitations which had been dormant for years.

Norwich being a very typical East Anglian town, it will be of interest to examine the figures given by Blomefield of fatal casualties from plague. The original outbreak in that city, or rather the first mentioned by historians, is that of 1104, but no estimate is given of the number of those who lost their lives. The figures for subsequent outbreaks are as follows. That of 1348, which is generally referred to as the Black Death, claimed 57,374 victims in addition to fatal casualties in monastic buildings and among beggars.

This figure is staggering when it is realised that the population of the city at that time has been estimated at 70,000 only. Blomefield may or may not have been accurate in his reckoning. But even allowing for possible error it can be seen that the mortality was disastrous to the prosperity of the city which never regained its previous position as the most densely populated town in the kingdom, London alone excepted.

The peak points for later generations were in 1551, when there were 960 deaths, forty years later, in 1591, when the deaths amounted to 667 and in 1602, 1635 and 1665 when the fatal casualties numbered 3,076, 1,431 and 2,251 respectively. These figures, although referring to Norwich specifically, do give some indication of the relative severity of the outbreaks in East Anglia.

It would serve no purpose here to enter into a medical inquiry as to the nature of the plague. Suffice it to state that the first known cases in the 1348-9 epidemic occurred in the Stour valley. There is a popular tradition that the disease was brought to Europe from the East where it had spread with alarming speed and intensity. Rats and other vermin probably carried the infection. The symptoms of all the plagues were similar and consisted of tumours in the groin or under the armpits, varying in size from that of an egg to that of an apple. After this, purple spots appeared all over the body and death usually occurred on the third day after sickening. There was no fever. The disease was most severe amongst the clergy and the peasants, but those of high degree were smitten also. Thomas Bradwardine, Archbishop of Canterbury, and Joan, daughter of Edward III were two of the earliest victims.

The unit used for discussing the effects of the plague will be the Diocese of Norwich, which at the time of the Black Death embraced the whole of Norfolk and Suffolk and part of Cambridgeshire. In passing it should be noted that certain authorities

A dead-cart depositing its load of victims of the Great Plaque at a common burial ground.

have pointed out that in many instances the village church is found at some distance from the settlement itself, and the reason assigned is that, after the Black Death, people were reluctant to return to inhabit their old houses and instead they built new ones. Whether this reluctance to re-settle in their old dwellings was due to sentimental reasons, the loss of their nearest and dearest having made their old homes abhorrent to them, or whether they or the authorities had the idea that infection might remain in the old buildings, is not stated.

In the peak year of the Black Death, 800 incumbents in the Norwich Diocese died. Their successors were equally unfortunate for 83 of them were carried off by the visitation within the same year. And of the 83 new parsons appointed to replace them, 10 died within the original year. From this it can be stated that in at least ten parishes three parsons died in the space of a year from this pestilence.

These figures refer only to beneficed clergy, but the details for the monastic establishments tell a similar tale. In Norfolk and Suffolk in 1349 there were seven nunneries, each of which lost its prioress. In the house of the Augustine Canons at Haveringland the prior and all the canons succumbed. The death of such a large number of beneficed clergy and monks was in itself a serious thing, but when it is realised that the masters who were needed to train their successors were also dying at an alarming rate, the critical nature of the situation becomes apparent. The high educational standards insisted on previously were waived and the Pope authorised the Bishop of Norwich to appoint to benefices sixty clerks who were only twenty-one years old and probably only in deacons' orders, so that divine service should not cease in the diocese. Furthermore, a number of older men who had lost their wives in the epidemic presented themselves for ordination. The post-Black Death clergy as a general rule were just as devout and conscientious as their predecessors but were not so well educated. It is impossible to say whether this made them any the worse as guides, philosophers and friends to their flocks. As regards the monasteries, they never were able, after the Black Death, to solve their manpower problems and drifted on like rudderless ships in a storm only to crash on the rocks of the Reformation.

The Plague had given the people a new angle on life and the hereafter and had made them less willing

NORWICH.
From the 8 of August to the 15 1666

	Bapt.		Bur	Pla.
St Peters at the Gates			3	3
St Audries			3	2
St Julians			19	18
St Peter per Mounter-gate			2[illegible]	25
St John Sepulchre			7	7
St Michael Thorne			26	24
St John Timber-hill			4	4
All-Saints			4	4
St Stephens			8	7
St Peters Mancroft			10	10
St Giles			6	6
Haigham			2	2
St Bennets	2		2	2
St Swithin			1	1
St Margaret			4	4
St Lawrence			6	5
St Gregories			2	1
St John Madre-market			6	5
St Andrews				
St Michael the Plea				
St Peter Hungate			1	1
St Georges Tomland				
St Symonds			2	3
St Martins Pallace			2	1
St Hellets			1	
St Michael Coslany			5	5
St George Colgate			3	3
St Clements	1		3	1
St Edmonds	1		1	1
St Maries			1	1
St Martins at the Oak			15	12
St Augustins			6	5
St Saviours			1	1
St Pauls			2	1
St James			14	14

Baptized		Buried		Pla.
Males	3	Males		
Females	1	Females		
In all	4	In all	196	177

And at the Pesthouse — 4
The total of the Burials — Whereof plague

The Great Plague: a Norwich "Bill of Mortality."

to support the old monasteries with financial aid. Instead they preferred to endow chantries in parish churches with priests in attendance who would pray for their souls after death. The terror of the pestilence was a means of putting new impetus into the work of the religious guilds which increased greatly in number between 1349 and the dissolution. These guilds had altars in the parish churches and guild chaplains who prayed for the souls of past and present members. Their organisation was very often connected with a particular trade or craft and membership generally carried entitlement to some form of sick benefit.

The deaths in the outbreak caused a severe labour shortage which resulted in the fact that no new churches were built until several years after the epidemic had subsided. With the loss of continuity a new style was evolved to give variation to the grandeur of our beautiful edifices. Prior to the coming of the pestilence a style now know as "Decorated" was in vogue, but this was now discarded for what has been subsequently labelled "Perpendicular." In at least one case buildings commenced before the outbreak were never completed. This is the traditional reason given for the fact that the tower of East Bergholt church was never finished. It is possible that the heavy casualties of the monasteries were caused by the crowds of frightened

The Great Plague. From an old drawing.

people who rushed to them for succour.

The deaths were so numerous that individual burials were out of the question and plague pits were dug for mass burial. Such a common grave was dug within the close of Norwich Cathedral, 'south of the nave of the cathedral and the Bishop's Palace on the east stretching as far as the Erpingham gate.'

One of the miracles of the Black Death was the survival of the then Bishop of Norwich, William Bateman, who moved about his diocese, endeavouring to reorganise it like a general trying to command an army 70 per cent. of whom are on the sick list. This courageous conduct is all the more to be admired, as his brother, Sir Bartholomew Bateman, Lord of the Manor of Gillingham, was one of the first victims of the epidemic.

The full economic consequences of the plague are too involved to enter into in detail but the salient points which led to the next phase of development are these. The serf and the manual worker realised that employees would be difficult to obtain, owing to the loss of life, and considered that here was an opportunity to gain higher wages. The government enacted a law which fixed the rate of pay at that ruling twenty years before the outbreak of the plague, despite the fact that one of the results of the pestilence had been to cause a sharp rise in prices. The eventual result of the clash of these divergent points of view was the Peasants' Revolt under Wat Tyler.

Another change arising from the new position caused by a depleted population was a new form of tenure. Farmers commenced to rent their farms instead of being owner-farmers.

So many teachers of French, then the language of polite society, died, that the native tongue came to be used for public business and thus prepared the way for the peculiarly English writing of Chaucer.

Owing to the invention of the printing press, much more is known of the 1665 plague, and an accurate calculation of the casualties is given in the Bills of Mortality which were then issued. Two examples of these, for Norwich and Great Yarmouth, are included in the illustrations. It will be noticed that on that of Yarmouth, John Johnson, the parish clerk, has written, "Three persons whereof there are not one of the Plague. The Lord's name be praised for our life and health."

Ipswich seems to have suffered very heavily from the 1665 plague which Defoe says was brought to the town through large trading vessels known as Ipswich Cats. In consequence of the outbreak the fair in the town was abandoned and a large number of people moved temporarily away. Consequently the authorities had some difficulty in financing the town as the rates due from those who had gone away could not be collected. An application was therefore made to the justices for authority to levy a rate on all persons living within five miles of the borough, for its upkeep. An arrangement was also made to borrow three hundred pounds from Mr. Robert Sparrow, Mr. John Wright, Mr. Henry Cosens and Mr. Robert Clarke for one year on the security of the lands at Handford Hall. Men and women were appointed to seek out people known to have plague and to render them all possible assistance. All funerals in public were forbidden and every measure taken to minimise the spread of infection.

Bury St. Edmunds appears to have had its worst epidemic in 1636, when owing to the shortage of labour caused by death, grass was for a time growing in the streets.

It is satisfactory to note that the only serious nation-wide epidemic which has attacked this country since 1665 has been the influenza epidemic of the last year of the First World War, which was in part thought to be due to what was then considered a diet inadequate to sustain healthy life. Since then it has been learnt by bitter experience that there is a yet lower standard on which existence can be maintained.

Chanting a dirge. (From a 15th century manuscript).

A Bill of Mortality (viz) *of all Perſons Buried within the Town and Pariſh of Great* Yarmouth, *from Friday* ffeb: 16 — to *Friday* ffeb : 23 *Anno Dom.* 1665

Aged	1	Impoſtum	
Ague		Infants	1
Appoplexie		Kingſevil	
Bruiſed		Meagrome	
Cancer		Pluriſie	
Childbed		Plague.	
Conſumption		Rickets	
Convulſion		Riſing of the Lights	
Cough		Scurvy	
Diſtracted		Sore legge	
Dropſie		Spotted fever	
Drowned		Suddenly	
Feaver		Surfet	
Small-pox		Teeth	
Flux		Thruſh	
Gowt		Tiſsick	
Grief		Ulcer	
Griping in the Guts		Wind	
Jaundies		Wormes	

3 psons whereof there are not one of the Plague the Lords Name be praised for life & Health - --

John Johnson Parish Clarke

A Gt. Yarmouth "Bill of Mortality," 1665. (Incidentally, the list of ailments from which one could die in those days makes interesting reading).

Rider Haggard with his wife, mother and three children.

A NORFOLK MAN

Being some part of the story of Henry Rider Haggard

by LILIAS RIDER HAGGARD

HENRY Rider Haggard first saw the light at the Wood Farm, in the village of Bradenham, Norfolk, on 22 June, 1856. The first sounds which he heard were the homely sounds of the farmyard beneath the windows, and his mother used to say that it was the accident of his birthplace (the Hall being let) which made the man who was to spend so much of his life in labouring for the betterment of agriculture.

Be that as it may, Rider was the only one of William and Ella Haggard's ten children who loved a rural life. Who knows what governs a man's destiny? Chance, inclination, opportunity, environment, heredity — they all have their say. The Haggards were good old yeomen stock, but a marriage into the Amyand family, brilliant but unstable, had brought with their vivid fair colouring a mental and spiritual unrest and a wandering spirit which warred with their love of the home acres, and sent them adventuring into the Army, Navy, Diplomatic and Indian Services. At one period all the seven sons were serving in different parts of the world.

Rider was the sixth son. His brothers had all gone to well known public schools and the universities, but Rider, never considered very robust nor very bright, had to be content with Ipswich Grammar School. It was a rough school in those days, and he distinguished himself not at all, partly perhaps because of what became a lifelong habit of day-dreaming, partly because he was a boy of slow development mentally, a disability not much allowed for in past years.

Ipswich left but little impression on Rider except that he was nicknamed "Nosey" because of the family feature, a large and impressive nose upon his thin boyish face, and that he occasionally excelled in original essays and Latin verse, which so astonished his form master that he was more than once unjustly accused of cribbing. They also laid the foundation of a lifelong friendship with Dr. Holden, the headmaster, a charming man and one of the most brilliant classical scholars of the day. It was he who in after years wrote the ancient Greek inscription upon the sherd

Rider Haggard at the age of fifty-four.

of Armenartas in *She*, a masterly imitation of the antique which is now in Norwich museum.

As a middle-aged man Rider went back to Ipswich to attend their speech day and found time to complete the last "h" of his initials, "H.R.H.," on the mantelpiece of his study. Afterwards he wrote of this visit:

"I know of no more melancholy experience than to return to such a place after forty years or more, and look on the old familiar things and find scarcely a living creature whom we knew. I remember telling my audience that to me the room seemed full of ghosts. Some of the boys laughed – they thought that I was joking – but a day may come, say towards the year 1950, when they too will return, and stand as I did surveying an alien crowd, and perhaps remember my words and understand their meaning."

When he was sixteen Rider left Ipswich for a Foreign Office Crammers, but three years later, William Haggard, hearing that his old friend, Sir Henry Bulwer of Heydon was going out to Natal as lieutenant governor, asked him to take Rider on his staff, which he consented to do.

The next four years of Rider's life laid the foundations of his career as a writer, although such things were far from his thoughts in the exciting and colourful days of the Zulu war and the annexation of the Transvaal. Looking through the little black notebooks which he always carried with him from boyhood, one comes across constant notes of people and scenes, sketches of plots for stories, and a ready instinct to note the dramatic in a conversation.

Those years saw his first efforts at journalism, which drew down upon him an amused but severe reproof from Sir Bartle Frere, another Norfolk man at that time High Commissioner for South Africa. He pointed out that Rider's habit of speaking the truth was not always politic, and had better be suppressed. Possibly the fact that Sir Bartle was an old friend of his mother's saved Rider from anything worse than a reproof. For Sir Bartle Frere, afterwards so much maligned, he had an unswerving affection and respect.

Those years, too, saw his friendship with Fynney, interpreter to Sir Theophilus Shepstone, who was twenty years Secretary for Native Affairs, and another member of the staff, Umslopogaas, a Swazi of high birth; a tall elderly man with a hole in his head, who carried a curved battle axe called Inkosikaas always in his hand. He became perhaps one of the most famous of all Rider's characters, and it was this remarkable man's tales of the early days of the Zulu nation which Rider used so largely in *Nada the Lily* and other African stories.

Later, owing to various events, including Rider's marriage to Louie Margitson of Ditchingham in South Norfolk, he left government service and started

Rider Haggard at the age of sixty-seven.

ostrich farming in the Transvaal. He took his young wife out to Hilldrop, as the farm was called, and his only son was born there, but after a few months, growing unrest and the disasters to the British forces in the first Boer war forced him to bring them back to England with the idea of emigrating to some other colony. Meanwhile he started to read for the Bar and incidentally to write his first books, which mostly barely covered the expenses of production.

The first successful effort was a boy's adventure story written in a few weeks and called *King Solomon's Mines*. It was refused by about half-a-dozen publishers before it proceeded to make history and break records.

It is not "literature." It never professed to be. It has, according to the views of modern critics, every conceivable fault of style and construction. But *it tells a story*. And the sobering and no doubt irritating fact remains that in the sixty odd years since it was written many so called "masterpieces" have been acclaimed and vanished as if they had never been, while K.S.M. still sells its annual thousands.

Rider's success with this and other books enabled him to return and live at his wife's home at Ditchingham, which in time he grew to love as much as she did, though first place in his heart was always kept for the home of his boyhood, Bradenham Hall. Later, tired of literary fame, making money, and the somewhat circumscribed life of a country squire, he left his three children with friends and went with his wife to Mexico. The plan was to join another adventurer, J.G. Jebb, and search for Montezuma's buried treasure, that fabulous fortune of gold and gems hidden by the Aztecs from the invading Spaniards. The death of his only son Jock within a few days of their arrival brought them swiftly home again, and was a shock from which Rider never really recovered. From that day he and his wife never left their children, and Rider determined to make the best of life in Norfolk.

In 1895 'utterly weary of a retired life and the writing of books,' Rider contested East Norfolk at the General Election and lost the seat by only 108 votes, a blow which since he had set his heart on politics, seemed to him 'about the most important thing in the whole world.' After that he turned to agriculture, and suffered all the tribulations, frustrations and annoyances well known to those who strove to make a profit out of what used to be erroneously termed a Pleasure Farm. The story of his labours is told in *A Farmers Year* and of his wider investigations in the momentous tome *Rural England*, a detailed agricultural survey of many of the English counties.

In after years his appointment to various government committees and royal commissions filled his days with incessant travelling at home and abroad, and besides this unrewarded, and alas, often unrewarding work, he had to find time for the writing of books and articles, and his duties as magistrate and many other forms of public service, for always he strove for the betterment of his fellow man. Through much rebellion of spirit he had grown to love the bonds which bound him to East Anglia, and he used to say that the view from the Vineyard Hills across the Waveney Valley was to him the loveliest in all the world.

One of the saddest days in his later life was when age, ill-health and conditions brought about by the first world war forced him to give up farming, and he stood in the auctioneer's waggon one sunny autumn day and watched his pedigree stock pass under the hammer.

Not long after, he died, and so passed not only the writer of many books but a Norfolk squire who, as he said of himself, was:

'A lover of the kindly race of men, a lover of children, of his friends (and no hater of his enemies), of flowers, of the land and all creatures that dwell thereon, but most of all perhaps a lover of his country.'

BRECKLAND - ALBERT RIBBANS.

These are the Times . . .

THESE *are the times that try men's souls . . . The summer soldier and the sunshine patriot will, in this crisis, shrink from the service of his country, but he that stands NOW deserves the love and thanks of man and woman. Tyranny, like hell, is not easily conquered; yet we have this consolation with us, that the harder the conflict the more glorious the triumph. What we obtain too cheap we esteem too lightly: 'tis dearness only that gives everything its value.*

THOMAS PAINE,
writing in 1776.

Take the juice of a rotten apple

How our forefathers cured their ailments—toothache, asthma, ringworms, smallpox, insanity, baldness.

by Olive Hemmant

AMONG my grandmother's treasures I found a book that was published in 1781. It is called 'Primitive Physic' and is by John Wesley. It is stated to be an easy and natural method of curing most diseases. Wesley started to collect these prescriptions in 1747 and no doubt his book was considered to be very up-to-date but I think he chose a very good name for it — his prescriptions are primitive indeed. I wonder that any of our ancestors managed to survive the queer medicines and treatments which were apparently used 200 years ago.

John Wesley made many journeys to all parts of England. He rode on horse-back and is said to have preached 40,000 sermons. He visited East Anglia several times and preached at Norwich, Yarmouth, Beccles and many other towns and villages. I expect he also sold his little book on medicine, for he tried to cure the sick as well as to prepare their souls for a future life.

Here are a few of the prescriptions which amused and astonished me. I don't advise you to try them.

TO CURE A STITCH IN THE SIDE:

Apply treacle spread on hot toast.

FOR THE AGUE:

Take a cold bath. To cure children of the ague let them wear a waistcoat into which bark has been quilted.

FOR APOPLEXY:

When the patient is in a fit take a handful of salt and put it into a pint of cold water and pour it down the patient's throat, when he will quickly come to himself if he is not already dead.

TO CURE THE INSANE:

Let the mad patient sit with his head under a great waterfall as long as his strength will bear it and give him nothing to eat but apples for a month.

TO CURE THE 'KING'S EVIL':

Drink for six weeks half a pint of a strong decoction of 'devil's bit.'

FOR ONE SEEMINGLY KILLED BY LIGHTNING OR SUFFOCATED:

Plunge him into cold water or blow strongly with bellows down his throat.

FOR ASTHMA:

Drink a pint of cold water every morning, washing the head therein immediately afterwards, and take a cold bath every fortnight.

FOR COLD IN THE HEAD:

Pare the yellow rind from an orange very thin, roll it up inside out and put a roll up each nostril.

TO CURE CONSUMPTION:

Cut up a little turf of earth and the patient, lying down, should breathe into the hole for a quarter of an hour each day.

FOR OLD AGE:

Take tar-water morning and evening or a decoction of nettles. Either of these will probably renew the strength for some years.

TO AID READERS OR WRITERS:

Those who read or write much should learn to do it standing, otherwise it will impair their health.

A TONIC AFTER RHEUMATISM:

To restore the strength after rheumatism make a strong broth of cow heels and wash the parts affected with it warm twice a day.

TO CURE RINGWORMS:
Apply rotten apples or pounded garlic.

FOR THE SCURVY:
Live on turnips for a month.

FOR BROKEN SKIN:
Bind on a dry oakleaf or put on a bit of white paper moistened with spittle. This also cures a cut.

FOR A SORE THROAT:
Take a pint of cold water lying down in bed or apply a chin-stay of roasted figs.

TO CURE STINGS:
Sting of a bee, apply honey. Sting of a nettle, rub with juice of nettle. Sting of a wasp, rub with bruised leaves of the house-leek, water-cress or rue.

TO CURE WARTS:
Rub them with a radish.

FOR DULL SIGHT:
Drop in the eyes two or three drops of the juice of rotten apples often.

TO DESTROY FLEAS AND BUGS:
Cover the floor of the room with leaves of alder gathered while the dew hangs upon them. Adhering to these they will be killed thereby.

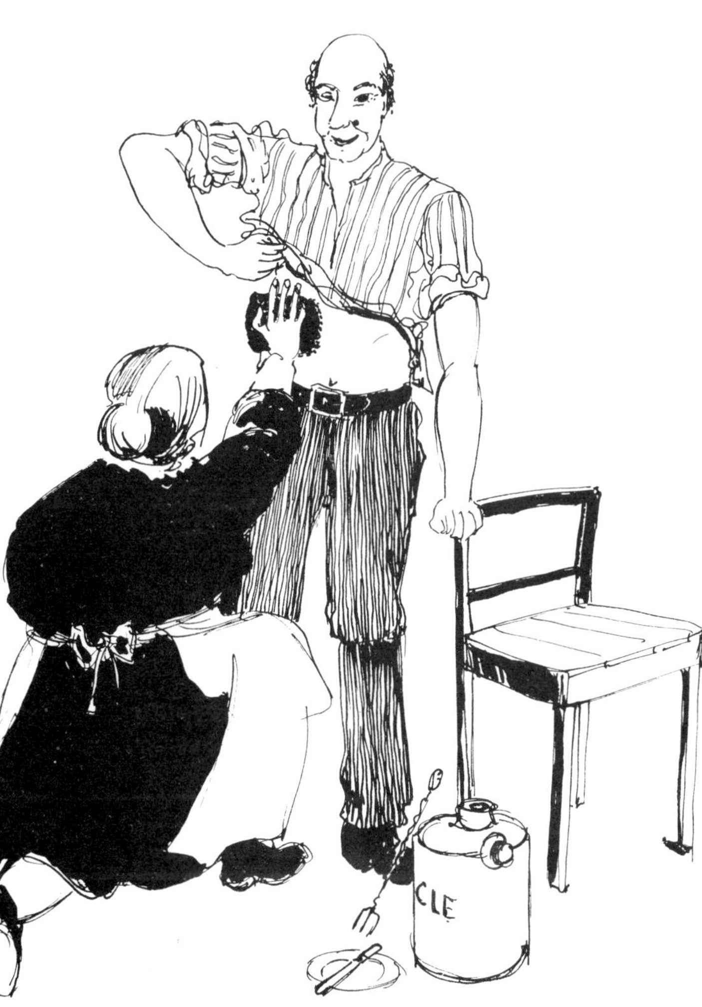

TO CURE BALDNESS:
Rub the bald part of the head morning and evening with onions till it is red and rub it afterwards with honey.

TO PREVENT THE PLAGUE:
Eat marigold flowers daily as salad with oil and vinegar. Or infuse rue, sage, mint, rosemary and wormwood, of each a handful, in two quarts of the sharpest vinegar over warm embers for eight days, strain it through flannel and add half an ounce of camphor dissolved in three ounces of rectified spirits of wine. With this wash the legs, face and mouth and sniff a little up the nose when you go abroad. Smell of a sponge dipped therein when you approach infected persons or places.

FOR PLEURISY:
Take half a drachm of soot. Or take out the core of an apple, stop it close with white frankincense and close with the piece you took out. Then roast it in ashes, mash it and eat it.

TO CURE DROPSY:
Drink five or six quarts of cider every day for several weeks.

TO CLEAN THE TEETH:
Rub them with ashes of burnt bread.

TO CURE TOOTHACHE:
Rub them often with tobacco ashes, be electrified through the teeth or apply to the aching tooth an artificial magnet.

TO CURE SHINGLES:
Drink sea water every morning for a week. Towards the end of the week, bathe.

TO CURE SMALLPOX:
Drink toast-and-water, also milk and apples. For violent cases bleed the feet, bathe the legs with warm water two or three times a day. Apply boiled turnips to the feet.

FOR VERTIGO OR SWIMMING IN THE HEAD:
On a May morning, about sunrise, snuff up daily the dew that is on the mallow leaves.

TO CURE AN ULCER:
Dry and pound a walnut leaf and strew it on and lay another walnut leaf over that.

TO CURE HYPOCONDRIAC AND HYSTERIC DISORDERS:
A cold bath and take an ounce of quicksilver every morning and 15 drops of elixir of vitriol in the afternoon.

The True and Proper Drink of Englishmen

Interior of an Alehouse by James Ward. *(Reproduced by kind permission of Sir Frederick Minter).*

by JOHN HALES-TOOKE

'Good ale is the true and proper drink of Englishmen. He is not worthy of the name of Englishman who speaketh against ale, that is good ale.' So wrote George Borrow, scholar, wayfarer and native of Dereham, Norwich.

Although ale was first discovered in Egypt, it was certainly known in this island at an early date. Brewing was one of the first by-products of a settled agriculture and probably existed in East Anglia as far back as 1900 B.C. An earthenware beaker of that period, discovered at West Bodney in Norfolk, is now in the Castle Museum at Norwich. Evidence suggests that it may well have been a Bronze Age beer mug.

The Romans had very little use for ale, for the mellow Mediterranean wines of their own latitudes were invariably found in their wake. These wines became a common feature in the counties of south eastern England whose inhabitants were of the same racial stock as the Belgic peoples of the continent. Not so the Iceni, the men of Norfolk and Suffolk, whose queen, Boadicea, had been particularly ill-treated by the foreigner. No new-fangled grape-juice for them!

'Water is our wine,' declared the queen in addressing her warriors before battle – and to impress her point on the Romans and their Essex satellites burnt to the ground Camulodunum, the forerunner of Colchester. Be that as it may, barley and its beer-making qualities had been known far too long for Boadicea's remarks to be interpreted too literally.

Neither the Saxons nor the Danes were unduly interested in water, save as a means of transport whereby they might plunder their neighbours the more easily. To them beer and paradise were twin inseparables, for ale was a pledge of the perpetual feasts of Valhalla, ever-present in the mind of the dying warrior – and seldom far from the reach of the survivor.

Souvenirs of their pastimes are plentiful. A Rhenish glass beaker of the 6th century A.D. was found on the site of a Danish camp at Caistor, near Norwich, whilst the silver mounts of oxhorn drinking vessels were but one of the many appendages to the burial ship of the Saxon chief excavated in 1939 at Sutton Hoo near Woodbridge.

It is reasonably certain that hop-brewed ale was known in East Anglia at this period, even though it fell into disuse in the Middle Ages. Not only were hops mentioned in the sagas or epic tales of ancient Norway but they grew wild in that country. The Northmen changed neither their tastes nor their habits when they settled in East Anglia. If they did not cultivate hops in this island it may safely be assumed that they imported hop-brewed beer from their own coasts.

The Norman Conquest made little difference to the ale-consuming propensities of the Englishman in general and none to those of the East Anglian. From an early date rules and regulations came into force to govern the trade. Thus Ipswich held an 'assize of ale' in the reign of the first Edward. Price control was not the only function of that assize for the bailiffs were equally concerned with the quality of the materials used and the fitness or otherwise of the finished product.

The pious folk of Fressingfield, Suffolk, disapproved of such festivals being held within the precincts of their church. Thus a deed of King Henry VII's reign contains a gift of land for the erection of a parish ale house wherein all future festivals might be held.

Hops reappear on the English scene at the end of the 15th century. Although they were then first cultivated by Flemings who had settled in Kent, they were extensively grown at Stowmarket in later times. Nonetheless, hop-brewed beer was long regarded as a Dutchman's drink 'which maketh man fat and inflateth the belly'.

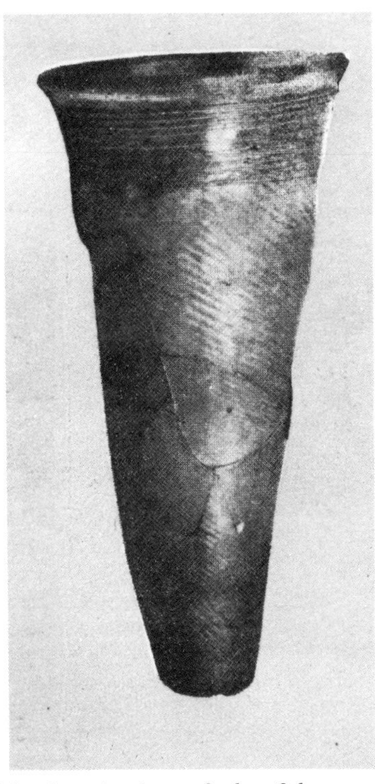

A Rhenish glass beaker of the 6th century found at Caistor-by-Norwich.
Photo by Hallam Ashley reproduced by kind permission of Norwich Castle Museum.

An earthenware beaker—most probably a Bronze Age beer mug—discovered at West Bodney, Norfolk.
By kind permission of Norwich Castle Museum.

In a later age the articles of the Free Fair at Yarmouth were noted for their rigour and under these regulations ale was divided into two classes. The best was to be sold at twopence per gallon and the second best at a penny.

In country districts ale was put to a great many diverse uses, often as a form of currency and more often as a means of raising money. In Bressingham, Norfolk, labourers were paid their wages in bread and ale on the 'ale-beeves,' or working days on which they carted the crops of the lord of the manor.

The Essex church of Thrope-Le-Soken, like many another throughout the land, owes its repair to the money raised at the Whitsun and other ale festivals. On these occasions villagers gave barley for the brewing of beer which was afterwards sold at a village ale feast. So pleased were the men of Sygate, Norfolk, with their new church screen that they inscribed the following rhyme upon it:

God speed the plough
And give us good ale anewe;
Be merry and glade
With good ale was this work made.

The brewer's lot was not invariably an easy one. When an exceptionally bad harvest afflicted the country in 1630 the brewers of Norfolk in general and Lynn in particular were among the first to suffer. 'Maltings were restrained. Brewers were not permitted to make, or the alehouse keepers to sell, strong beer.' And for strong beer Lynn was justly famed.

A Lynn merchant, Thomas Wale, who had established himself in Riga some years previously, returned home to England in 1776. While visiting Everard's brewery near Baker's Lane in his native town, Wale was justifiably amazed at the quantity and quality of the beers there stored. One vat contained upwards of 200 barrels. Wale recovered his wits sufficiently promptly to order 50 casks of pale ale – 'nicely good like Burton' – and 25 casks of porter, all of which earned him a handsome profit on his return to Russia.

It was during this latter part of the 18th century that the whole tenor of brewing changed. Beer-making ceased to rate as a domestic accomplishment and transformed itself into an intensive struggle between competing organisations and ever-expanding territories. If, as George Borrow maintained, beer is the good and proper drink of Englishmen, the breweries of East Anglia have always been to the forefront in providing it.

GEORGE CRABBE

by RONALD BLYTHE

The details of Crabbe's life are too well known to require much further elucidation. How he was born on Christmas Eve, 1754, at Aldeburgh, a decaying and forsaken fishing town midway up on the Suffolk coast, of his haphazard schooling at Bungay and Stowmarket and his fruitless efforts in the less reputable side of medicine, has been dealt with fully and well by Alfred Ainger and later biographers.

It is to his poetry, lately offered a bright renaissance in the music of Benjamin Britten, that we would go; and his poetry is intensely Aldeburgh which, when Crabbe knew it, possessed but a shadow of its Elizabethan prosperity. The sea which two hundred years previously had swollen the fisheries and brought favour and royal charters to the town, then prevailed upon its former benefactions, and the Aldeburgh which Crabbe knew consisted of "two parallel and unpaved streets, running between mean and scrambling houses." It was in this remote and lonely place that the best of his work was inspired.

Crabbe's vision was enormous. Little escaped it. Aldeburgh lay, like Lilliput before Gulliver, completely revealed to his stern, discerning eyes. From the parson to the troll, every vestige of petty passion and human goodness to be seen inverted upon itself by the geographical isolation and poverty of the little fishing community, was noted by the thoroughgoing poet.

But this great field of rustic emotion had no patron to foster a writer, and little money and less time to give to a poet in exchange for a frighteningly truthful portrait of itself, often displayed in unflattering candour. So with three pounds and a surgeon's bag, Crabbe sailed for London where he was fortunate enough to gain the patronage of Burke. (Those interested in the often commendable state of patronage would do well to read the letter Crabbe thrust through Burke's letter-box with his own hand. It is the epitome of courage and faith in one who has no doubts as to his own abilities, given a fair chance to display them).

Under the kindly Burke the poet met literary London, wrote copiously, "burning much in the fire," was ordained a priest of the Church of England and obtained independence and laurels in his own life time. Crabbe was a success. Dr. Johnson spoke well of him. He went to Holland House and Jane Austen was said to have declared "that he was the only man she would care to marry . . ."

His output was prodigious but its quality was often marred by the unbending requirements of the heroic couplet. Crabbe used practically no other poetic pattern than the one used by his master, Pope. Often to the rigid limits of the Augustan pedagogue he had to sacrifice grace and charm. Yet his nature was such that he was never so blinded by formal requirements as to present anything other than fruit of his own discerning in the light of the most stringent truth. This rough honesty savoured a little of upbraiding and even of brutality to many of his contemporaries.

With little doubt *The Borough*, an epic and all-embracing picture of 18th century Aldeburgh, is Crabbe's greatest poem. Written in twenty-four "Letters" and beginning with the church, it moves inexorably and with microscopic intentness over the vices and virtues of the little town. The heroic style, imperfect in the earlier "Library" where often banality and clumsiness usurp the place of intended gaiety and lightness, becomes flexible and accomplished in *The Borough*. The entire poem is filled with deep understanding and with the happy assurance of one who is privileged to know his subject and gifted sufficiently to portray it.

There is little hesitancy as Crabbe moves from house to inn, from shopkeeping to lovers and from gossip to its terrible consequences. In spite of the dreary first years and a certain amount of finger pointing when he returned to address his resentful neighbours from the parish pulpit, he wrote of Aldeburgh with that affection which can only be justly interpreted as being in love with a place.

Surveying his work now through the privileged glass of time we are able to see exactly what happened to the countrywide familiarity and general respect that once attended it. We are able to observe the approach of something Crabbe could scarcely have been aware of; the great, golden flower of the Romantic Revival opening with a glory which had not been equalled since Tudor days. This dazzling barrier, coming at the turn of the 18th century, was to confine Crabbe for a long time in the austere precincts of his cynical age.

Admittedly his poetry was often reprinted throughout the Victorian period. But the answer to this apparent devotion is easily found in the moralising prologues and in the woolly admonitions adhering to these editions, making them, one feels, depressingly suitable as a minor prize for elegiacs.

It was not until our own day that George Crabbe, realist, was belatedly discovered and then, curiously, in the vicinity of Little Gidding.

Aldeburgh early in the 19th century.

DEDICATION CEREMONY, BURSTON 1978

In 1914, the children of Burston Village School, supported by their parents, went on strike in support of their teachers, Anne and Tom Higdon, who had been unjustly dismissed. No fault was found with their teaching but the local Establishment resented their active support for agricultural workers—wages 14 shillings a week—who were struggling to establish the Agricultural Workers' Union in the area. Much bitterness followed, including the punitive evictions by the parson, but the school—and the church—were left almost empty, while the Higdons taught their pupils on the village green, in a carpenter's shop and finally, in 1917, in the new Burston Strike School, subscribed nationwide, especially by the trade union movement. Villagers' confidence in the Higdons resulted in The Strike School continuing throughout their lifetime, closing in 1939, but used ever since as a village social centre.

BBC 2 made a programme about it, and Bertram Edwards wrote a book, soon to be filmed. In May 1978 he dedicated memorial gravestones to the Higdons, a ceremony attended by the surviving Strike School pupils, including their leader, Violet Potter. Pupils from the Hewitt School weré present.

May sun shines on the green candles of the chestnuts,
On the church with its wire-meshed door,
Only half-shut today, as if some late breath
Of humanity and love had touched it.
The older tombstones stand, silent, in the knee-high meadowsweet,
And the old folk sit, silent, in two rows of schoolroom chairs.
Behind them stand the youngsters from the city school,
Seeing, with clear eyes, that history is people.

The Man Who Wrote The Book is reading;
He is accepted, pleasant, unassuming, part of this village,
His labours and his caring have bound him to their lives.
'I love this old world,' he says, 'I am not a dreamer,'
But he reads us old Tom Higdon's words, not his own.

Tom and Annie Higdon loved this old world;
They saw the meanness, the oppression, and the heavy press of greed
Tread out and drown the wine of young hopes,
Leaving poverty, sour as vinegar,
And unrealised talent withering on the vine.

Not for them force-feeding sterile words, facts, figures,
Unrelated mumbo-jumbo, neatly packed in a pill-box
Labelled 'This is what Teachers Teach'.
For them a deeper caring for these, once their students,
The clarity of thought that led the way,
And struggled for the quality of life.

This small, sturdy school looks towards the green,
Turns its back upon the church; by chance, or by design?
Those glebe-land tenants, by the parson harshly thrust aside
For no sin but being loyal to the Higdons,
Do their sighs lie on the wind blowing through the empty church?
They should be here, half a century on, and more,
To see these young ones, round-eyed in the schoolroom,
Speaking with Violet, immortal Violet Potter,
Who led her classmates into history.

The old echoes die; the railmen's tread, the miners',
The marches and the banners and the bands;
A voice only, reading; and in a distant tree
A wood-pigeon, softly calling in the sun.

JOAN CUBBIN

Sutton Hoo Ship-Burial

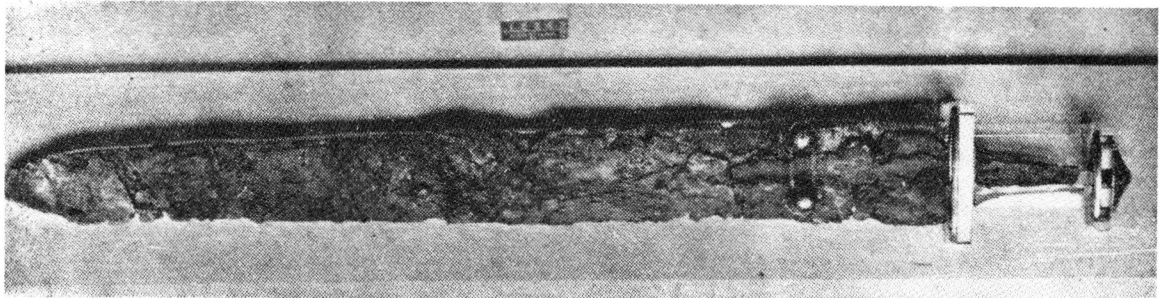

The Sutton Hoo sword, with jewelled gold pommel and handle fittings set in a perspex mount.

by R.L.S. BRUCE-MITFORD

Assistant Keeper of British and Medieval Antiquities, British Museum.

SEVEN years have elapsed since public and archaeologists alike were startled by the discovery in a tumulus at Sutton Hoo of the funeral ship of an East Anglian King, buried about the year 650 A.D., complete with the jewelled gold trappings of a royal harness, with insignia, weapons, armour, and an astonishing array of more domestic grave furniture. The Sutton Hoo ship-burial, in spite of six years lying dormant, has already won recognition, in England and abroad, as the most important document that has as yet come down to us from the era of the Teutonic migrations.

The officers of the British Museum upon whom the care and interpretation of the treasure now rests are fully alive to the great responsibility they bear, not only to East Anglia, but to the world, to whose common heritage of history Sutton Hoo belongs. As soon as the war ended, the Trustees augmented the Laboratory staff for the specific purpose of dealing with the Sutton Hoo find, securing the expert services of Mr. Herbert Maryon.

As a result, many of the objects are now included in the Museum's general re-opening exhibition in King Edward VII's gallery. You may see there all the gold jewellery, the splendid sword (here illustrated at full length for the first time), the Byzantine silver dishes, bowls, cups and spoons, the great ceremonial whetstone weighing 6 lbs. 4½ ozs., the pottery bottle, some remains of the warrior's mail-coat, and the bronze bowl with drop-handles that seems to be a provincial (? Central European) version of the familiar bronze bowls made in Egypt and found in Saxon graves.

By the time this article appears, the helmet, brilliantly restored from hundreds of rusted fragments, and the large hanging-bowl, the finest of the series of such bowls found in Saxon graves yet to be discovered, will probably also be on view.

The helmet, like the sword, the great gold buckle, the shield and the ship-burial itself, bears a remarkable similarity to finds of the same period in the Uppland province of Sweden, not far north of Stockholm. Yet none of the Sutton Hoo objects can definitely be said to have been made there. It is only now becoming possible for the Museum's officers to begin research work on the Sutton Hoo material, but the Scandinavian and in particular the Swedish affinities of much of it are bound to prove of the greatest significance. This would be so if only for the fact that we have here a specific archaeological connection parallel to that implied by the famous and much studied epic poem in the Anglo-Saxon tongue, Beowulf, which, as is well known, deals with events from the folk-history of Scandinavia. Beowulf himself ruled the Geats, a people located in the southern part of Sweden.

The restored helmet convincingly shows the outsize-shape of the padded crash-helmet, a feature which, judging from available photographs, it seems that all Swedish helmet-reconstructions have failed to achieve. Its main features are cheek-pieces, a neck-guard canted out at an angle, silver crest and eyebrows inlaid with nielloed lines, a face-piece in the form of a mask, with nose and close-trimmed moustache. The helmet seems never to have had any boar or bird figure standing on top, like those familiar in Anglo-Saxon literature and in representations on contemporary bowls and helmet-panels. The silver eyebrows, however, each terminate in a gilt-bronze boar's head. Running like a hat-band round the base of the crown were a series of bronze plates embossed with pictures of warriors and combats. These for the most part together with the interlace ornament on the bronze plates that covered the rest of the crown, are very nearly all lost through rusting and decay. Certain very interesting details, however, are pre-

Jewelled gold purse-lid with sliding catch.

Procession of Animals from the inside of the "Coptic Bowl".

served. Some idea of the achievement represented by the reconstruction of the helmet may be had when it is realised that it is the product of six months' continuous and full-time work on the part of Mr. Maryon.

The large hanging bowl is of thin bronze and is decorated with eight enamelled escutcheons, six on the outside round the bowl, one underneath, and one, bearing the unique feature of a fish in the full-round supported on a pedestal rising from the middle of the escutcheon, on the bottom of the bowl inside. The bowl was extensively repaired with silver patches, and so must have been already of some age when it was placed in the grave.

When the bronze bowl with drop handles was cleaned for exhibition a few days ago, Museum officers were astonished to discover in its interior an engraved procession of animals, naturalistically drawn, a donkey, a lion, a camel and a second large feline.

The purse, the lid of which is illustrated, was probably a hanging pouch or bag worn at the waist, with this heavy lid lifting about its hinges, which were riveted either to leather straps hanging from the belt or to the belt itself. The frame and the ornamental plaques are of solid gold set with cut garnets, and, in the case of the frame, with squares of blue and white and red and white mosaic glass. In the lid as exhibited the frame is filled with modern white board, in which the plaques are set. It was possible from the condition of the rivets by which the plaques were fixed to the original lid to deduce that this had been of some substance harder than wood, and therefore, almost certainly, bone or ivory. The modern white board is meant to suggest this. The purse-lid, like much else at Sutton Hoo, is unique.

On the pair of hinged and jewelled gold clasps, which are of great importance, I will now draw attention only to the remarkable design of inter-linked boars that appears at either end of both clasps. They are perhaps not very easy to see, but once recognised become obvious. Their crested backs and lowered heads make them strikingly similar to the sculptured boar on the late Saxon (11th century) tympanum at St. Nicholas' Church, Ipswich. A simplified drawing may help to make the design clear.

Great quantities of material from the ship-grave still await laboratory treatment and archaeological study. As may be deduced from the excavator's plan, this includes iron-work (badly rusted), fragments of buckets and bronze cauldrons, and remains of textiles. There are also various gilt-bronze mounts and fittings, the remains of a small stringed musical instrument, two smaller hanging-bowls with enamelled escutcheons, leatherwork and other things. The work of detailed study has only just begun, and it will be some years yet before the Museum can issue the full account of the find that it is our duty to produce. Meanwhile, however, an interim description of the find, with as many illustrations as possible, has been prepared. This should be on sale at the Museum from about September.

Since the war it has been possible to make a second and more leisured examination of the 40 gold coins that were contained in the purse. These were struck at many different mints all within the confines of the Merovingian Kingdom in France. Coins from the mints of two of the Merovingian Kings have now been identified, and other new evidence has been produced, and I do not think it possible, or even desirable, to reject the collective verdict of the coins, which is that the burial could not have taken place before 650 A.D., and might be as late as 670.

This rules out the view generally held in 1939-40 that the grave was that of Redwald, the East Anglian High King, since he died about 623. As we might have expected from literary sources, however, the grave contained many heirlooms. Besides, the hanging-bowl, the shield, and the gold jewellery, not to mention the ship itself, all showed traces of repair, and must have been of some age when buried. Thus the Saxon antiquities may still largely represent the archaeology of the earlier days of East Anglian political greatness under Redwald.

If the burial is not that of Redwald the question "who was he?" comes to the fore again. Following Professor Chadwick's 1940 analysis of the various possibilities, we may say that failing Redwald, the only two candidates that seem possible are the East Anglian Kings Ecgric and Aethelhere. Of these two, Aethelhere, who died in 655, is much the more likely. In his one year's reign he showed that he had

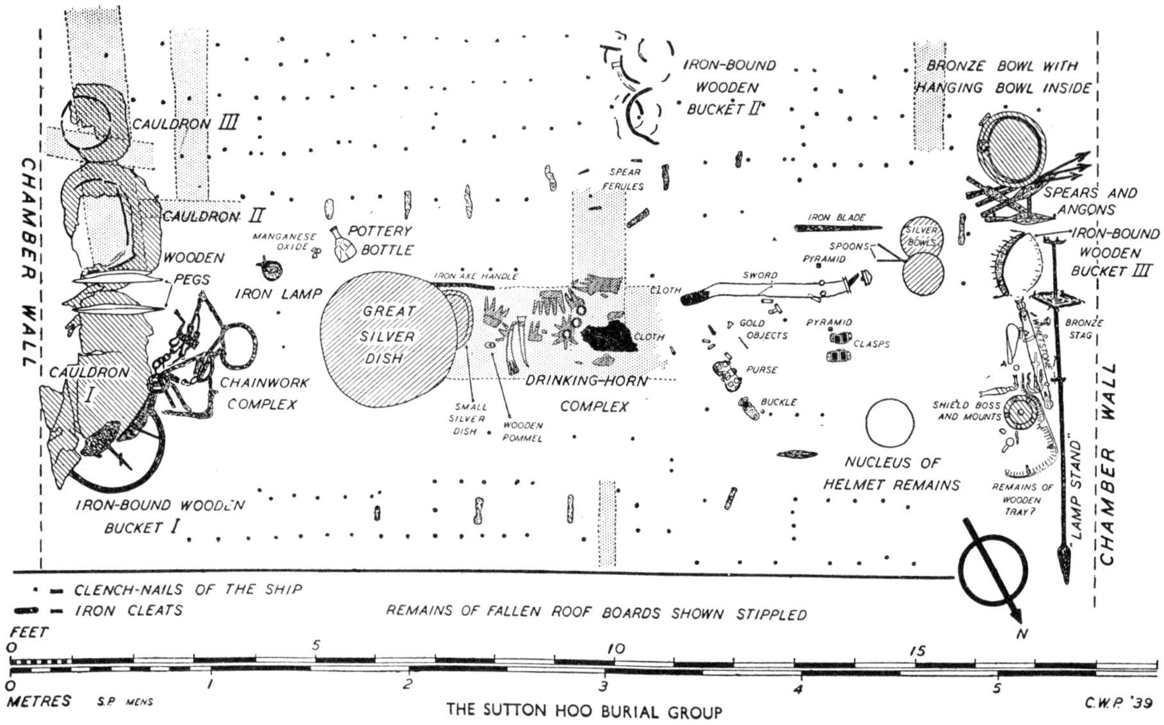

The excavators' plan showing the relative positions in which the various funeral deposits were found.

personality and a clear-cut policy of his own. There is some justification for thinking that he may have been a pagan; and we know that he was on the losing side, and met his end, at the Battle of Winwaed in Yorkshire, where, Bede states, many more were drowned in floods in the flight than were killed in the fighting. The excavators of the Sutton Hoo ship are agreed that it was a cenotaph, and had never contained a body. Aethelhere's claims at least have the merit of providing an historical explanation of this puzzle.

An interesting aspect of the find, noticed by Mr. Guy Maynard in his 1939 article in the *East Anglian Magazine*, is the various signs and indications, direct and indirect, of Christianity in a burial wholly pagan in its general character. There are the spoons inscribed with Saul and Paul, a direct reference to conversion. There is a fish, a Christian symbol, in the hanging bowl. Its naturalism (a fisherman tells me it is quite recognizable as a rainbow trout) breaks with the ornamental traditions of the hanging bowl escutcheon series, and suggests it had a more than ornamental significance. There is the set of silver bowls, each chased with ornament in the form of a cross, and paralleled in silver treasures such as that from Lampescus that have a specifically Christian character. It would be unwise to stress as reflecting Christian ideas the east-west orientation of the burial, which may be purely coincidental, or the plaques on the purse lid showing a human figure between two beasts, which may prove to be connected with pagan subjects known in Swedish archaeology, rather than with the Frankish versions of "Daniel in the Lion's Den." These signs of Christianity amongst the treasures and heirlooms of the East Anglian royal house are only what one would expect if the burial took place as late as 655, for most of Aethelhere's predecessors since Redwald were Christians. The mixture of Christian and pagán is typical of the seventh century, in the earlier part of which one finds grave goods deposited in the pagan manner in graves in Christian churchyards, and at the close, the Franks Casket with its strange mixture of Christian and heathen subjects, and the production of "Beowulf," in which Christian ideals transmute the subject-matter of a heathen epic.

Merovingian gold coins, blanks and ingots from the Sutton Hoo purse.

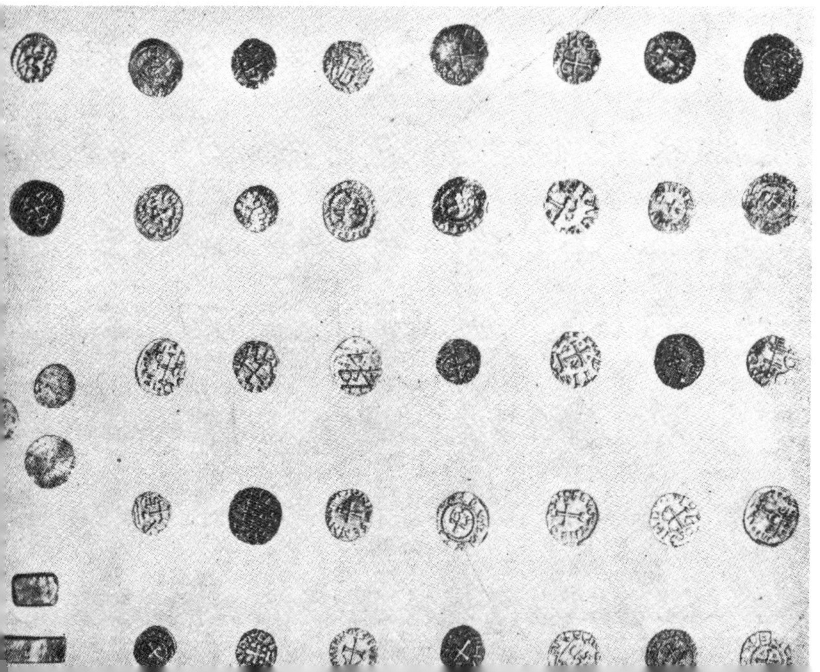

Design of inter-linked boars on the ends of the pair of gold clasps.

Pair of jewelled gold clasps.

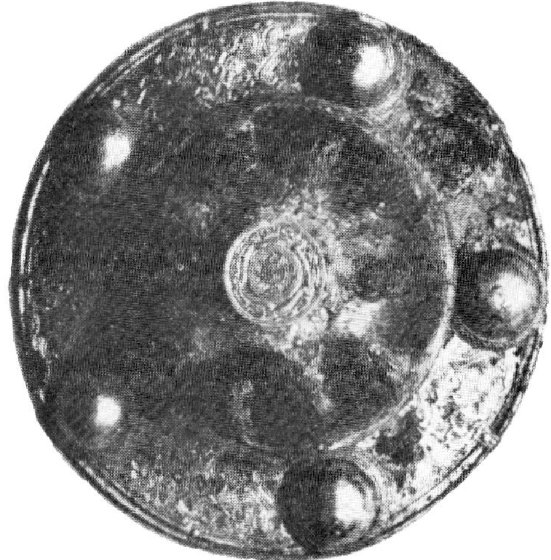

Iron and bronze boss from the Sutton Hoo shield.

The study of the Sutton Hoo ship itself has not progressed beyond the point to which it was taken by Mr. C.W. Phillips, F.S.A. in 1940. It was an open, sea-going rowing boat, rather over 80 feet in length and with a beam of 14 feet, without sail, propelled by thirty-eight oarsmen. It was clinker-built, the strakes being made up of lengths of wood riveted together at overlapping joints, a technical advance on the methods of the builders of the famous Nydam ship (400 A.D.) in the Museum at Kiel. In this the strakes were made up from single pieces of wood running the whole length of the ship (73 feet). The Sutton Hoo ship had probably nine strakes a side, more than in the Nydam ship. The later Viking ships had a greater number of strakes a side and were propelled by sail as well as oars. The Sutton Hoo ship lies between the two.

Many other features of the ship, that cannot be gone into here, have also been recorded. The amount of detailed information that it has been possible to recover, in spite of the fact that the timbers had completely perished, is largely due to the care with which the early stages of the excavation were conducted by Mr. Basil Brown and the Curator of the Ipswich Museum, Mr. Guy Maynard.

Saxon archaeology of the Pagan period, before the age of churches and high crosses, is an archaeology of small and generally insignificant looking things. From these, the Sutton Hoo ship stands out as a monument, the greatest of the period yet to come down to us.

So far only three ship-burials of the Saxon period are known. All have been found in this small corner of Suffolk, two at Sutton Hoo (a small 18-ft. boat was found in one of the other tumuli there in 1938) and the third at Snape, in the last century.

In conclusion I would like to make it clear that in the opinion of the Museum, in spite of the many importations and foreign connections represented in the find, the burial is not that of any foreigner — adventurer, visitor or guest. However novel many of the aspects of the find appear at first, and in spite of the close affinities already noticed for example, with Swedish finds, the Museum is of the opinion that the Sutton Hoo ship-burial is a natural and acceptable part of the archaeology of this island. And Suffolk men will be glad to know that there can be little doubt that the almost incredible masterpieces of goldsmiths' and lapidaries' art that make up the harness-fittings are the products of a hitherto unsuspected East Anglian workshop.

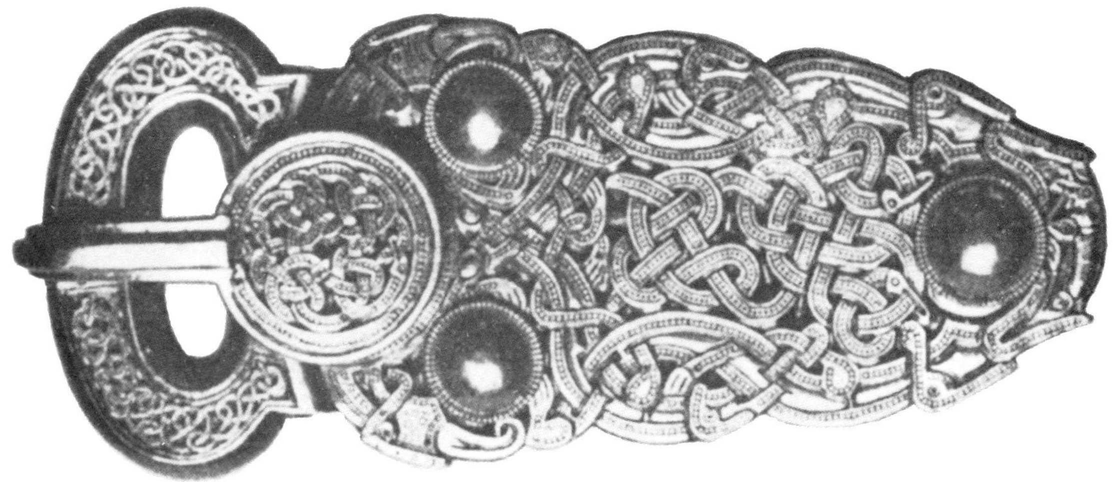

Gold belt-buckle with nielloed animal interlace.

THE EAST ANGLIAN AND HIS HUMOUR

'I like the way they refer to themselves as the egg producers!'

THE WHEREABOUTS OF THE LORD

About 50 years ago in Norwich there lived an old man called Cranfer. He was inclined to be religious and would give away tracts on 'the Walks'.

One Sunday he confronted a young man who was approaching with his girl, held up his hand with the tracts in them and said:

'Young man, have you seen the Lord?'

'Blarst no, bor,' said the young man.

'Whoi, hev you lorst Him?'

Miss. Elizabeth Marks, The Firs, Sahill, Thetford.

BIGGER THAN IPSWICH

The time: The Twenties: The Place: Coddenham.

Will had been to London for the first time and was undergoing the usual cross examination in the local.

'You say it's a grut old place,' said one little man who had been no further than Ipswich during his three score years. 'Is it as big as Ipswich?'

'Big as Ipswich?' said Will, with a look of withering scorn. 'Blarst, boh, it's twice as big as Ipswich—nearly,' he added, fearful of being thought guilty of exaggeration. —

C.E. Runeckles, 7 Watering Close, Somersham, Suffolk.

NOTHING SERIOUS

I can still remember the answer given me by a Suffolk man at Hawkedon in 1920 when completing a life assurance proposal form. Receiving a negative reply to the question 'Is your father living?', I asked what was the cause of his death.

That true, honest face looked at me for a couple of moments and then he said:

'T'wern't nothing serious, bor.'—

Herbert S.H. Rolley, 4 Daisy Street, Hamilton, New Zealand.

INDIGESTIBLE

A man felling out of sorts decided to visit his doctor about two miles away. The doctor examined him and said:

'Well, have you passed anything this morning?'

The man thought for a moment, then brightened and said:

'Oh, yes, doctor. A steamroller.'—

Kathleen Reeves, 14 Clarendon Road, South Woodford, E. 18.

GUIDED TOUR

The time: The twenties, the place: Baylham.

Joe, a much travelled man in his 60s, had been to Ipswich several times and had persusded old Henry who had never ventured so far, to accompany him to Ipswich on their next Saturday off. They walked, Joe leading the way, into Ipswich, down Westgate St., Tavern St. and into Carr St., where Joe stopped and, sticking his thumbs into the armholes of his sleeve weskit, turned to Henry and said: 'Know where y'are now, fellah?'

'Danged ef I dew,' replied Henry.

'Y'ar outside Woolworths,' said Joe.—

C.E. Runeckles, 7 Watering Close, Somersham, Suffolk.

THE TRAIN THAT SHRUCK AND BOLTED

In the early days of railways in Norfolk a train was to run for the first time near a certain village, passing through a tunnel under the road.

Many of the villagers had never seen a train and as most of the men would be at work they told the oldest inhabitant to go to a certain spot not far from the tunnel, where he would have a good view.

When they wanted to know all about it in the village inn that evening he said:

'Well, nor, Oi caern't tell ya for sarten 'cos that come rushen round the bend and when that see me that wholly shruck and rushed inta a burrer.'—

Mrs. E.K. Matheson, 277 Colchester Road, Ipswich.

PHLEBITIS

The local baker called at an old lady's house and, getting no reply, opened the door and went in. He found the old lady sitting in a chair with her stocking down and examining her leg with a torch. Said the baker:

'Whatever are you doing?'

She replied: 'The doctor says I've got phlebitis so I'm looking for the varmints.' —

Mrs. M.E. Clowes, Thatched Cottage, Caston, Attleborough.

RUM OWD WEATHER

by ALLAN JOBSON

THE weather was an all important factor in the life of an East Anglian since agriculture was the chief pursuit, as in that too of a countryman generally. Its significance to-day is still with us, considering there is to be a world weather watch organised by the World Meteorological Organisation.

Foreknowledge of an impending change was an essential in the cultivation of crops and a successful harvesting. Barometers, both home-made or acquired, were to be found in the cottage homes, cow-houses (known as a nettice), stables, the Manor House and Hall alike. I have one of the primitive variety, which is a clear glass bottle with a bulbous flask stuck in the neck. The bottle was filled with water and this would rise and fall in the neck of the flask as the atmosphere changed. My grandfather would always tap his mahogany banjo barometer to see which way the mercury took the pointer.

Added to these were the weather-vane that adorned the gable-end of the barn, and the golden cockerel on the church tower that, so they believed, had been there since the days of the Conqueror. Yet another forecaster could be made by drawing a line on the stable wall, suspending a cord of flax from a nail above, weighted by a stone with a hole in it. This acted as a bob that rose or fell below or above the line.

But there were a number of other guides to storm or fair, such as the eccentric movements of animals, the peculiar flight of birds, the activity of insects, the unfolding of flowers, cloud formation, distant sounds; and above all the moon. They could read and understand these things in a lore which has been passed on to them by their ancestry. However, they were not mindful of that bit of wisdom contained in the old Book: 'He that observeth the winds shall not sow; and he that regardeth the clouds shall not reap.'

In my grandfather's native village of Middleton-cum-Fordley, three sounds bore significance. One was the firing of guns at Landguard Fort, some 30 miles distant southwards (his boyhood days had been punctuated by fear of Napoleon); the trains passing over an old pile bridge westward; and the roar of the sea eastward. But then, of course, their fields were strangely quiet, a peace such as we do not understand in these days of stress and strain.

The aerobatics of rooks circling in the air portended stormy weather — 'Ta rooks be windin' ooop ta clock,' or when they played football. Again, when a robin sang at the bottom of a bush it betokened bad weather but if it sang at the top it would be fine.

Animals, especially the cottager's pig, contributed their premonitions. If they moved about with straws over the head it was a sign of change. Or when a cat wiped its face over its ears, it was a sign of fine weather; but when it sat with its back to the fire it was a sign of frost.

Of insects the following is most probably unique. A.G. Bradley writing in *Other Days* of his Suffolk grandfather has this: 'His bailiff, Tom Doddington, came to him in fine weather just before harvest, full of gloomy prophesies of a wet autumn culled from the manifestations of Nature revealed only to the rustic close to the soil. His desire was to begin cutting at once, even if a little premature. "Them spiders, rot 'em, have been pushing about and filling their webbes," was one portent. His master acquiesced, and almost alone in the neighbourhood saved his grain in good condition, the spiders and the bailiff proving correct. It was a frightful harvest and most of the grain sprouted in the shock.'

Cloud formation, which could be read by all, was quite picturesque in its description. Streaky clouds were 'Colts' tails', small clouds were 'Water-carts'; but small clouds, thick in the centre and tapering at the ends, were 'Soles', and an indication of bad weather. 'Noah's Ark' was a cloud resembling an overturned boat: 'Noah's Ark' from south to north, Rain till it froth.' However, 'Sheperd's flock' were white fleecy clouds, indicating fine weather.

Of flowers, the Scarlet Pimpernel was both the 'Shepherd's Calendar' and his clock.

References to the moon are legion, many of which are still well known. It governed their life not only in the pursuit of agriculture but in their domestic economy. 'Soon seen, seldom seen,' was said of a new moon, because if seen too early it was likely to be clouded over.

Saturday new, Sunday full,
Never was good and never wool.

But it was lucky to see the moon over your left shoulder. When the crescent moon was in a certain position it was said 'ta mune lays waterchutin'; but as soon as it had passed the 'full' it was said to *dreep.*

Naturally, the elements of such significance to general welfare called forth a considerable vocabulary. All the same they were guarded in their speech. 'Do you think it will rain today?' 'I don't know as it 'ont. It maay an' it mayn't. I don't know but it will.' And when it did they said: 'That dew rain a suffen.' *Wet* was rain: 'Dew it wet?' 'Iss ta dew.' 'Tittley weather' was inclined for occasional drizzling or small rain. However:

Happy is the bride the sun shines on,
Happy the corpse the rain rains on.

Dag was the morning dew; but in Norfolk a shower of rain was noted as a 'dagg for the turnips'. *Dingin* was an alias for showery, also called *falling* or following weather; but *dribble* was a drop or small light rain. *Leasty* was dull wet weather, *mizzle* was mist or small rain: 'Dews it rain?' 'No, ta mizzle.' *Smur* had a similar meaning: 'Ta smur with rain.' But curiously enough *smear* was marsh land, as 'down by the carnser and over the smear'. *Stingy* was sharp, unsettled weather inclined to rain, *rafty* was raw damp, coarse and smelly, *roke* was a mist: 'Thass a nasty roke com' oova ta maashes.' *Water-eynd* was sea smoke, or a dense vapour from the sea. *Following Time* described a wet season, in which showers follow each other in quick succession, and *thredigal* was a term for unsettled weather, and never applied to anything else. 'Ta weather fare ta look thredikal, and the clumps of the evening are coming on.' *Tempest* was used only of a thunderstorm but a *thunder-pipe* was a meteorite and a *thunder bug* was a midge in Essex.

Of all the terms, that of *Roger's Blast* appears to be the most interesting. It was also known as *Sir Roger.* It applied to the sudden mysterious manner in which on an otherwise perfectly still and calm day in summer a gust came sweeping and whistling across the fields: 'Thar goo Roger's blast acrost ta fild a twizzlin' ta barley.' This phenomenon was credited to the icy breath of Sir Roger Ascham in one of his moods, but it might have described one of the Bigods. However, *gushy* and *gussock* was a sudden blowing of the wind: 'Ta wind blew gushy last night.' *Snaggy* was snappish snarly: 'How is a' this marnin?' 'Kienda snaggy.'

A 'weather breeder,' a term still used, described a beautiful summer-like day or week during winter or early spring, supposed to indicate the approach of very bad weather. But *weather-head* was a secondary rainbow and to be *weather-laid* was to be stopped on an intended journey by stress of weather. 'Lamb storms' were so described by the shepherds as happening about the time that lambs fall. 'Winnol-weather', was applied to the stormy weather common at the beginning of March, the third day of that month being the anniversary of St. Winwaloc, a British saint. And 'so many fogs in March, so many frosts in May'; but foggy was *misky* or *mullicky* in Essex.

Billows of snow were snowdrifts but a 'blunt of snow' was a heavy fall. *Frawn* was frozen: 'I'm frawn ta dead amost.' But *frize*, which rhymed with prize was the colloquialism for freeze. *Forgive* was when it began to thaw, although 'Ta blew, an' ta snew, an' ta thew all at once.' *Water frost* was ice but *frosted* described the action of turning down the hinder part of a horse-shoe in cold weather.

Thongy, a word peculiar to Norfolk, was descriptive of the oppressive heat which sometimes occurs between summer showers. We might end this symposium with the *Seal-of-the-day*, which is still given by old inhabitants. 'Do you know so-and-so, John? Is he a friend of yours?' 'Waal, sir, he aint much of a frind, but I giv' him the seal of the day when I meet him.'

But Grantchester! Ah! Grantchester

Written and Photographed by
ALASDAIR ALPIN MacGREGOR

A FEW years ago, those of us with intimate Cambridge associations learnt with considerable disquiet that the Cambridge Town and Country Planning Committee had scheduled for building purposes that veritable Elysium of our youth, the celebrated tea-garden at Grantchester known as The Orchard. This filled us with alarm and despondency. Did it mean that no longer would there be 'honey for tea' under the apple-trees there? Such a prospect disturbed thousands to whom this setting has meant something very special ever since Rupert Brooke immortalised it with his poem *The Old Vicarage, Grantchester,* which he himself described as 'a long, lanky, lax-limbed set of verses'.

It made its first public appearance in 1912 in the King's College periodical, *Basildon.* Since 1918, when it was included in the larger collection of Rupert Brooke's poetry, for which his friend, Eddie Marsh, was responsible, this poem has occupied an assured place in our literature, ranking high in popularity with such of it as emanated from the First World War. It has also bequeathed to Grantchester the stature of a place of poetic pilgrimage.

The announcement involving The Orchard's destruction precipitated a spate of protest from every quarter. For 60 years, it was pointed out, it had functioned as the very special tea-garden of Cambridge undergraduates and townspeople. During the May Week Balls, when traditional punting parties arrive at dawn by Cam and Granta, as many as a thousand breakfasts have been served there; and all throughout those years countless visitors from other parts of the country and from abroad have sipped tea under its apple-trees. We were all immensely relieved to learn in 1960 that a local landlord, anxious to retain The Orchard as formerly, had bought it and had leased it to Mr. Sydney Wells, conditional upon his maintaining it in its traditional style and spirit.

The Orchard at Granchester has been a tea-garden since 1897, the year when J.W. Stevenson and his wife opened it as such, in response to the requests of Cambridge undergraduates who punted upstream from the city and enquired whether they might be given tea under its apple-trees. That year the Stevensons erected in The Orchard what has been known ever since as the Pavilion, which, for many years now, has been used as a deck-chair shed. It was Mrs. Stevenson who, with her own fair hands, and on

Wright's Row as I first knew it.

more than one occasion, served Rupert Brooke, with the honey so felicitously remembered in the concluding couplet of his Granchester poem.

Incidentally, John Drinkwater was among those who insisted that in 1912, the year Rupert Brooke wrote his poem, the clock had been standing at ten to *five*. Poetic license, therefore, would seem to have justified the alteration. And why not? A pity to have forfeited that ever mellowing honey-at-tea-time touch for a couple of immaterial hours.

When visiting friends at Grantchester the other day, I could not but notice that the church clock recorded the correct time.

Rupert Brooke, born in 1887, went up to King's College in 1906. In the summer of 1909, having taken a Second in the Classical Tripos, he went to live with the Stevensons at The Orchard. 'I'm in a small house,' he wrote to his cousin, Erica Cotterill, 'a sort of cottage, with a dear, plump, weather-beaten, kindly, old lady in control. I have a perfectly glorious time, seeing nobody I know all day. The room I have opens straight onto a stone verandah covered with creepers and a little old-fashioned garden full of old-fashioned flowers, and crammed with roses. I work at Shakespeare, read, or write all day, and now and then wander in the woods, or by the river. I bathe every morning and sometimes by moonlight, have my meals, chiefly fruit, brought to me out-of-doors, and am as happy as the day is long. Every now and then, dull, bald, spectacled people from Cambridge come out to take tea here.'

From The Orchard in 1911 he moved no farther than a couple of hundred yards to The Old Vicarage, then occupied by his friend Dudley Ward, whose widow I myself knew, and whom I used to visit

Byron's Pool. 'Still in the dawn-lit waters cool His ghostly Lordship swims his pool, And tries the strokes, essays the tricks, Long learnt on Hellespont or Styx.'

Porch of the Parish Church.

The Old Vicarage.

Rupert Brooke in the garden of The Old Vicarage. 'The room I have opens straight onto a stone verandah covered with creepers.'

there when convalescing at Cambridge after a long bout of incapacity arising from the trenches.

The Old Vicarage Rupert Brooke knew in those ecstatic Grantchester days of his was less tidy, and its garden less trim, than at this time. From 1919 onwards, and still in Mrs. Dudley Ward's time, the garden glowed with everything the reader of his Grantchester poem would have expected to find there. I remember particularly its wallflowers and, later, those blooms recalling his lines:

And in my flower-beds, I think,
Smile the carnation and the pink;
And down the borders, well I know,
The poppy and the pansy grow.

While at the Old Vicarage he wrote many of his best poems. The letters he wrote to the late Frances Cornford, as she herself told me, were often accompanied by a poem or two, on which he solicited her comment. Some of his poems, and for the same reason, reached Wilfred Gibson and Jacques Raverat in the same way – if not actually submitted on postcards. Eddie Marsh, whose opinion Rupert valued so greatly, and who, without a doubt, encouraged the poet in him more than did all his gifted friends put together, was likewise the frequent recipient of them. Eddie by this time had made those criticisms of D.H. Lawrence's work which had won for him in Cambridge the soubriquet of 'the policeman of poetry'.

By the spring of 1910, Grantchester had become very much a part of Rupert Brooke's being. Its apple-blossom, its mill and mill-pool, its quietude at sundown had so ensnared him that he found it impossible to read more than a hundred lines of poetry a day, or to think very much about anything else. This setting, in all its natural loveliness, and especially when peopled by the few he loved and admired, held him in thrall.

He wasn't much concerned with the village folk: and the village folk weren't much concerned with him. To them, he was a rather odd, long-haired undergraduate who happened to be lodging with the Stevensons at The Orchard, or staying indefinitely with the Dudley Wards at The Old Vicarage. They knew, however, that he had something to do with poetry. *'I dunno nawthin on 'im, 'cept he were a-stayin' yon way. He wuz one o' them rum booeys what writ po'try loike.'*

Grantchester, of course, has earlier associations with the poets, as Rupert was clearly aware:

Dan Chaucer hears his river still
Chatter beneath a phantom mill.
Tennyson notes, with studious eye,
How Cambridge waters hurry by.

One other poet falls to be mentioned, namely Byron. He gave his name to the pool on the Granta situated above the sluice at Grantchester:

Still in the dawn-lit waters cool
His ghostly Lordship swims his pool.

Men and women of Olympian stature in fields other than poetry have known Grantchester too. Alfred North White, Bertrand Russell's collaborator in the *Principia Mathematica*, lived there about 1910, as did the American novelist, Mary Ellen Chase, roughly 20 years later. Sir James Frazer of *The Golden Bough* had known it since his college days at Cambridge. I used to meet him there when for a time he occupied part of the Old Mill House, owned by my friends, the Winters.

The Winters! The dear Winters! What pleasant memories I have of ploys at Grantchester and on the Granta during their years at the Old Mill House! I recall particularly a few days' sojourn there in the spring of 1920, during a brief interlude of extreme happiness in my life — an interlude when the flower-beds at The Old Vicarage, just over the wall from us, sent waves of fragrance over to us as we played croquet on the Winter's lawn — an interlude when the wistaria at the Old Mill House vied with the lilacs flowering profusely on every hand — when the grey pussy-willows dropped buoyant catkins into the quiet and almost imperceptibly moving stream, and the water-meadows between us and Cambridge, criss-crossed by the long, lambent shadows of poplar and willow, were knee-deep in the gold of king-cup and the pinky mauve of cuckoo-pint.

Birds were nesting everywhere around us; but not numerous enough in the Winter's quite extensive garden to satisfy one or two of the younger members of the family and their bird-nesting contemporaries. In mischievous mood I purchased in a Cambridge confectioner's an assortment of sweetmeats resembling a variety of birds' eggs. These I dropped surreptitiously into a number of old nests in the Winters' shrubberies, and also into those I found among the dense boscage behind the 'Folly' at the foot of The Old Vicarage garden.

When the young, bird-nesting enthusiasts turned up the following morning to continue their quest, lo! they discovered some very remarkable eggs, the like of which had never been laid in Grantchester before.

Confusion ensued. Bird books were feverishly consulted to discover whether thrushes sometimes nested on the ground, and larks in lilac-trees. You see, I had deposited my eggs with little reference to ornithological exactitude.

Among those quietly witnessing my little bit of wickedness was an interesting undergraduate of 21, then in his fourth year at Trinity. Being the close friend and college contemporary of John Winter, he just happened to turn up at The Old Mill House that morning. In the years that were to follow, he was to earn for himself an international reputation as an artist and naturalist. His name — Peter Markham Scott.

A quiet backwater of the Granta, behind the Old Vicarage and the Old Mill House.
'The chestnuts shade, in reverend dream,
The yet un-academic stream.'

Grantchester Church 'Stands the church clock at ten to three, And is there honey still for tea?'

The House known as The Orchard, where Rupert Brooke lodged with Mrs. Stevenson.

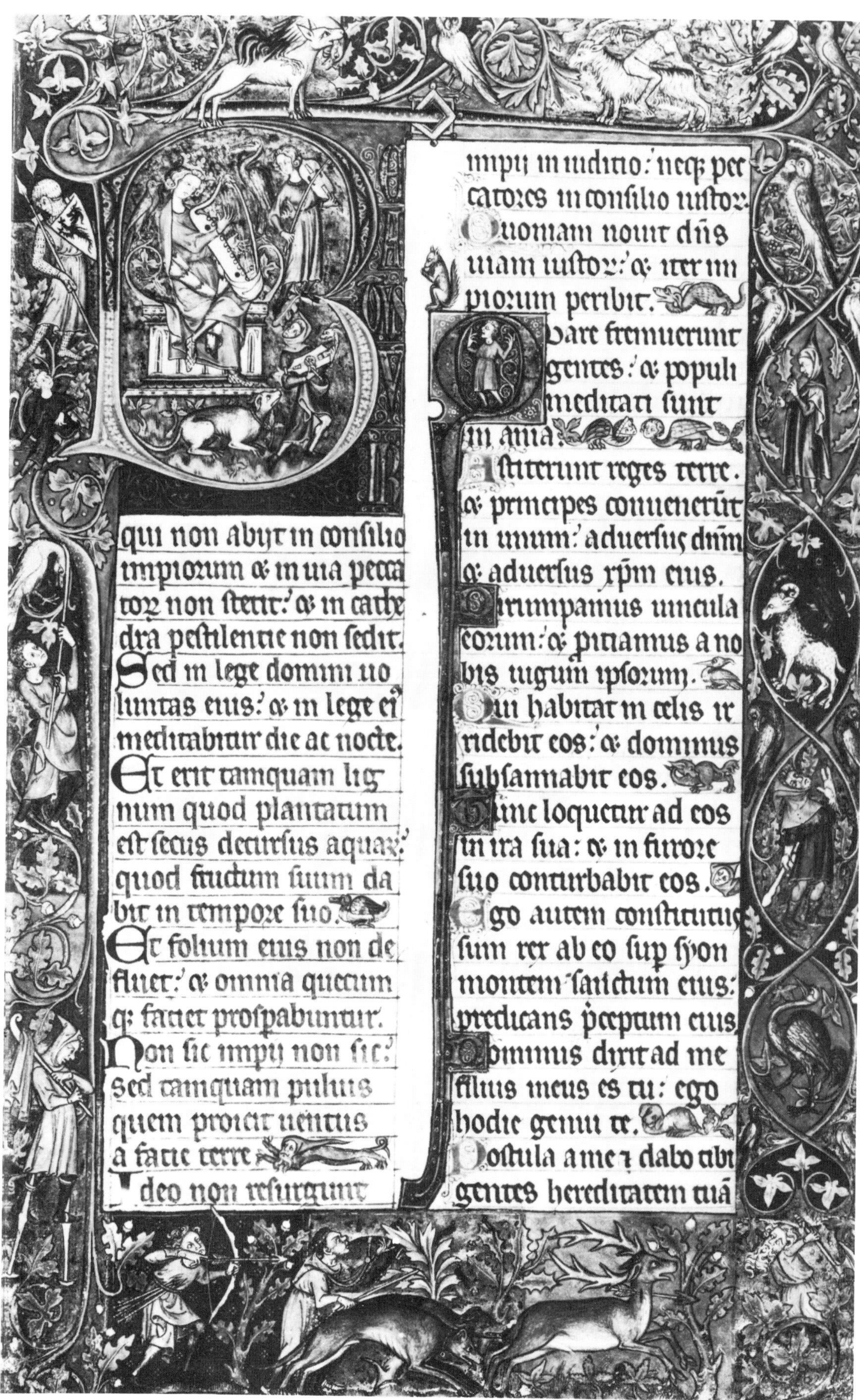

The Beatus page from the late 13th century Peterborough Psalter. David and his musicians are in the 'B' and there is a series of marginal grotesques, including a hunting scene at the foot.
Royal Library, Brussels, photo.

EAST ANGLIAN ILLUMINATED MANUSCRIPTS

Infinite riches in a little room:

by JANE A. WIGHT

A sowing scene from Queen Mary's Psalter, f. 80b. British Museum photo.

INK and razed sheepskin, gold leaf and vivid water-colours were used for the finest East Anglian work: the illuminated manuscript Psalters of the later Middle Ages. Those that survived time and use and Reformation are treasured in Ranworth and Norwich, in Cambridge, Oxford and London, in Brussels and New York. Their aesthetic and actual value is, perhaps, astronomical.

The Psalters were the service-books of the laity, providing both status symbols and an amiable distraction for the wealthy. They were in a tradition soon to be superseded by considerably smaller, more convenient and prettier Books of Hours, which were analagous to present day prayer-books, containing the different church services as well as the Psalms but, still, all in Latin. The great *Luttrell Psalter* (British Museum) is a weighty 309 pages of parchment, in size about 10 by 15 inches. This is the most famous and the most interesting of the group but it is by no means the most beautiful, being of the period of decadence. It was commissioned by Sir Geoffrey Luttrell of Irnham in Lincolnshire, who is shown on one page with his wife and daughter-in-law. Luttrell sits on horseback – himself, the horse, the weapons being emblazoned from top to toe with his arms, silver birds on a blue ground. Nor is the boast of heraldry absent from the other books.

The 'limners' of the East Anglian School worked, for the first quarter of the 14th century, at the centres of Norwich, Gorleston, Bury St. Edmunds

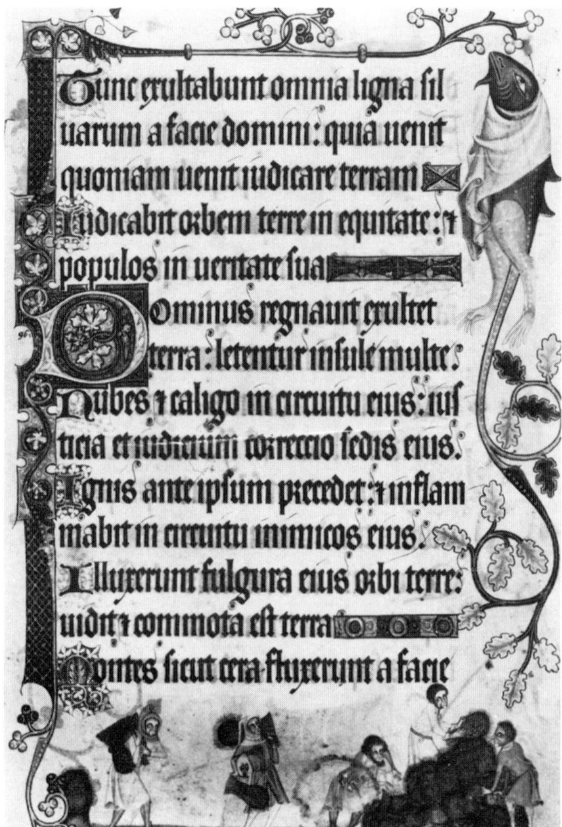

Psalm 96 in the Luttrell Psalter, f. 173, showing a harvest scene. Three men stack the sheaves while two others bring them in from the left. British Museum photo.

and Peterborough. They were patronized by ecclesiastical foundations and by the nobility, the most skilled workers being reputedly those of the diocese of Norwich. The style later spread beyond East Anglia, the differences being due to local provenance and more, or less, French influence. Apart from the distinctive spare lines of the drawing, their manuscripts can be recognised by narrative in the illuminations; by detailed subjects from natural history; by fabulous beasts wandering through genuine foliage; by – a characteristic detail – the 'East Anglian Daisies', which are the ordinary English daisy reduced, for the purposes of ornament, to a rounded pinkish tip and green calyx.

It is worth pointing out that, although Latin is the language of these books, English (or Norman-French) makes a very occasional incursion. One can cite a duck in the *Gorleston Psalter* (British Museum), which cries 'queck' as the fox runs off with it! More important is the dialogue in English in the *de Lisle Psalter*, between the Three Living Kings and the Three Skeleton Dead Kings, who frighten them with the evidences of mortality. 'Ich am afert' (I am afraid) says one of the living.

The manuscripts can naturally be assoicated with mural paintings and retables of the same date, although the association is general rather than in depth. The retable at Thornham Parva, Suffolk, with its figures of saints, has been compared with the *Arundel Psalter* (now bound up with the de Lisle Psalter, and in the British Museum), while the wall-paintings at Longthorpe Tower, near Peterborough, can be compared with the *Queen Mary's Psalter* group and the *Peterborough Psalter;* this last in Corpus Christi College library, Cambridge.

The best way to treat these marvellous manuscripts is, perhaps, simply to place and characterize a few, and hope that people can see them or, anyway, facsimiles.

A beautiful service book, following the Use of Sarum, is the *Ranworth Antiphoner*, preserved in the church at Ranworth, Norfolk. This was made by the monks of Langley Abbey about 1400, being bequeathed to the church in 1478, to which it was finally returned after a lengthy disappearance. It is a MS of 285 pages, size about 20 by 15 inches, with a text in small, neat and delicate script, written on fine pared sheepskin. Apart from the floreate scroll borders and other decorations, it has some 20 initial miniatures, delicate and small, which take one from Nativity to Crucifixion – with flashbacks to the Old Testament: King David the Psalmist, Jonah and the Whale. There is musical notation throughout, for chants and psalms, and music links the manuscript uniquely with Ranworth Church: where survives, with pasted music sheet, a Cantor's Desk of 1500, as pictured in one of the illuminated initials. The colours of the Antiphoner are fresh, but pale in tone; blues, greens and pinks, heightened with yellow, red, dark green and burnished gold.

In the style of Peterborough is the *Queen Mary's Psalter* (British Museum), which is outstandingly well *illustrated*, rather than merely decorated. It dates from the early 14th century. Although all the monsters and animals of the medieval bestiary romp through its pages, there are also numbers of tinted drawings, and paintings on gold or diapered backgrounds, which illustrate Old and New Testament history – as well as the traditional Calendar series of occupations of the months. 223 tinted drawings, for instance, are dedicated to Old Testament stories from the Fall of Lucifer to the Death of Solomon, and in the Psalter proper there are 87 large coloured miniatures. In the lower margins are 463 small tinted drawings. These last are of hunting scenes, sports, grotesque creatures and scenes from the Miracles of the Virgin and the Lives of the Saints. Apart from the famous series of the months – feasting in January; picking flowers in April; pig-killing in December – one must cite the scene of Adam and Eve, gloomily delving and spinning in the harsh world outside Paradise.

The double but incomplete *de Lisle Psalter*, also in the British Museum, is fascinating study. The *Arundel Psalter* is perhaps 25 years earlier than the second half, the *de Lisle Psalter*, which was finished by 1339. This part has only a few folios, including a second Calendar, but it mainly consists of pictures – sometimes four to a page. There is a full-page miniature of the Virgin and Child, who holds a goldfinch apparently, accompanied by censering angels and female saints. A grimmer subject is the traditional late medieval story of the Three Living and the Three Dead. This appears over a Norman-French poem of their dialogue, a short version of which exchange is also given in English. This representation of the frightened living kings and the crude, ominous, brown skeletons seems to have been used as a model for church murals in East Anglia and Lincolnshire.

Finally we come to the great *Luttrell Psalter*, which should really be seen to be believed, that proudly states: 'Galfridus louterell me fieri fecit' (caused me to be made). The style is much the same throughout the book but the second and third hundred pages have much less decoration; the colours change to some extent and the ubiquitous monsters become larger, clumsier and more grotesque. The date is about 1340, and the Psalter has been much used for illustration of costume and social customs. Although the illuminations take us from Nebuchadnezzar to the martyrdom of Thomas à Becket, from the golden city of Constantinople to the Trinity, two types of illumination are outstanding in their vigour and profusion. Firstly, there are the monsters: the blue-tailed merman; the unicorn charging a crowned lion; the dragons; the obscene beasts. Secondly, there are the scenes dedicated to rural life, and these predominate. Admittedly, there are rather more kings and queens and fabulous beasts than an East Anglian peasant, or even a minor landlord, might hope to see in a lifetime but even in the religious element we find the predominant rural culture – for St. Francis preaches again to the birds.

The main colours used are blue, pink, mauve, orange, these being lined and dotted with white and gold. Later, we find green, much more orange, pale brown and pale blue.

We see the soil ploughed and harrowed; the corn harvested and stored, by small, stocky peasants. Away from the toil of the fields, they play musical instruments, wrestle or watch bear-baiting. The pages are bordered with oak and sycamore leaves. Horses (characteristically Suffolk Punch) and hens, sheep and swine appear, but also wild life: robin, bat, squirrel, Red Admiral butterfly, snails. People pick cherries; the windmill turns; fish-traps are sunk by the watermill; bees buzz round the hive.

There are passing strangers: female royalty in a travelling coach or a pilgrim with the badge of Santiago in Spain. Disaster strikes: horse violently throws rider; someone's blood is let; here is a greying corpse in its coffin. To console the living an archery contest is held or a spitted roast sizzles over the fire. We are absorbed into a lost world of realism and powerful imagination.

Four examples of decoration from the Gorleston Psalter, showing two half naked wrestlers; a slinger about to deal with a bird; a groteque bird with the head of a man; and a blacksmith shaping a horseshoe.
British Museum photo.

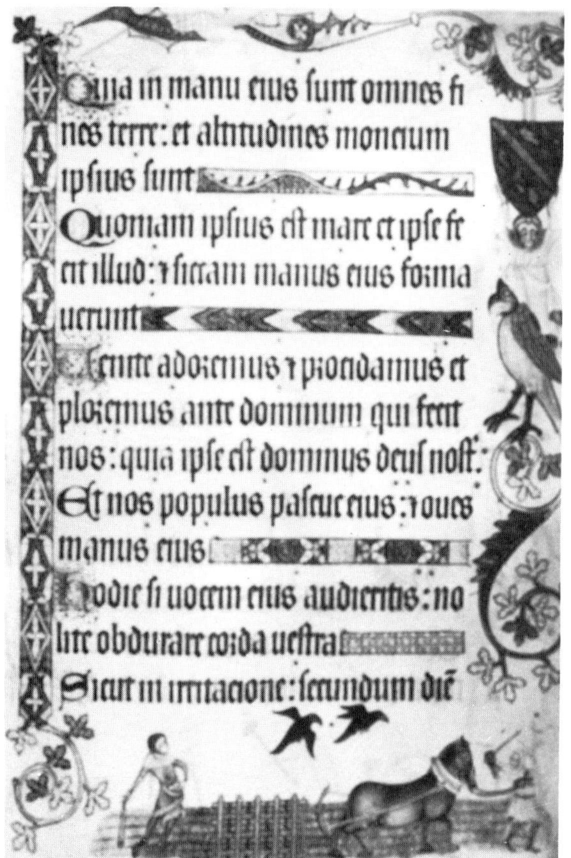

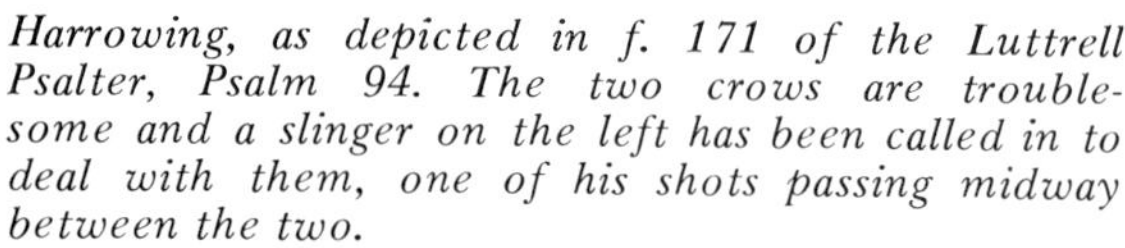

Harrowing, as depicted in f. 171 of the Luttrell Psalter, Psalm 94. The two crows are troublesome and a slinger on the left has been called in to deal with them, one of his shots passing midway between the two.
British Museum photo.

Illuminated letter from the Ranworth Sarum Antiphoner, 1400. Photo courtesy Rev. E.D. Everard.

The frontispiece of the Ormesby Psalter, depicting the Tree of Jesse. It dates from the opening years of the 14th century, though the kneeling ecclesiastics were added over text c. 1325.
Bodleian Library photo.

Fourteen Days by

These extracts from the diary of a 13 year old, written 130 years ago, are reproduced in their original spelling and punctuation. — M.W.

First Day — Wednesday, 30th August, 1865

Got up very early, and, after breakfast Mary Maltster fetched a cab which took us, one large box, one little box, one carpet bag, one railway rug and cloaks, some umbrellas, one handbag and Joey; to the Bishopgate Street Station for 3s. and 8d. — there, after a little delay, Mamma procured three 2nd class monthly return tickets for 'Dovercourt' 16s. apiece. We found a nice carriage, and in company with a widow and 4 men we drove to the junction where we changed for Harwich, and got into another train with a lady bound for the 'Cliff Hotel' Dovercourt.

She told us the charges there were very high. At our journey's end we got out; and having seen us Joey and luggage in the waiting room, Mamma left us to seek for lodgings. No easy task however, for after an hour's absence she returned with a doleful tale of the malhousing in the little unattractive town. Nearly all of the few unlet habitations being from 23s. to 26s. and 30s. a week the former, none of the best houses.

Mamma had seen a very nice two rooms in 26 Victoria Terrace, a Mrs. 'Young's', it was 23s. a week. Then, taking only Joey we salied forth and 'marched through the town' and up a road where we saw a cottage — owneress a 'Mrs. Inwards', who was eager to receive and attend us for 10s. a week, but the house was very odiferous and certainly a woman with 9 children, and 'a bad knee' however cheap was very unprepossessing so bidding her good-day we departed.

We went to the 'Cliff Hotel' but found the prices quite exorbitant, 2 guineas a week each for board only, and everything else extra, so we retraced our steps and feeling hungry, entered one of the eight or ten shops in the 'high street'.

the Seaside

by MAUD G. HOMER

An old man, rather deaf, and crossgrained pawed four buns (?) and gave them us to 2d. also a loaf 6½d. and we have futhermore a long roll of tallow meant for butter a 'pint' 1s 9d. We returned to Mrs. Young's (we had visited her opposite neighbour number 18 – previous to 'Mrs. Inwards' – her lodgings were not quite so nice but 20s. a week). Alas, hers were taken, so there was no alternative but to cross the road, and fairly establish ourselves at no. 18 which we did.

* * *

Friday, 1st September, 1865, our third day

Down at 7.40.

After breakfast we went to the beach and after paying five shillings for one dozen bathing tickets we secured a machine which was let down into the water and Mary (who was much better with no headache) and I had a regular good bathe. I was in 2 minutes. Mary tried to swim and float much to all our amusement.

We find the smells from the marshes very disagreable. Those closed our third day by the seaside.

* * *

Saturday, 2nd September, 1865

Everybody is social here the bathers speak, and smile to each other and warn one of the jelly fishes that Mary finds sting horribly.

The postman is a woman with a basket instead of bag. Had a very nice roast fowl for dinner, we got it at Watt's – 2s 9d. Afterwards we stayed in till after our shrimp tea and then strolled on the slopes and loosed our sea stock till supper time 8.30 when we eat a curlew 1s 3d. and so ended our 4th day by the seaside.

* * *

Sunday, 3rd September, 1865

Went to church at old Dovercourt where Mamma received the communion, we stayed in the church-yard. Received a letter from Miss S with other enclosed in it. In Dovercourt we fell in with a little girl who was the granddaughter of Dr. Coglan's Mrs. Johnson, so we went with her to the cottage and saw her mother and the remains of the 'fushia hedge'. After tea we walked to Harwich church where a lady and two dear little children invited us into her pew: the church was very full. We heard rather an emphatic discourse on Corinthians XV 52, 53, and 54 verses, from Mr. McDugel.

* * *

Monday, 4th September, 1865

Had a delicious bathe, tide coming in, afterwards went thro the Spa to the breakwater where we took a boat for an hour. The boatman was a very chatty fellow and spoke of the cattle plague and price of milk very sensibly.

* * *

Tuesday, 5th September, 1865

Waited a long time for a machine. Had a very good long bathe, although the tide had turned.

* * *

Wednesday, 6th September, 1865

Had a beautiful bathe, the best we've had. Went to the station and met Aunt Carry and Mr. Downs who engaged Mrs. Young's apartments, and dined with us, on roast meat and peaches. Joey laid on her lap and Mr. D... read the Times. O. I forgot to say that I rode a donkey who hurt Din's foot.

* * *

Saturday, 9th September, 1865

Arrived at Harwich a man acosted us with tickets for the 'Queen' the best boat on the river, he declared. Mr. D. . . wished to take them, but Mamma knew that the Stour, or Ipswich were the right boats, and we finally seated ourselves in the saloon cabin of the former. It was a very hot day, but the awning protected us from the sun. We passed the Queen it was brim full and not a nice boat. I did not feel at all well having suffered since Wednesday from staying in the sea too long that day.

We found the Orwell a little disappointment to us as the scenery was not so very lovely as it had been represented to us. When we got to Ipswich we steered to the old House and I felt 'so bad' that Mamma asked the other three to go on and stopped with me at a chemist's at the corner of Silent St., He gave me a delicious glass of pepiment and told us to come back if I was no better.

We went about the town which is a clean, well shopped one. We saw the old house and got a photo of it for Aunt Charlotte, and Aunt Carry gave us two pretty view pincushions. Opposite we got a vase (in lieu of one I broke) for Mrs. Cox. We walked about the town and up to the free Aboretum or pleasure ground where we found a seat and rested.

We found Mr. D. waiting to show us old Wolsey's gateway and to conduct us to the steamer landing place. There, we waited ever so long, and we wished to sit in an old man's cushioned boat till it came, but Aunt Carry feared the paddle wheels.

* * *

Sunday, 10th September, 1865

After tea we all went out and M read 'Juvinile tales' a book Mrs. Young lent us. We girls supped and went to bed which closed our 12th day by the seaside.

* * *

Tuesday, 12th September, 1865

After breakfast we set off for the bathing, but found the tide very low, and so walked thro' the blackberry lanes to Upper Dovercourt, and called at Mrs. Johnstones as we meant to. We sat there some time, and saw her 11th child, a baby of 8 week's old. She promised to send us down a basket of fruit and some fushias for Dr. C. . . in the evening.

When we came to the beach the tide was still low so I took off shoes and stockings and walked out into the sea. Then we took a machine and all 3 got in, it was just over our ankles, and so Din walked on her hands when suddenly, our mirth stopped, Mamma had lost her guard ring, and only just saved her wedding.

All the afternoon and up to 6 p.m. we searched the beach but in vain, the tide would not go out. Din offered 5s. and came in where we found Esther Johnstone with the fruit. Darkness finished our 14th night by the seaside.

IN A MANNER OF SPEAKING

by DENNIS HAZELL

Illustrated by A. Brown

EVEN though the old Suffolk countryman's knowledge of the world outside his own district was inevitably limited, this did not prevent him from applying his hard won knowledge of the practical side of life to good advantage. Slow of speech and movement he may well have been — but never slow of native wit.

The examples of home-spun proverbs which follow, and their likely interpretation, are a reminder of the pungent way the inhabitants of 'Silly Suffolk' of yesteryear gave voice to the truths of life in their own inimitable and colourful idiom. The old race of sons and daughters of Suffolk will soon all be 'sleeping abroad'. But the basic wisdom embodied in their quaint sayings will always be with us, imperishable as the soil which nurtured them.

'Whin yew lay a gowden egg, doon't cackle.'

(Don't boast about your good fortune.)

'Doon't be rude, give what corst narthin.'

(Be civil, it pays in the long run.)

'She's crab atoom and apple away.'

(Said of young 'mawthers' (teenage girls) who are unco-operative at home but show up to advantage in company.)

'Dawgs what'll fetch'll carry.'

(Beware of tittle-tattles; they will tell tales about you, as well as taking you into their confidence.)

'Doon't tairk more'n yew can carry, and if yew dow make tew journeys on it.'

(Know your capacity for alcohol; moderation in all things.)

'Money what go down the red lane is lorst for ever.'

(Drinking is a waste of 'spondooliks.' This applied specially to 'bought' beer in the days when there was 'hoom brewed' ale in most households.)

Times have . . . . Changed

'She's loike owd Jonathan's goose, never happy less she be where she bain't spoozed ter be.'

(Said of a meddler or poke-nose.)

'That family doon't brew no small beer.'

(They think a lot of 'theirselves'; an allusion to the weak beer which resulted from the third brewing. This was also known as 'arms and legs', that is it had no *body*.)

'Good ook boards'll last yew a loifetime.'

(A pertinent reminder of man's mortality.)

Corruptions and malapropisms, although not ranking as pure dialect, are very much a part of it. Unlike Mrs Malaprop's 'nice derangement of epitaphs', the corruptions and other verbal solecisms common in bygone Suffolk had little connection with social pretensions. Rather were they an unconscious reflection of rural isolation and the absence of educational opportunity.

Times have changed. The Suffolk Punch has been supplanted by the internal combusiton engine; 'muck' has been largely replaced by artificial fertilisers. The educational developments and social changes which have inevitably followed, and which themselves have helped to bring about even more radical changes in farming methods, have done much to eliminate the natural malapropisms formerly common parlance in Suffolk. Even so 'book learning' is not yet entirely respectable, with the result that certain distinctive corruptions and quaint words can still be heard in the speech of Suffolk people in diverse walks of life.

Thus a modicum of the untutored yet colourful speech of earlier generations lives on, not merely with 'th'owd codger and his missus', but often in the most unexpected quarters. Of course, the full-blooded colloquial manner of speaking is fast vanishing, yet most of the words which follow can still be heard in various parts of the county. They are a heartening reminder that the muted overtones of standard English still fall on some deaf Suffolk ears. Long may it be so.

Bronichal: Bronchial. Life in Suffolk would hardly be the same without the 'corfs' and 'tizzicks' caused by 'bronichal' disorders. (*Tizzick:* A dry, troublesome cough.)

Certified: Certificated. 'She've had a swelled hid (head) ever since har daughter wor certifoied.' (Said of a Suffolk mother who was over-proud of her 'skulema'am daughter.)

Christyanthems: Chrysanthemums.

Epidemic: Emetic. 'Oi give him an epidemic but Oi coon't make him gag (retch) nowhow.' (Said by a Suffolk mother whose young son had swallowed a piece of silver paper).

Exceptionable: Exceptional. Often used when referring to extremes of weather. It has also been known for Suffolk shopkeepers to display sale tickets offering 'Exceptionable Bargains'.

'Morfeydite: A corruption of 'hermaphrodite'. A 'crorss a-tween' a wagon and a tumbril made by joining two carts together. Hence it was 'noither one thing nor t'other'. (This word, like the unusual vehicle itself, is now almost obsolete. However, until quite recently a well preserved morfeydite could be seen standing in an agricultural contractor's yard at Farnham on the A.12)

Ought: Nought. 'Th'owd Town oonly drawed ought-ought, though they had three parts of the play.' ('Drawed' for 'drew' is still fairly common; as also is 'shew' (rhyming with 'hue') as the past tense of 'to show'.)

Obstropolous: Obstreperous; noisily resisting control. 'Owd Hinry git hully obstropolous when he've had more than he can howd.'

Plumpandikkalla: Perpendicular.

Reach: Retch. 'She felt that bad, poor little mawther, that she kep' a-reachin' all noight long.'

Shiver: A splinter. 'Oi've got a shiver in moi thumb and thass suffin' tender.' (Also used to denote a small slice or piece of food. But a 'shiver o' pork' is a joint of meat from the thick end of a fore hock.)

Susstifikit: Certificate. 'They rackon they're sploiced, but Oi doubt they hin't got noo sustifikit ter prove it.'

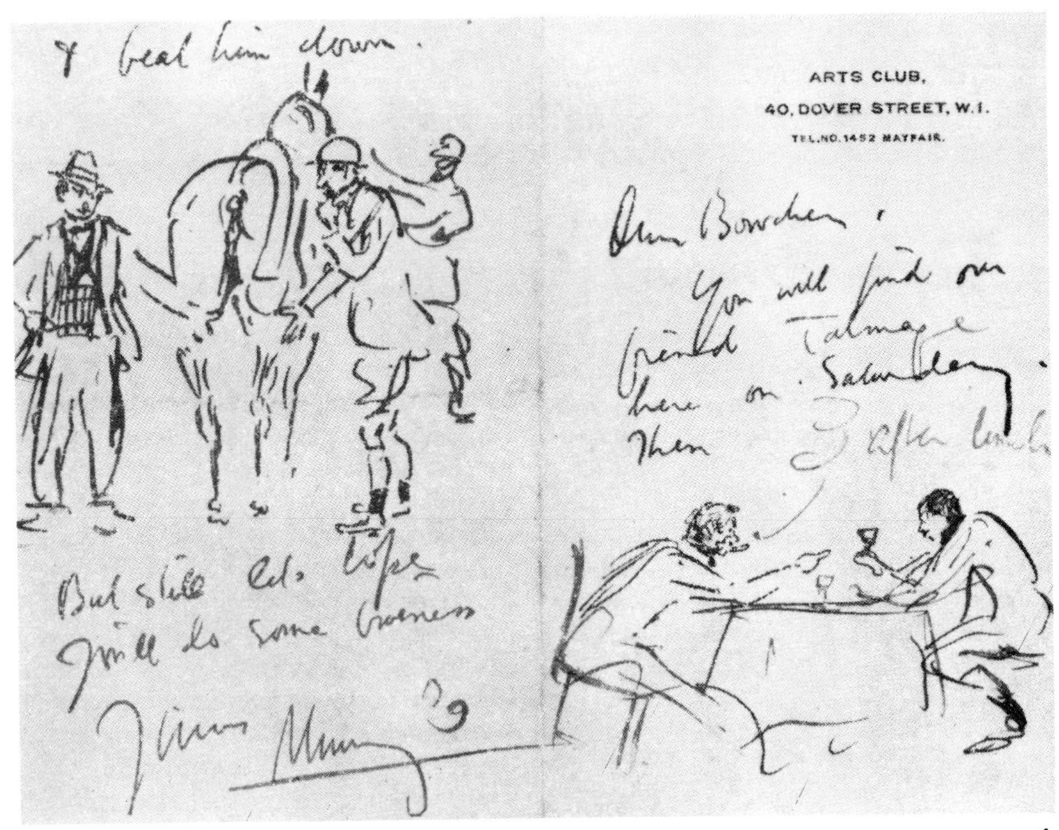
& beat him down.

But still [illegible]
you'll do some business

Yours A Munnings 29

ARTS CLUB,
40, DOVER STREET, W.1.
TEL.NO.1452 MAYFAIR.

Dear Bowcher,
You will find our
friend Talmage
here on Saturday.
Then after lunch

4 1

MUNNINGS AND BOWCHER

I enjoyed reading your article about the late Fred Bowcher (*EAM* February). He was one of the true characters of East Anglia. Perhaps your readers would be interested to see the enclosed letter written by Sir Alfred Munnings to Bowcher. It is an example of the bond of sheer *fun* which existed between the two men.—*Stanley Olsen*, *Orchard House*, *Hintlesham*, *Suffolk*..

2 3

you'll go to Hounslow
in the train

Then you'll be
shown the mare

After that you'll
be told the price
& then you'll try

The Future of our Churches

by WILHELMINE HARROD

THERE ARE 659 medieval churches in Norfolk – and that is not counting 245 substantial (and fascinating) ruins, a few good Georgian churches, and some Victorian ones, now being properly appreciated again. Of these medieval churches, 32 are within the city walls of Norwich. There had once been many more – folk-lore says there used to be a church for every Sunday in the year – 52 – and a pub for every day – 365. But both have dwindled now – and for the same reason. People moved out of the middle of Norwich. So the Norwich city churches became a problem; and Bishop Launcelot Fleming set up a commission under Lord Brooke of Cumnor to see what could be done about them. This commission published its report in January 1970. I shall never forget the shock and horror of those press headlines: 'OLD CITY'S TOO MANY PARISHES – 23 TO BE RE-ORGANISED INTO FOUR MAJOR PARISHES, 24 CHURCHES REDUNDANT'

All this was terrifying; and made more so by a study of the Pastoral Measure 1968. Under this act a church may not be left to moulder quietly – but one of three things must happen. *One* – it can be put to a suitable alternative use – *two* if, but only if, it is of *national* importance it can be handed over intact to the Redundant Churches Fund – and *three*, if those two schemes fail, it must be demolished. Several of the Norwich churches had alternative uses already – St. Peter Hungate is an ecclesiastical museum, St. Swithin's, St. Mary Coslany and St. Edmund's stores of various kinds, St. Simon and St. Jude a Scout headquarters. But this left at least 20 unwanted churches in the city, all of interest, all at least 500 years old, and all with their monuments, furnishings, wall-paintings and so on, inextricably bound up with the history and life of this fine city.

In 1970 these churches were in grave danger; many of them could, quite legally, have been pulled down to make car-parks or provide building land for offices, or just roundabouts for 'road-improvements'. So the Friends of the Norwich Churches was started

Vandalism at Corpusty. Photo: Roger Last.

Bircham Tofts. Closed since the war
Photo: Dominick Harrod.

and Sir John Betjeman, now Poet Laureate, came and made a splendid and much-quoted speech in the Assembly House. One way and another – the highest points were two auctions at the Easter Antiques Fair, and the premiere of the film *The Go-Between* attended by the Queen Mother – the Friends raised £10,000 in two years, and as the money rolled in it was immediately applied to first-aid work on the most needy churches. This had saved the fabric of some of them, but did not solve the problem of their future.

But now the whole situation has changed, and in October 1972 the Corporation of Norwich announced that it had set up, with the Friends, a Norwich Historic Churches Trust, to which the city has subscribed £50,000, spread over five years. By an enormously complicated legal process involving the Church Commissioners, the diocese hands over the freehold of these churches to the trust, which has undertaken to preserve them all. This is splendid, though the form this preservation will take is still problematical. But at any rate their physical presence is assured, and Norwich will not lose its most valuable asset and tourist attraction.

The rest of the 659 churches are scattered about the county and here the problem is different. As in the city, there have been population shifts, though these have worked both ways, and the 'dying villages'

Left: North Barningham, the Palgrave monuments. Church closed. Photo: Dominick Harrod.

St. Michael (Coslany), Oak Street, Norwich.

St. Michael at Plea, Queen Street, Norwich.

are filling up again, not just with holiday-makers nor even retired people, but with the many who have left the rat-race of the towns and want to lead the more civilized life of the villages, which often includes an interest in the parish church. We have in Norfolk the largest and best collection of medieval churches in England, larger even than Suffolk, and they, as much as the Broads or Yarmouth, are what bring the holiday-makers here.

Most of our churches are in good order though of course they all need money to keep them so, just like old, or even new, houses only on a bigger scale. But it is not lack of money which closes the churches and causes them to decay; money is always available from one source or another, though it may be hard work getting it. What is closing the churches is lack of interest; although they are endlessly visited by holiday-makers, Pevsner in hand, and by brass-rubbers, so that throughout the summer the naves and aisles are full of kneeling figures, when it comes to Matins or Evensong the congregation is often (though not always) thin, and the parson discouraged; then he feels that it is not his job to sweat away propping up a building which no one appears to want.

As a solution to this, parishes are 'grouped' and although in some cases every church in the group is

Barmer: Former parishioners and friends have raised the money to restore it. Photo: Dominick Harrod.

used in turn, in others one or two will be chosen and the others 'phased out'. Alternative uses are hard to find for remote country churches and the current suggestion of using them as houses may well fall foul of the Planners, as well as being repugnant to many people who feel that the sacred association of centuries should not give way to materialism.

In any case this sort of alternative use can preserve little except the landscape value of the church. Its contents, furniture, and monuments must go; and few people would like to eat their dinner under a stained glass portrayal of the Crucifixion. The interest and the atmosphere of the church must be totally lost.

Really the only way to preserve them is to use them for the purpose for which they were built, which is also the only one for which they are suitable. Obviously regular services are out, but an occasional one keeps the church alive, and what is more it keeps the vandals away; it is noticeable that as soon as a church is abandoned they move in.

In the city parish life hardly exists any more; in the country it is still there though it needs encouraging. The Norfolk Society (Norfolk branch of the Council for the Protection of Rural England) has formed a Country Churches Committee to help rural parishes to keep their churches *as churches;* they offer guidance through the legal tangles, practical help in raising money, manual labour in clearing churchyards and scrubbing church floors, and even money to prime the pump. They see the churches as England's greatest asset, spiritual as well as aesthetic, and they will work all out to keep them.

Right: The Norman door at Hales. The church was closed in 1971. Photo: John Piper

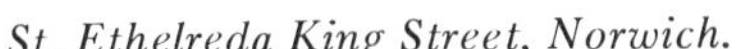

St. Ethelreda King Street, Norwich.

OPERA AT ALDEBURGH

by MARION HAREWOOD

Daughter of a distinguished musicologist, a concert pianist of rare talent, the moving light behind the Leeds Festival, Marion Harewood has been a close friend of Benjamin Britten for many years (he shared a London flat with her father towards the end of the war and he wrote a Wedding Anthem for her first marriage, to the Earl of Harewood, in 1949). She has been associated with the Aldeburgh Festival since its inception and is a council member of the recently formed Snape Maltings Foundation, whose aim is to develop the great potential that exists at this magnificent site.

She can, perhaps, lay claim to having suggested to Britten, during an Austrian skiing holiday in 1952, the idea of the composition of 'Gloriana'.

THE STORY OF opera at Aldeburgh is so closely linked with the story of the English Opera Group that perhaps something should first be said about the function and aims of this company. So exactly does it fit the scope and size of the festival that one might assume it to have been created especially to suit the festival's circumstances. But it is in fact the other way round: the group was formed two years before the festival, and it is almost true to say that Aldeburgh invented the festival to give the group a regular platform on which to work and perform.

In Red Square, Moscow, 1963. Left to right: Peter Pears, Galina Vishnevskaya, Mstislav Rostropovich, Benjamin Britten, Marion Harewood.
Photo: by courtesy of Aldeburgh Festival.

The story is also a personal one, for both the group and the festival were the brain-children of a small group of artists, the central figures in both instances being Benjamin Britten and Peter Pears. In 1945 immediately after the end of the war, Britten had an overwhelming success with his opera *Peter Grimes,* the story of which is actually set in Aldeburgh. The general operatic situation in London was only just beginning to take shape, and Britten soon realised that, whatever the future held for Sadlers Wells and Covent Garden, he would have to be independent and therefore need smaller, more flexible machinery for the kind of operas he had in mind to follow on the success of *Grimes.* Instead of writing another 'grand' type of opera he wanted to explore the medium of chamber opera. Whether this decision came from practical and financial considerations, or from an inner urge to find new forms for what he wanted to express, perhaps even he does not know exactly. But the moment seemed ripe for a small, mobile, economically viable opera company to be formed and in 1946 it gave the first performance of Britten's *Rape of Lucretia* at Glyndebourne.

When the association with Glyndebourne came to an end the following year, after the production there of *Albert Herring* the group was without a permanent base from which to operate. That summer of 1947 it toured in Holland and Switzerland, and it was during this journey that the idea of starting a festival in Aldeburgh came to the group's artistic directors, Benjamin Britten, Peter Pears and Eric Crozier. Eric Crozier writes in the introduction of the first year's Aldeburgh programme: 'During our stay in Lucerne we discussed this idea – analysed, criticised, objected, amplified – till it was agreed that if the stage of the Jubilee Hall proved large enough to accommodate a simple form of opera, we would try to plan a festival for 1948.'

The Jubilee Hall was indeed a very simple affair, hardly more than a village hall: a small stage, a strip of an orchestra pit, very basic lighting equipment, only two dressing rooms, an unraked auditorium. But local interest in the scheme was so encouraging that a committee was formed, the artistic direction of the festival was entrusted to the English Opera Group and plans went ahead for 1948. 'A modest Festival with a few concerts given by friends' was Peter Pears' description and these friends included Clifford Curzon, the Zorian String Quartet, Joan Cross, Nancy Evans. To raise the extra money needed to engage a chamber orchestra for the opera, Peter

Benjamin Britten conducting a Promenade Concert.

Benjamin Britten, left, leaving Orford Church. John Shirley Quirk walks beside him.
Photographs by courtesy of the Decca recording company.

Pears and Benjamin Britten gave a recital without fee in the Parish Church, and by June 7th *Albert Herring* had arrived in his native parts.

Frederick Ashton's brilliant production of this piece was fitted on to the tiny stage, John Piper's sets had successfully been adapted down to size, the orchestra somehow managed to avoid each other's bow arms and a first-class, highly polished performance conducted by the composer was presented. The humour of the libretto, its local character and the allusions to nearby place-names (for example during the search for Albert, 'They've been phoning around to Ufford and Orford, Iken and Snape', and Lady Billows' 'A detective inspector won't accept less, Dispatched by the Liverpool Street express') was not lost on the audience, nor on the performers, and the result was one of the funniest, most brilliant 'Comic Opera' performances I remember. The musical characterisation and acting of Joan Cross as Lady Billows, Peter Pears as Albert, Gladys Parr, Margaret Ritchie and Norman Lumsden will long remain prototypes of their kind.

Since this highly professional village hall beginning, opera at Aldeburgh has gone a very long way. The first steps were to improve the facilities at the Jubilee Hall, and after various minor adjustments the hall was drastically rebuilt in 1959. The stage and orchestra pit were enlarged, more adequate dressing room accommodation was added, the seating capacity of the auditorium was increased to about 300 and proper ventilation was put in. To celebrate the extension Benjamin Britten composed *A Midsummer Night's Dream;* it had its premiere in the 1960 Festival, and John Cranko who produced and John Piper who designed the sets made full use of the improved facilities.

However, there had been various plans afoot to build a special theatre for the festival for, whatever the possible improvements to the Jubilee Hall might be, the seating capacity could never be large enough to accommodate the growing demand of audiences. Not only was it unsatisfactory to turn people away, but economically so small a house could never be a paying proposition. In 1954 the festival even bought some land and plans were drawn up for a theatre to hold approximately 600 people. For various reasons this scheme could not be carried out, and the Jubilee Hall remained the centre of the festival's operatic activities.

When, however, some buildings in the disused maltings at Snape came up for sale in 1965, this seemed too good a chance to miss. Here at last was an opportunity to build, for a not impossible sum, a hall specially designed for the festival's purposes. In less than one year these buildings were converted into a concert hall holding 800 people. The provision of a good orchestra pit made open stage opera production possible, and the first of these was a most interesting performance of *A Midsummer Night's Dream* with sets, lighting and costumes, but no curtain.

The possibilities of this glorious new hall seemed endless, for not only was it acoustically a triumph, but the stage would obviously lend itself to many different uses. 1968 saw a performance of the Sadler's Wells production of *Gloriana,* and for 1969 a most exciting staging of Mozart's *Idomeneo,* conducted by Benjamin Britten, was planned. Everyone knows of the disaster which then struck: on the first day of the festival the roof and auditorium were completely destroyed by fire. This tragedy was at the same time the greatest challenge the festival had had to face, and emergency arrangements at once went into operation. It was an historic moment when, a few days later, the performance of *Idomemeo* took place in Blythburgh Church, on an improvised stage, the audience sitting on improvised seats and the orchestra squeezed into a part of the aisle. It was a great performance, and almost miraculously was repeated a year later in the rebuilt hall at Snape.

Since then, Britten's *The Rape of Lucretia* and *The Turn of the Screw* have been performed at Snape, and a spectacular production of Purcell's *King Arthur* had its successful premiere in 1971. The hall has been put to use outside the festival season, and in the last three years there have been performances of opera in the summer months. Apart from being used for recording purposes, it has also been turned into a television studio – the television performances of *Peter Grimes* and *Owen Wingrave* were rehearsed and filmed there.

Not only has opera at the Maltings now become

The Maltings, Snape. Photo by Flt./Lt. Michael Marson, M.O.D. (Air Force Department) Crown Copyright reserved.

Rehersal of The Burning Fiery Furnace.

very much part of the East Anglian scene, but opera at the Jubilee Hall and at Orford Church continues to thrive. Many operas by young as well as established English composers have had their first performances at the Jubilee Hall. The most recent was last year's premiere of John Gardner's *The Visitors*, and the list includes work by Arthur Oldham, Gordon Crosse, Harrison Birtwistle, Malcolm Williamson, Lennox Berkeley and William Walton. Since 1948, 21 new English operas have been given at the festival and there have been productions of 10 other operas ranging from Monteverdi to Poulenc.

There is no other festival which has regularly provided a platform for so much new material, which has encouraged British composers to write new operas and has given native artists the opportunity to work and perform under the most favourable conditions. Britten's own output would never have been so prolific without the possibility of long periods of planning and preparation and of close association with producers, singers and designers which the unrushed atmosphere of Aldeburgh affords.

In fact there are five pieces which almost certainly would not have been written without the inspiration of the particular character of the Festival — the two Children's Operas and the three Church Operas. *Let's make an Opera* is, like *Albert Herring*, set in Suffolk and full of local allusions. The audience songs, rehearsed in the first part and sung by the audience during the actual opera of *The Little Sweep* in act two could only have been written for the special intimate atmosphere of the Jubilee Hall.

The other four operas — *Noye's Fludde* and the Church Operas proper, *Curlew River, The Burning Fiery Furnace* and *The Prodigal Son* — were, on the other hand, conceived to be performed in church. Again one wonders whether Britten would ever have evolved this completely new style of church opera if he had not been forced, through lack of space at the Jubilee Hall, to make frequent use of the local churches for concerts. The shape of Orford Church particularly seemed to lend itself remarkably well for mounting platforms to form a stage, still leaving enough room in the width of the aisle to seat a large orchestra. *Noye's Fludde* employs large forces of children both in the orchestra and in the chorus, the audience or congregation joins in the hymns, and I think it can be claimed that Orford Church inspired the conception of this remarkable, movingly innocent and gay opera for children.

The list of artists who have over the years taken part is equally impressive. The festival and the English Opera Group have made full use of all the best talent available in this country and have given opportunities to many young and less experienced performers. It is not uninteresting to recall, for example, that Janet Baker's first professional appearance on the operatic stage was as Dido in 1962, and that she and Heather Harper were respectively Polly and Lucy in *The Beggar's Opera* the following year. It is impossible to give a complete catalogue of all the many distinguished names, but it is nice to note that Frederick Ashton, himself a native of these parts, will return to the festival to participate in the production of *Death in Venice*, which will have its premiere this June.

The strong musical personality of the festival's artistic direction continues to exert its influence and is an inspiration to all who work at Aldeburgh. Britten has created an English style of writing and performing opera, and through his personal involvement with other artists he has laid the basis of a native operative tradition. Without Aldeburgh and its festival this would not have been possible.

God, the Queen & Mr. Smith

'Mr. Smith,' she say, 'do you pray about your ploughs?'

This unusual story was sent by Mr. Bernard Goodall. He writes: "This somewhat weather-beaten typescript was discovered amongst literary remains of my father, Mr. John Goodall. I believe it was conveyed to my father by Lady Helen Ramsey, from whom he used to receive communications in my remote youth."

MR. SMITH OF DICKLEBOROUGH, in the county of Norfolk, was a simple-minded, earnest Christian who lived through those glorious times for the British farmers when Napoleon turned all Europe into a vast battlefield, and wheat was selling at from 15 to 20 shillings per bushel. He was a genius, too, in his way, and invented a plough which was a great improvement on the cumbrous implement then in use.

His invention came under the notice of Prince Albert, who took great interest in agriculture and sent for him to explain certain matters connected with this plough. The old farmer accordingly journeyed to Windsor, no light undertaking in days when the railway had not altogether supplanted the post-chaise, the stage-coach and the carrier's cart.

He reached Windsor in the twilight of a summer's evening and reported himself at the Castle. A gentleman of the household came to him and told him he would have to present himself at 10 o'clock the following morning. 'Yes, that's all right,' said the farmer, 'but what am I to do for a bed?'

'A bed? A bed?' said the colonel. 'You had better go to an inn,' and he mentioned one where he would be made comfortable for the night; but Mr. Smith did not take kindly to the suggestion.

'Wul, there now, Cunnel,' he said, 'that deu seem mighty quare, that raly due. Go to an inn – that very ill-convenient and costyve (costly) place? I didn't come here 'cause I want to come, I come 'cause you axed me, and I had to come, and the laste you can deu is to give me a bed. If you was to come to Dickleborough, my missus she'd find you a bed. I know right well she would, especially if we had axed you to come; and if you was hungry as I be, I warrant she'd find you suffen to eat in the bargain.'

Old Smith said this in his pleasant way, and the colonel was taken by storm. He brought him up to his own room, had a good supper put before him, and gave orders for his accommodation for the night. The two spent a very pleasant evening together. As Mr. Smith reported it, 'Then the Cunnel, he say, "I'll ring for your candle, Mr. Smith, and the man he'll show you to your room." "Thank'ee, Cunnel," I replied, "but there's one thing I always deu afore going' to bed – I have family prayer. I know my missus is having it at Dickleborough, and it won't do for her master not to have it because he happens to be away from home. Will you let's have your Bible, if you please?"

Mr. Smith speaks with the royal children.

'The Cunnel, he say, "Oh, certainly, Mr. Smith," and he put it on the table, and I say to him, "Well now, will you rade and I pray, or shall I rade and you pray?" He made answer and say, "I think I had better do the reading, Mr. Smith"; so he read a psalm, he did, a buttiful psalm it was, tew, but one of the shortest in the book; and arter he'd done it we knelt down and I prayed, and I axed the Lord to bless him and the Queen and the Prince and the dear babes.

'He took the candle that was browt, an' he show me to my bedroom his own self; a rare good grip he gave my hand when he bid me good-night at the door.

'Well, in the morning I had a rare good breakfast, and at 10 o'clock I was took to see the Prince. He shook hands with me quite friendly, and he got a-talking about my plough, and I show him how it worked. Arter we had bin a-talking for a bit the door opened and a big man with his head powdered and a uniform on, he says, "Her Majesty!" in a loud voice, and out came the Queen. When I saw her I was right stammed (astounded). I thought she'd have a goold crown on her head, and a goold sceptre in her hand, and her gownd all a-trailing behind, same as we see her in the picters. But there she was, just a plain, simple woman with a kind look on her face.

'She spoke to me quiet and friendly like, and she was very glad to see me, and what a long way I had come to show them my plough. She hadn't spoke them words afore I was no more afrad of her than I am of my neighbours' wives, not half so much as I am o' some on 'em. She was just as simple and kind as if she warn't no more nor nobody. There wasn't no mucky pride about her, but when I had to speak to her I let her see I respected her. She saw right well, she did, that John Smith of Dickleborough wasn't the man to take no liberty because she was kind to him.

'Well, we had a rare pleasant talk arter we'd done with the plough. The Queen asked me a lot of questions about the farmers in our parts, and the poor folk what wages they got, were their cottages comfortable, did they go to church reg'lar, and all manners o' that, and I told her the best I could. Bye and bye I began to get a bit onasy.

' "Smith boy," I say to myself, "you're broght before kings and princes, and you must testify." I said, "I ool (will)," and I looked to the Lord for an opening, and it warn't long afore it came. The Queen say to me, "Mr. Smith," she say, "however did you come to think o' this clever invention o' yourn?" "Well, your Majesty, mum," says I, "I had that in my head a sight o' days afore that come straight – I see what was wanted plain enough, but I couldn't make out how to get at it. I thought and I thought and I better thought, but that did not come clear no-how. So at last I made it a matter o' prayer, and one morning that came into my mind like a flash, just what you see in that there model."

' "Why, Mr. Smith," she say, "do you pray about your ploughs?" "Whu, there now, your Majesty, mum," says I, "why shouldn't I? My Father in heaven, He know'd I was in trouble about that plough, and why shouldn't I go and tell Him? I mind o' my boy Tom – he's a fine big man now, keeping company along o' my neighbour's datter, he is, and a rare good gal I know she to be – but when he was a tiny mite o' boy, I bowt him a whip and rarely pleased he was with that.

' "Well, he came to me cryin' as if he little heart was bruk. He'd bruk that whip, he had, and he came to me with it. Well, now, your Majesty, mum, that whip warn't nithin' to me, that only cost 1s 6d. when 'twas new, but it was suffen to see the tears a-runnin' down my boy's cheeks, so I took him on my knee and I comforted him. 'Why, don't cry, Tom my boy,' says I, 'I'll mend that whip, I ooll, so that'll crack as loud as ever, and I'll buy you a new one next market day.'

' "Well, now, your Majesty, mum," says I "don't you think our Father in heaven, He cares as much as I care for my boy Tommie? My plough warn't of much consekence to Him, but I know right well my trouble was."

'Would you believe when I'd said that, the Prince he tarns, and he wiped his nose with his pocket handkercher, and the Queen she had tears in her eyes and I see one on 'em rolling down her cheek.

"You're a good man, Mr. Smith," she say, "I'm glad to have such subjects as you." Them were her very words; I'm proud on 'em. I have told my son Tom he's never to forget 'em, and he's to tache 'em to his children, if so be God give him a family.

'When the Queen say them words to me, I say to her, "Your Majesty, mum," I say to her, "I ain't got nothing good about me but what comes from

God." "No more ain't none of us, Mr. Smith," says the Queen. The Prince he joined in, and we had a rare good talk. 'Twas for all the world like a band meetin'. Folks may say what they like, but it ain't no use o' them sayin' to John Smith of Dickleborough; he knows and he says to all the world Queen Victoria is a right good godly woman, and Prince Albert he's another – leastways – well, you know what I mean.

'It was getting well on noon by this time, and the Queen at last she say to me, "Mr. Smith," she say, "you will find lunch provided for you, and the man who waits upon you will take you over the Castle if you wish. There are some fine paintings and other things you might like to see." "Well, your Majesty, mum," say I, "I ain't much of a judge of picters, but there is one thing I should raly like to see." "What is that, Mr. Smith?" she say. "If I might see the dear babes." The Queen she laughed and she looked right tickled, and she say they out a-walking in the park and someone should go with me and show me the way. So she bid me good-bye, and so did the Prince; and a man came and took me away.'

Mr. Smith was taken to the park, and there met the royal children. His conductor said something to the lady in charge of them, doubtless telling her of Her Majesty's commands. The good old man talked to the children in his kindly way for a few minutes, then he took off his wide-brimmed hat, and standing bare-headed in the sun, he prayed that the blessing of God might rest upon them and abide with them. Then he turned his face homeward and back to the simple everyday life of a Norfolk farmer.

Not long after, he received a box which was brought from London by the carrier, and in it he found a most beautiful 'family Bible' with a note explaining it was a present from the Queen and Prince Albert. Mr. Smith carefully packed it up again, and returned it with a letter to the Queen, asking her if she would be so good as to put her name in it. The bible came back in due time, with the autograph signature, not of Her Majesty only, but of the Prince also, and all of the children – even the baby's little hand had been guided to write his own name. Under the signatures the Queen had written with her own hand, 'A memento of the visit of a good man.'

Drawing by Albert Ribbans, Thaxted, Essex.

by J. J. Maling

illustrations by Zelma Blakeley

I Remember The Example

EVERY TOWN which calls itself a town needs a shocking example; and in the 1920s we had one in Diss — Bob Stevens.

'If you don' wash your neck . . .'

'If you don't do your homework . . .'

'If you don't go straight down to Easto's for the fish and chips without dawdling. . .'

The chorus was always the same. 'You'll end up like Bob Stevens.'

A mile or so up the Heywood Road there was a meadow on the banks of a little stream, a place much frequented by gatherers of primroses and cowslips and bulldaisies in their various seasons, a place where mavises sang in the hawthorns and the long grass was full of skylarks and partridges.

In the corner of the field stood a black barn and it was there, they said, that Bob Stevens slept.

Some of the boys were afraid of him and, if the black barn had been the notorious red barn, they couldn't have looked at it with greater awe.

I could never see much harm in the man. He was quite young, a ragged figure in an old army overcoat and a battered pointed hat, dirty and stained, but with a jaunty pheasant's tail feather stuck in it. He made his living by begging round the town; and it was certainly true that he often swore at those children who shouted insults at him. Perhaps he was justified in doing so.

Yes, Bob Stevens was our horrible example and hardly a day passed during which our sins were not likely to land us up in the same boat as Bob.

There could have been worse fates, I thought. Bob never seemed to go hungry and he never did any work. I wish he'd taken me on as an apprentice.

It was often said that he was the son of a well-known local business man who was supposed to have thrown him out for some unspecified misconduct, unspecified to us at least. Our elders discussed the matter with many winks, nods and shushes-the-child-will-hears.

So perhaps Bob Stevens could have been rich if he had wished. If that was true, it only made him the more romantic. We admired and envied him for his carefree life.

Bob never swore at me. Once or twice I stole bits of bread and cheese out of the pantry and gave them to him. He always accepted politely but I had the feeling he was accustomed to better fare and that, if he could have declined my offerings without hurting my feelings, he would have done so.

So for several years of my childhood Bob Stevens slouched round the town, always happy at least to outward appearances, always dirty, always ragged; and even if he did sleep in a barn up The Heywood, it didn't seem to do him any harm.

One day we heard that Bob had been found dead in a ditch. What a day that was for our parents!

The coroner made a little speech in which he said all the right things and drew all the right morals and what-did-we-tell-yous flew thick and fast.

And somewhere, no doubt, Bob was thumbing his nose at the lot of them. But not, I think, at me.

In a strange kind of way we understood one another.

ROAD TO NOWHERE

by JAMES WENTWORTH DAY

OLD NANNY HOWLETT, who lived in a tiny, thatched cottage with walls of clunch and wattle-and-daub at Wicken Lode on the edge of the old, undrained, mysterious fen, where night-winds ran like mice through the reeds and the bittern boomed his ghostly love-song under the stars of spring, looked like a kindly witch. She was, in fact, a wise old woman. When I lay sick and 10 years old, under the whitewashed, wavy ceiling of my bedroom, shuddering with whooping-cough, Nanny produced, on a plate, a tiny, golden-brown object, sizzling from the oven. It looked like a minute suckling-pig.

'Do you walk that down on ye,' she commanded. 'That'll cure ye. That's a roosted meece.'

The thought of eating a roasted harvest mouse was heavenly. Down went the exciting morsel. I am not sure that it was not followed by another one the next day, in response to clamour for more mice. In any case, the whooping-cough went.

For that matter, if the wise woman tied horsehair round warts and then anointed them with seven drops of blood from the snout of a fresh-killed mole, they went too.

Another witch of a very different character lived under a hood of thatch in that tiny hamlet of ancient cottages, crouching among their hollyhocks and willows at the head of that old shining waterway, Wicken Lode, where barges, pulled by donkeys harnessed to long dripping ropes, unloaded their towering grey-black cargoes of turf cut from the peat-diggings on Adventurer's Fen. The old turf sheds, where Mark Bailey, old Norman and John Butcher, the turf merchants, stored their pre-historic stocks of cottage fuel, stood, weather-boarded, tarred and thatched until a few years ago. Then fire destroyed one of the last monuments of the workaday life of the now-vanished turf-diggings of Burwell Fen.

Just below the turf sheds, beyond the little dyke choked with reeds and water-lilies, where my father kept his floating live-bait box, there stretch the Ten Acres. A triangle of soggy peat, dense sedge and innumerable deep little death-traps of pools. It is part of the Poor's Fen of Wicken, still parish property but now included in the Wicken Fen Nature Reserve.

The poor of Wicken have held the right, for centuries, to dig turf and cut sedge on the Ten Acres on a certain day in the year. The first man on the spot naturally claimed an undug area of turf or the best growth of sedge. As soon as light dawned you would hear the ring of the stone on the scythe blade of Bob ('Fal-Lal') Simpkin, long, rangy and bushy-browed. He usually beat the rest of them to it by a short head.

So when, in the last century, Tom Dennis, a farmer who held the 500 acres of Spinney Abbey

Illustrations by Jennifer Kent

from our great-aunt, sent his men down to dig turf and cut sedge on the Ten Acres, he broke not only the law of the land, the custom of the village and the canons of decency, but he broke also the future of his own family. For the witch of Wicken Lode issued in wrath from her cottage door between the hollyhocks and laid a curse upon it.

'That curse shall lay on you, Tom Dennis,' she screamed from beneath her sun bonnet, 'and on your childer that come arter you.' And, says village legend, it did. Tom Dennis did not prosper. His children were born deaf and dumb. Tom Money still tells the tale.

A much more recent witch was Old Mother Redcap from Horseheath, in Cambridgeshire, who died in 1926. Many local people went to her to be cured or be given charms. It was said that, when young, a 'tall black man' called on her. After he had talked to her, she signed a paper and he promised to send her five imps who would perform anything she asked them to do. The tall black man, it was whispered, was the Devil. At any rate, Mother Redcap was seen soon afterwards walking down a lane followed by a cat, a ferret, a mouse, a rat and a toad.

Tom Money, now 83 or more, has worked all his life for the Fullers of Spinney Abbey. The Fullers, who have been in the parish for more than 300 years, have lived at Spinney and at Field Farm on the by-road to Upware for the last 80 years or so. They own and farm a good deal of land. Hard-headed, practical fen farmers, with down-to-earth values and a great love of the land. Yet they are the last to disbelieve the local stories of hauntings in the abbey – where members of the family have heard inexplicable noises over the years.

Now at that end of the parish an old green Roman road known as Fodder Fen Drove runs from High Fen Farm, which 80 years ago belonged to my grandfather, Luke Staples, to Upware on the Cam. From his day to this, Fodder Fen Drove has had the reputation of being a queer place after dark. There were childhood stories in the village of the coach and headless horses which were seen at night in Red Barn Lane but not in Fodder Fen Drove. The latter had an intangible haunting. Something odd but no one knew what it was. For that reason few villagers went there after dark except the hardy poacher with his gun.

Upware, where the Drove terminated, is a tiny riverside hamlet with the faint remains of a Roman Villa in front of the school-house – inexcusably destroyed and ploughed over a few years ago. Nearby, on the river bank, can still be seen the last crumbling brickwork of a Roman landing-stage. This may well have been used for the unloading of stone brought from the village of Reach by barge down Reach Lode, a Roman waterway, to Upware where it would be trans-shipped and taken either to Cambridge or Ely.

Be that as it may, during the 1920's two Cambridge undergraduates, Lord Cawdor and Tom Lethbridge – now the eminent antiquary – were said to have unearthed the complete skeleton of a Roman soldier which they found buried a few feet below the surface on the edge of the Drove where it skirts the deep Fodder Fen Pits, now a jungle of reeds, water and trees. One heard at the time that they had bundled the bones into a sack and bicycled all the way to Cambridge with them, about 17 miles, including some appalling rough-riding over a black, peaty, rutted cart-track from Upware Ferry to

Waterbeach Road. Their find was hailed by the fenmen as proof positive of the fact that Foddler Fen Drove had long been haunted by the ghost of 'an owd Rooman sojer'.

Some years afterwards, another skeleton of far more recent date was dug up when a new pit was excavated less than half a mile from High Fen Farm to provide ballast for the embankment which carried the new road over the 'washes' of the Cam to the new bridge which connects Wicken with Stretham and the main Cambridge-Ely road. Before this bridge was built Wicken was virtually at the end of nowhere. There was one road into the village and that was the only way out of it. It was an island, or rather the end of a peninsula, surrounded on the one side by wild undrained fens and on the other by the wind-swept dry beds of Soham Mere and Burwell Broads. Fodder Fen Drove was, and still is, the Road-to-Nowhere in the loneliest part of the parish.

That was why, for centuries, the gypsies, the genuine East Anglian Romanies whom Borrow loved and Munnings painted, came every winter to pitch their great hooped tents on the grassy Drove between tall hedges which sheltered them from the sharp wind off the fens. As a boy I visited their camp and had my first – and last – taste of roast hedgehog. Very like chicken.

The gypsies had been long accepted by the parish. My uncle and grandfather gave them freedom to camp provided there was no poaching. Dead piglets thrown out in the muck-heaps and dead calves were their perquisites. You might be sure that their rough-haired lurcher dogs snapped up a hare or two. On the whole they were a well-behaved race, with a cheerful sense of humour.

Then came the night, perhaps 20 years before the bridge was built, when a fen farmer, living in the little one-storey riverside farm house known as Dimmock's Cote on the opposite side of the river heard the most appalling row. Shouting men and screaming women rent the night silence. A first-class fight was on among the gypsies. It culminated with a long shuddering scream as a man being murdered.

The farmer set off at the crack of dawn to fetch a policeman from some miles away. When they arrived at the gypsy camp, tents, caravans, horses, men, women and children had vanished. They had packed up in the dark hours and gone before the first streak of dawn lit the wide fen skies. They never came back.

Twenty years or more later the new bridge was built. The new road to it cuts straight across Fodder Fen Drove. A great pit was excavated by the side of the Drove. There they found the skeleton. No one has ever identified it.

Now comes the sequel. In 1966 I was shooting with my friend Frank Fuller of Field Farm, who also owns Westmere Farm and lands which border Fodder Fen Drove. Tom Fuller of Spinney Abbey and his two sons were with us.

We reached Fodder Fen Drove in the dusk, to wait for duck flighting in on the flooded 'washes' of the river. As we stood in the half-light on the glimmering grass of that old silent road of mystery, Frank Fuller said to me: 'I never told you, Wentworth, about the funny thing that happened here a year or two back when we came through the hedge on to this old Drove after shooting, just as we've done now. We were walking along the Drove, Tom and myself and the two boys and our retrievers, when suddenly the dogs all bristled up. They snarled and growled and advanced in that creepy sort of way when they are about to spring at someone.

Then to our absolute astonishment the three dogs all sprang up and attacked a man! They went for him tooth and nail, springing up again and again, growling and biting. *But there was no man!* And it's not the first time it's happened. Ask the boys.'

Fodder Fen Drove keeps its secret.

Drawing by Albert Ribbans

A Medieval Immigration Problem

by H.O. MANFIELD

Norwich Bailiff's Seal
(Courtesy of Norwich City Museum)

WHILE POLITICIANS WRANGLE over our modern immigration problems it seems only fair that the individual should be able to air his own prejudices, his fears and heartbreaks, when an alien people appears on his very doorstep. Is he correct in his conviction that the leaders of policy do not understand his personal problems, do not see his dilemmas and perplexities? Has the alien always been regarded with suspicion?

Perhaps it is hard for us in the east of England to answer these questions. The problem is not an immediate one for us; we are able to take an academic view of events that in other parts are at the moment cutting into the roots of social life. Yet in the past Norwich has had more than its fair share of immigration. Apart from the great migrational waves of Saxon, Dane and Norman that, intermingling, made today's East Anglian what he is, there have been others whose impact on the community has at times outlasted its temporal memorials.

One in particular, bearing something of the stamp of our present day problem, was that of the medieval Jews. Just as the initial flow of Commonwealth immigrants to Britain has been in the main government sponsored, so too, the influx of Jews after the Conquest was the direct result of William of Normandy's own planning.

He was poor, he was ambitious and above all far-sighted. His invasion was a commercial enterprise on a large scale and for it he needed money; so he turned to the Jews. Immediately following his success, his rewards were naturally in land and we know he granted the Manor of Herringfleet to a Jew, Renaldus Aurifaber, who had lent him great quantities of gold to further the expedition.

Some scholars maintain there is no evidence that Renaldus Aurifaber was a Jew and they can give several good reasons for thinking that he was not one; but men such as Renaldus were the proud spearhead. Where the great first trod, others later planted their more humble footmarks. Norwich was to wait for the years between 1100 and 1140 before it was to have a ghetto of its own.

That first Jewish settlement was where Littlewood's Supermarket stands today. A more wealthy

The martyrdom of St. William.

Photos courtesy of The Colman and Rye Libraries of Local History.

Isaac's Hall, or the Music House, Norwich, built by the first Jurnet.

member of the group, one Abraham, had his hall on the site of Peter Robinson's store.

It was not long before the citizens began to take exception to these strangers with their peculiar customs, outlandish speech and distinguishing dress. But action revealed that they had a mighty hard nut to crack for these Jews were not citizens; they were the 'King's Jews' and the King's Sheriff in his castle just above their ghetto was responsible to the King for their safety. In his archives at Westminster the King held an inventory of the wealth, possessions and transactions of every Jew. Often the wealth of the country was in their hands for only they, under Christian law, could manipulate money for interest.

This was put to the proof in 1140 when the Norwich Jews were accused of ritually slaughtering a boy – later to become little St. William – on Mousehold. The Prior of the Benedictines issued a warrant. The Sherrif rejected it. The Prior again served the summons at which the Sheriff in a rage gathered his Jews together and took them to the monastry. After a day of legal wrangling he took them back to the castle and kept them there until danger had passed.

Two years later Sir Simon de Novers, one of the Prior's knights, slew a man called Deusadjuvent ('God help him'). His name is also given as Eleazar, which is the possible rendering in Hebrew. Sir Simon may have borrowed money off the Jew and felt this to be a way of clearing the debt but it was not overlooked by the King. Thereon for 40 years the Norwich ghetto prospered and the Jews owned quite a considerable amount of land in the city. But in 1190 some Crusading knights awaiting embarkation attacked the ghetto and murdered every Jew found therein. Luckily some had been warned and had escaped to the castle.

Following that event Norwich Jewry shrank to fewer than a hundred. It was, of course, the humbler Jew that had suffered. The wealthy had seldom lived in the ghetto and of them, particularly of the Jurnet family, we possess plenty of evidence of all five generations. The first Jurnet built possibly the only stone house in Norwich other than the Cathedral and the Castle. And the Prior's masons helped in the building because they left their marks on the stone of the crypt.

The last Lord Mancroft reckoned Isaac, the second Jurnet, was so favoured because, though forbidden to trade, his skill in cutting lenses made him useful to the monastery where short-sightedness could be a drawback.

Legend has it that the first Jurnet had the temerity to marry a Christian heiress and that the fine for this sin was 6000 marks, paid by the Jewry of all England. Modern scholarship has disproved the legend – but not the feeling that lay behind it.

There is no record of Losinga's borrowing money to build the Cathedral but the Jurnets certainly lent money to the church. Bury St. Edmunds Abbey was in debt to the tune of £1200 and we are told that the interest charged was 2d. per £ per week. Granted, a high rate but the Jew seldom got his capital back in full, sometimes not at all.

By the mid 13th century the safety of the Jews was becoming tenuous, for the King's cloak no longer adequately covered them and the claws of the Church hovered close. Their religion and way of life remained bars to any assimilation into the community. Within a hundred years acceptance of their presence under duress turned into active hatred. Their wealth and ostentatious bearing were no help in a city where many lived in squalor. The situation became inflammable and was only waiting the match.

Edward's *Statutum de Judaismo* of 1275 forbad the Jews to lend money at interest. It made real the wail of Shylock that 'you take my life when you do take the means whereby I live'. In 1290 a mere handful of Jews were expelled from England and their descendants were not to return for 350 years. They went with what property they could carry and what they left behind was the King's. In Norwich a deed of 1292 records how Peter de Bumstede built a house and solar on land 'acquired of the Lord King' which once belonged to Elyas the Jew. So ended a medieval immigration problem.

THE SUFFOLK BIBLE—CHRISTMAS

BY F. ROBINS

St. Luke and St. Matthew

GOD, 'E SAID t' one 'f 'Is angels, Gabriel, 'is name wuz, 'Oi want yew t' goo down t' Naz'reth,' 'E say, 'Oi want yew t' goo 'n tell 'at noice little owd mawther, Mary, 'at Oi want har t' be th' mother a moi Son.'

Gabriel, 'e did what 'e wuz towd, an' 'e fetched up at Naz'reth an' went an' towd Mary what God 'd said. Mary wuz whully s'prised! 'Whoi,' she say, 'how c'n Oi hev a son when Oi een't even married t' Joseph yit?' (Joseph wuz har fiancy y'see). 'Don't yew worrit,' Gabriel say, 'this on't be no ornary babe, this babe 'll be th' Son a God. God c'n dew anythin', yew wait 'n see.' Then orf 'e went.

Mary wuz still reg'lar dawzled, an' she thought she'd goo 'n see har cousin, 'Lis'beth who wuz hevin' a babe tew. When she come in, 'at babe a 'Lis'beth's jumped insoide 'er, an' 'Lis'beth say 'Ass fer sartin yew fare t' be a woman blessed boi the Lord.' An' Mary, she jest got down an' prayed, she wuz s' happy. Free munce Mary stayed with 'Lis'beth, 'en she went hoom, an' soon arter, 'Lis'beth had a little owd booey an' called 'im John.

One day, owd Caesar, he say 'at ivryone gotta be taxed — even in them days — Joseph, he hatta goo t' Bethlehem t' pay, an' 'e took Mary with 'im although she han't got long t' goo afore har toime. Wal, there wuz s' many fooks in Bethlehem there worn't no place fer 'em t' stay, so they hatta sleep in th' stable at th' inn with all th' animals. Blow me if she din't goo 'n hev har little owd babe 'at noight, an' 'e han't got no crib, so she put 'im in th' manger.

In th' filds cloose boi, a lot a sheppuds wuz a-lookin' arter th' sheep, when all 'f a sudden, a whul hoost a angels lit up th' skoi. Por owd sheppuds han't niver seed th' loike afore! Scared 'em t' dead 'at did! 'En one 'f th' angels, 'e say, 'Don't yew be frit t'gither, we come t' tell ya suffen marv'llous. Down in Bethlehem's jest bin born a little owd booey who's goona be th' Saviour 'f th' whul world. 'E's th' Son a God, 'E is, an' 'E's down there a-lyin' in a manger.' 'En they all sung a hymn an' flew 'way. Them sheppuds 'd bin knocked alluva heap, an' when they come tew a bit, they thought they'd better goo an' see this 'ere 'mazin' babe, an' they went an' found 'Im, an' they jest *knowed* 'E wuz th' Son a God, an' went an' towd a lot a other fooks an' kep' praisin' th' Lord. An' Mary an' Joseph, they coon't hardly b'lieve sech a wunnerful thing 'd happened. Whoi t' them? An' they called the babe Jesus, an' ivrybody what seed 'Im knowed 'e wuz a Holy Babe. Even th' animals seemed t' know tew.

Presen'ly, free woise min from th' East come 'long. They'd seed a broight star in th' skoi an' follared 't all th' way t' Bethlehem. 'Where's 'iss new King woss bin born?' they say, an' 'en went an' found 'Im an' took 'Im some rare foine presents, an' they wuz real pleased t' see 'Im. 'En they went hoom th' long way round without tellin' Herod th' King, cooz 'e moight a bin a bit jealous.

Musta bin whully grand t' be in Bethlehem 'at fust Chris'mas. Jest a little owd babe loike 'at, an 'E wuz reely th' Son a God, come t' save 's all.

Wunnerful thing. . . wunnerful thing. . . . Een't no other word for 't.

Chris'mas be a lovely toime, Oi reckon.

For me, Peggy Cole personifies the East Anglian countrywoman. Sane, reliable, endlessly helpful and inventive, her role in *Akenfield* went far beyond her memorable performance on the screen. We meant it when we said, 'What would we have done without her?' I had privately considered Peggy as ideal for the part before the main auditions but had somehow convinced myself that she was unobtainable. So when I took Peter Hall to see her at the flower-show it was just to suggest that we should try and find somebody like her. But, walking home, he said, 'She's the one.' Long after the filming had ended I heard her giving a lecture with slides about the experience and was again impressed and delighted by her humour, steadfastness and grasp of things. I have long thought myself fortunate to have her as a friend and neighbour.

RONALD BLYTHE

Peggy Cole.

'Tom went and got wed in the middle of harvest'

A part in

by PEGGY COLE

'One day a year we all went to Southwold'

WHEN I MET Ronnie (Mr. Ronald Blythe; we all call him Ronnie) at the Church on February 4th, 1973, he came over to me after the service and asked for a great favour: would I play the part of the Mother in his film 'Akenfield'. I replied that I would have to discuss this with my family – Ernie, my husband, and two sons, Allan, a police cadet, and David. They were all very enthusiastic at the idea and encouraged me to have a go.

The next thing I heard was when Ronnie 'phoned me and told me that arrangements had been made for me to go up to London, to see what I looked like on the screen. I went to London and met Garrow Shand from Pettistree. I knew of Garrow as his Nanny and my Mother were great old friends. In the film Garrow plays the part of my son, Tom.

In London I also met Rex Pyke, editor and producer, in his home, and a girl from Beccles, Barbara Tilney. She was to play the part of the school teacher and Tom's girlfriend.

Peter Hall soon turned up. I first met him at our local Flower Show in August, 1972 and I then thought him to be a great Gardening Professional. We soon started to chatter away and find out about each other, with a pot of tea on the table, which we sat around.

'Akenfield'

INTRODUCTION by RONALD BLYTHE

PHOTOGRAPHS PETER HALL

Peter and Rex then said ' . . . now you are a family, imagine your son has come home very late and you are anxious and want to know where he has been.' We talked about this for a couple of hours, 'running on a lot of grunt'; well, that's what I thought.

On February 19th, I heard that I had got the part and from then on the work began. They did not start filming my part until 15th April which began with the 'Breakfast Scene'. But just the same we were always busy as we were being called on from time to time to help the film unit. They would 'phone before they came down to Suffolk and ask me to find some 'extras' or props. For instance, one week they asked for a baby. I remember saying on the 'phone 'It takes nine months for a baby in Suffolk'.

I also cooked food for the film crew, which they liked. I didn't mind doing this as I like cooking. I did practically all the baking of the food which was used in the film. I also did a lot of research into 'Old Suffolk Recipes' for the Harvest Supper, but as I do my own baking every week, it was normal routine for me. I also provided the meals for the crew and cast in the Harvest scene.

I used to prepare my family's weekend lunch in midweek, then put it into my deep freeze, because I lead a very busy life in the summer with flower shows, as well as acting as judge at shows. We also have our Council Garden open to the public during the Summer. I work on a local farm, but I did manage to fit in all my hobbies as well as the filming.

I will always remember April 15th, the first day I was filming, when we eventually finished the Breakfast Scene. I was nearly a nervous wreck. I think we must have done the scene eight or nine times I kept thinking to myself, 'I'm doing it wrong', but now I see what Peter Hall wanted. He would pick the best 'take' from each scene.

Mr. Blythe wrote a big script. The cast did not have to learn this; we just had to be ourselves. It was a joke amongst the cast. We used to ask each other and wonder what was in those books. (There were a few copies of it, about 120 pages long.) I'm glad we didn't have to learn any of it. Ronnie just told Rex and Peter about Suffolk traditions and how Suffolk ways were, and they would then stop and discuss the next scene to check and see that everything was right.

The art directors were very kind and I went and helped them to set up my 'little cottage'. This was a vacant cottage which had to be furnished. Some of the accessories in the cottage had come from my own home. Once the art director sent me flowers for helping him. I remember when we had finished doing a scene in the cottage, and we had cleared out all the accessories; then we had a 'phone call asking us to get the cottage ready again as they wanted to do a kitchen scene, so we had to return all the furniture and put everything exactly how it was when they finished the last scene. It was hard work replacing all the furniture but it was worth it in the end.

I remember too that the garden was wilderness and my husband laid this all out in two days.

Rex (Mr. Rex Pyke) and Ronnie used to go around the country looking for locations, and when Rex was busy in London getting ready for next week's filming, Ronnie would go around on his bicycle looking for suitable farmyards, meadows, etc. (He doesn't drive.)

'Charlotte was in service at the rectory. . .He wasn't always about, the vicar'

Tom the horseman – the best job on the farm.

The funeral was one of the biggest scenes for me, one which I shall never forget. Nobody in the film, not even Ronnie, knew that my father worked as a farm labourer next to Hoo Church, and it was there I used to go to Sunday School – so you can imagine my feelings when we did the scene at Hoo Church.

I wore the same clothes which I wore for my father's funeral. We also had the same hymns. The tears rolled down my face and they were not artificial. The service was so touching, especially when Ronnie (the Vicar in the film) spoke some lovely, comforting words to me which he had written for this part in his script, and when he quoted from the Burial Service in the Book of Common Prayer.

Another big scene was the funeral tea-party, in which we used my own homemade wine. After several takes, the wine got less and less and the cast got a bit merry. I remember I had to kiss all the men good-bye, and this was done several times. You can understand how happy everyone was, even the crew had a few bottles.

The crew of the film were marvellous and very kind to us. This was one of the best things in the making of 'Akenfield', a great friendship soon developed among us all. I have now got a great many friends from the film.

Now we are all back to our every day life. Garrow to his ploughing, Barbara to her teaching, Rex to another film, Ronnie to writing another book, Peter to his theatre. My family and I still have many a laugh about the film, but now I am going around showing slides on 'Akenfield' which I took during the making of the film, to groups throughout the district (Women's Institutes etc.) and am kept busy with my job on the farm and my work about my home and family.

The commital of old Tom.

LIMERICKS

There is a young lady of Clare
Who dearly loves pink underware
Trimmed with Sudbury lace,
As it improves her bace
Which isn't quite nace if it's bare.
—P. F. COOK

There was a fair maiden from Hadleigh
Who loved a young Chinaman madleigh,
But her shots at chow mein
Made him take the next trein
For Pekin—and she misses him sadleigh.

There was a young farmer from Hoo
Who fell for a girl dressed in bloo,
Her praises he hymned
But his vision was dymned
By his love—what he'd wed was a shroo.
—JOY WESTENDARP

A pilfering poacher at Rougham
Adored to hunt pheasants and scougham,
Then, quiet as a mouse,
He'd return to his house,
Where he'd pluck, disembowel and stougham.
—D. R. BUTCHER

A young woman dwelling in Costessey
Rejoiced in the sweet name of Flostessey
But chaps called her Flo
As they thought to do so
Would possibly make her less bostessey.
—MISS E. G. WILKINSON

A large footed farmboy from Falkenham
Bought new boots and then couldn't walkenham
So his mate said: 'My lad,
My new teeth are as bad.
I'll swap with you if you can talkenham.'
—MRS. LOUISE DAWSON.

illustration by Margaret Blake

A lady from Morley St. Peter
Complained that her stepfather beter.
But the old villain cried:
'She has patently lied.
You couldn't find anyone sweter.'
—RONALD MANLEY, *who started it all*

and from his 12 *year old daughter, Karen:*
There was a young lady of Cromer
Whose scent had a sickly aromer.
I smelt it one day
And near fainted away
But instead I went into a comer.

IT WAS RAINING when I left Wells' dead and going-derelict railway station, once the terminus of the Fakenham line, and the grey skies were still weeping when I got off the bus at Blakeney quay. The horse-shoe shaped creek waters gleamed dully amidst the flat marsh and the sandhills; canted-over boats were lonesome and unattended; and there were puddles everywhere.

Once, corn barges used to load at this quay and then be towed down the creek to schooners anchored at the mouth; and Blakeney even had a Guildhall. But where that stood, I never found out for there was no one to ask and it was too wet for me to look. And so I stumped up the curling high street, keeping a wary eye on the puddles, towards St. Nicholas' which loomed through the greyness on the other side of the Sheringham Road.

The church of St. Nicholas has a single hammer-beam roof, a tower 104 feet high, a small turret which used to display a beacon light for mariners, and a 15th-century octagonal font where I knocked a pot of flowers over looking for St. Peter's sword which was supposed to have the ear of the servant of the high priest stuck on it.

I tried to mop up the water and fallen petals but only seemed to spread the mess further, so I departed through the glass fronted porch before anyone arrived. All I hope is that the church council haven't started repairing a perfectly good roof.

Car tyres hissed on the shining road, leaves bent at right angles to their stalks in the wind; and the sea, a mile or more distant across the marshes, was a depressing slate colour and apparently congealed. The aggravating thing about it all was that, south-wards, there were sun-tinged clouds and turquoise skies.

Cley-next-the-Sea — next the sea? it is over a mile away — was just as wet, with bockety cobbled side-ways, doorways that opened straight on to them, and a Women's Institute that looked like a fortress. No two houses seemed alike; and there were a number of archways, including one with four, rather in-distinct orders of carving, a flat timbered roof, and a high tide-mark of 1953. According to that, every-one at that end of the street must have had about five feet of sea-water in their front rooms, with its grievous aftermath of sludge.

Actually, it was another high tide, of 1897, which really finished Cley as a port, washing furniture out into the streets, drowning hundreds of chickens, and crumbling many a cottage. A reminder of the days when Cley was really next the sea is the Custom House with its elaborate carvings, and the church of St. Margaret which lies a full half-mile southwards from the village.

It has two ruinous transepts, a quite magnificent porch, a brass of a priest and five choristers, another of 1512 depicting John Symonds and his brood.

A corner of the front.

NORFOLK

St. Margaret's stands on very high ground. I never found the tomb of James Greeve who, for burning ships 'in ye port of Tripoli in Barberri' in 1276 was awarded a gold medal and command of the Orange Tree of Algier.

JOURNEY

by ERIC RAYNER

Whoever cut the brasses must have got a bit confused for the inscriptions and the *'Now Thus'*, issuing from everybody's lips are upside down.

Meanwhile, my innards, protesting at so much wet walking with nothing in them to sustain them, began to rumble in a most rude manner. So, at Salthouse, a scrap of a village with a triangle of rough green, the *Dun Cow*, and a post-office, I assuaged them with a bar of chocolate. Then, consulting a time-table between the drops of rain running down the glass I saw, with a little leap of joy, that a 36 bus would be along at 1655.

The five minutes to 1655 went by, plus another 10, and so I went and read the time-table again; and saw that the column was marked *F*, and as this was *S*, I had waited in vain.

And so I stomped on, occasionally hopping on to the bank when two cars wanted to pass each other and me too: a contingency for which this A.149 road is not really fitted. But never mind, half a mile off Weybourne, I did the same for a bus going the opposite way, received a salutation from the driver, and a lift with a married pair who considered my life was at risk. Thus did I arrive in Sheringham, at a railway station as derelict as the one at Wells which I had left at noon.

On the station walls notices advise that the M. & G.N. is the only preserved Standard Gauge Railway in East Anglia, and pose the question 'Why not call in one weekend?' However, this weekend all the doors were locked and so, like a minature Tarzan, I plunged down the bank through lots of nettles and weeds to the rolling stock drawn up alongside one of the three platforms.

Back on the road where ordinary citizens walk I consulted a notice advising me that all details of this *Midland and Great Northern Railway* could be obtained at the present Sheringham station on the other side of the level crossing. But there, oh dear, another notice declared that it had been an unmanned halt since May 1968; and so I finished up no wiser.

A small seaside resort is a sad place after dark when the holiday-makers have gone. The noisy little amusement arcades are in darkness, many restaurants are closed, and the streets, except for an occasional car with dimmed headlights are empty. B & B signs disappear from windows and, when I did find one, my ring on the doorbell evinced no response. When I looked up at the windows there wasn't a light glimmering anywhere.

However, in Victoria Road, in a house with a small garden in front where the last roses were on their stems, I did find a bed, a big, soft, smothering affair followed, next morning by a breakfast that left me full up until dinner time.

On the Cromer Road, opposite the Catholic Church of St. Joseph which, over the years, has 'growed' from a small chapel, is the Methodists' St. Andrews'; a place of flint, yellow brick, and a slender open tower with some lace-like filigree work. Inside, the leaded windows, divided in various angular patterns, are filled with the most gorgeously coloured glass. The circular Communion rail is stainless steel, the font, rather like an egg-cup, of aluminium; beaten from one piece or block without a brack or a join in it.

The benches, upholstered in black, are so comfortable that I fear the combination of a dull sermon and a warm day may send weaker brethren nodding off. They won't even have the fidgetings and prattle of those youngsters who think hymnbooks are only

St. Andrew's Methodist Church. The 12 ceiling lights on the left represent the 12 Apostles; the one over the pulpit or reading desk Our Lord.

for dropping on the floor to keep them awake: there is a glass-fronted, sound-proof chapel at the west end for parents with very young children.

In every way this church with its vivid colouring, its lighting, and its angular designs is full in the 20th century: as modern as its opening day, Saturday, 22nd June 1968, suggests. Its cost? £38,000 and all paid off.

In 1673, when the Dutch were rampaging up and down the North Sea, the inhabitants of Sheringham were much put out at the thought of invasion because their houses, very close together, were thatched with straw, and because, as they put it 'our Towne joynes upon ye Main Sea . . .'

Well, there isn't much thatch in Sheringham now; but the town still 'joynes upon ye Main sea' with a series of ramp-like walks which form an esplanade, where no car can get. There is also a pier where the lifeboat, 38 feet long with a weight of 9½ tons, and powered by twin diesel 43 h.p. engines in housed.

Its cost was £29,000 and, as the Manchester Unity of Odd Fellows raised £18,500 of that outlay, the lifeboat bears their name.

In a weather-beaten shed at West Cliff is the pensioned-off *Ramsey Upcher* lifeboat: a sail and oared thing which for a small entrance fee is open to the public. However, when I stopped by the guardian was away somewhere else; and he was still away when I stopped back. So, as I was, apparently, the only would-be visitor, and not wishing to interrupt an animated conversation amongst some rotund salts, I marched off to Upper Sheringham: with the sun streaming down, and trees and girls looking gorgeous. And my shoes still wet from yesterday.

Engines and rolling stock of the M. & G. N. Railway. Beyond is the level crossing, and beyond that the present un-manned station.

A Suffolker Visits Mine Host

by Simon Dewes

MY old friend Mrs. Pearl of the Rose and Crown, Elmsett, has recently died and, for the first time in nearly 200 years, Elmsett's local has passed out of Mrs. Pearl's family. She herself lived there for 72 years and, for most of that time, she was the landlady. It is more than 50 years since I first met her and I was in the Rose and Crown a week or so before her death.

Yet, in our 50 years' friendship, I never once got into the bar; for my father was, for years, the Pearls' doctor and, to a lady of Mrs. Pearl's generation, that would have been unseemly. So, first with my father, later with my wife and many friends, we would sit in the kitchen (which could only be approached through the cellar) and have our refreshment. There was another reason that precluded our presence in the bar, for there our conversation would have been inhibited by the company of others and I should have missed many a tit-bit of gossip or scandal, so that it was better that we kept ourselves to ourselves.

A neat, spare little woman who, in later years, became dreadfully shrunken and bowed, Mrs. Pearl never allowed circumstances to overtake her and she had much to contend with, culminating in the fact that, for the last 21 years of her life, she had to run the pub totally unaided; for Alf, her husband, had the misfortune, all those years ago, to injure his back and spent the rest of his life upstairs in bed, where I saw him whenever I was in the Rose.

With all his helplessness and the pain he must, from time to time, have had to endure, he, too, was ever cheerful and I would look with wonder at the dazzlingly white sheets (changed three times a week), the polished brass and the washing utensils. The jug was always filled with water, the commode was always in order, and all the water had to be carried upstairs in jugs by Mrs. Pearl, just as she had to carry the commode receptacle downstairs.

She regretted not one moment of her hard life; and looked back with nostalgia to the days when Mr. Scratchly was Rector of Elmsett and kept a carriage and horses and coachman. 'He was a real gentleman,' Mrs. Pearl would say, 'not like the one that followed him.'

I, too, can remember Mr. Scratchly, more particularly because he suffered from eczema and went about in summer under a green umbrella to protect himself from the rays of the sun; for his name, I thought, was singularly appropriate.

I knew too, his coachman, a great bearded fellow whose wages were, believe it or not, 10s. a week.

But long ago as I first met Mrs. Pearl, I knew another publican (not counting Miss Spooner at Hadleigh Lion, who attended my christening) even earlier.

This was Mr. Wix, who kept the Ram in Hadleigh Market Place. It was my father who, when I was about seven, first took me into the Ram.

'What will you have?' he demanded.

'Bass,' I said stoutly, for I had seen it advertised.

I had it. It was disgusting. But I got through it manfully, little realizing the agony I would have to go through before the next interval. I have, however, persevered and, as the years have passed, the taste of Bass has, to memory's mind, improved.

In later years Mr. Wix, whose complexion was the colour of the belly of a frog, suffered from gout and spent his days (and, for all I know, his nights) in the back room, where he sat on a high chair at a round table with a bottle of port and glass to hand. On this table there was also a pile of silver and copper, so that the habit was that the customers helped themselves to their drinks, adding a shilling or so to the pile from which they then took their change. Somehow, I do not think that Mr. Wix really benefited from this arrangement, for the poor man ended his days in the Almshouses.

Among Mr. Wix's customers was a revolting little man named Teddy Norford. Mr. Norford was, ostensibly, a greengrocer; and he had, when I was very small, been good enough to allow me to water his ponies, for which service I was rewarded with a penny a week. I was also allowed to exercise his dogs; but I didn't get paid for that.

In my ignorance I always supposed — for I was a simple soul — that Mr. Norford came to the Ram, like my other friends, to quench his thirst and enjoy good company. But this, indeed, was not the case, although he always bought a drink just for the look of things.

Mr. Norford came, in his pony trap, on business, for it would never have done had all those with whom he had transactions called at his house. His pony trap — as I had early discovered when cleaning it one day — had had a false bottom put into it; but I, thank God, had had the sense not to ask what the false bottom was for: for, had I known and said nothing I should, sure enough, have been compounding a felony.

The truth of the matter was that all these good fellows who came to the Ram to see Mr. Norford brought him clutches of pheasant or partridge eggs for which he was obliging enough to pay them ninepence or a shilling a dozen as the mood took him. In addition to bringing the eggs, these purveyors had to secrete them in the false bottom of the trap, for Teddy Norford was not going to know anything about it. *He* was no receiver of stolen goods.

Then, twice or three times a week, he would trot off to Ipswich and put up at the Half Moon & Star (having called at Hintlesham George first for further transactions) where he stabled the pony and left the convenient trap in the yard. While Teddy was in the Snug, a varied collection of gamekeepers or their nominees, who were a bit short of eggs, made cautious calls at the trap, collected what they wanted and placed 3s 6d. or 4s 6d. a dozen (it depended on the season) in the receptacle provided. Here again Mr. Norford had no apparent part in the proceedings; and, his business at the Half Moon & Star completed, he harnessed his pony and trotted off to deliver his apples or turnips or whatever it was.

But the chaps at Hadleigh got wind of the vast profit he was making, while most of them were on the dole and taking the risks: and they bided their time to take their revenge. They had to wait longer than they had expected for Teddy, trusting no one, never took a chance.

But the day did arrive when Teddy, in the odour of sanctity and gangrene (for his leg had gone rotten and he had refused to have it off) put off corruption and put on incorruption.

He was buried, with suitable ceremony, though there was no one to mourn him, at three o'clock one wet afternoon. There were a few wreaths, most of which, we were told, Teddy had paid for himself, for he was a man who liked things done decently and in order. And my good friend, Mr. Stephenson (with whom I had once gone fishing, when he fell in the river) was the undertaker. And Mr. Stephenson had, in his cups in the Wheatsheaf, let slip that Teddy, who trusted no one, was to be buried with his gold watch and chain and his diamond rings.

(It may, indeed, have been that, with these offerings, he would be able to square up the Doorkeeper.)

Word flashed down Benton, up George Street, across the Bessles and down Angel Street. On the day of Teddy's funeral all his old business associates stood butterflies in their stomachs.

And, at about midnight, dim figures might have been seen — but weren't — sneaking across the cricket field, nipping over the wall into the cemetry and, armed with pickaxes and shovels, assembling round Teddy's grave. They carefully removed the wreaths and, in no time, they had Teddy unearthed and, in less than no time, they had him unscrewed and the bribes to St. Peter were no longer Teddy's passport.

He was screwed up again, dumped in his last resting place, earthed up and the wreaths replaced.

There were better Sunday dinners that week-end in Hadleigh than there had been for years; and, to think that, if Teddy hadn't been so mean, he might have had a brick-lined grave.

What a good thing he didn't.

The White Lion, Hadleigh.

Associated Press photo

A Giggle at Walton

by ROY LACEY

HE HAD been to the seaside only once in the nine years of his life and that was to Walton-on-the-Naze on the village school outing two years ago. He lived only 20-odd miles from Walton: a mere nothing to us in a car or a coach or on a scooter. But those miles were a great divide to Peter, eldest of four children with a widowed mother and a family budget trimmed finely to the necessities of feeding, clothing and warming.

He had spent a short seven hours on the sand; but the sights and sea-smells of that day haunted him more and more strongly as the freedom of the long holiday palled, day after heat-heavy day.

Now, sleepless, with his five year old brother snoring gently at his side and moonlight flooding their room, Peter awaited the dawn of Saturday and his return to Walton. He had saved five shillings over eight months from his infrequent earnings. Sixpence would go on his bus fare to Colchester, and then he would hitch-hike to Walton. There he would buy ice-cream for himself, sticks of rock for his brother and sisters, and for his Mum he would buy the brooch with a flower made from sea-shells at the centre he had seen on the stall that sold beach balls and shrimping nets, buckets and spades. It was his Mum's birthday on Sunday.

His eyes smarted with tiredness — but to stay awake was important, for his plan was to be up before the family, to eat a plate of corn flakes and to walk the two miles to the Colchester road to catch the half-past six bus.

* * * *

He awoke and for moments his heart pounded with the thought of failure. But his brother was still asleep and there were no sounds of movement in the house, no indication that the day had begun for his Mum.

He dressed briefly, noiselessly. He took his small cache of money wrapped in a piece of rag from the hiding place under the mattress and crept to the kitchen. There the clock showed five minutes past six. No time for breakfast; time only to take two apples from the larder and to scribble a pencilled note: '*Mum. I have gone to the sea for the day. Love, Peter.*'

Although he jog-trotted most of the two miles to the main road, he missed the half-past six bus and had to wait nearly an hour for the next one. He was glad of his jersey, for the sun had yet to dismiss the early morning mist.

The bus dropped him near the roundabout and the road to the coast, already busy with the cars and coaches of day-trippers to Clacton, Frinton and Walton. They failed to stop for the small boy on the grass verge, despite the urgency of his thumbing.

The cars and coaches were followed by wave after wave of motor-cycles and scooters, their riders and pillion passengers in the uniforms of their chosen tribes: jeans and sweaters for the Mods, jeans and black leather jackets for the Rockers.

It was a youth riding a scooter solo who gave Peter his lift to Walton. He pulled into the kerb with sparking-plug trouble, a pleasant-looking though shaggy-haired Cockney lad with STEVE embroidered in maroon letters on his white sweater.

Peter watched as Steve changed the plug. Then he asked: 'Are you going to Walton?'

'That's right, kid.'

'Will you take me?'

'What for?'

Peter hesitated. 'I want to buy my Mum a present.'

Steve grinned. 'O.K., kid,' he said, 'hop on and hold tight. But keep out of me hair when we get there, see? There's gonna be a giggle at Walton today.'

* * * *

So Peter's day at Walton began at a little after 11 o'clock and it seemed that the gulls wheeling overhead cried welcome back, and the salty smell was sharper, the water wetter and the sand softer than he had so often remembered.

For several hundred holidaymakers that day at Walton was ruined. But Peter was neither dismayed nor deterred from his enjoyments by the activities of the long-haired brigades who battled with each other through the long, hot afternoon.

Walton is too small a town to accommodate those who wanted to do no more than relax in the sun and watch their children paddle in the water as well as those who wanted the beach for a battlefield. So the day-trippers were returning home early as the police reinforcements moved in.

* * * *

The last of the sunlight was reflected in the pool Peter had dammed from the sea as the tide ebbed. It had held his attention for much of the afternoon, starting as a fort built with the firm, moist sand and becoming a lagoon, his own piece of shimmering sea with a navy of empty match-boxes.

The policeman stood over him and said: 'You'd better run along home now, sonny. This is no place for you.'

This was authority, to be obeyed, so Peter picked up the spade and bucket which early that day he had intended to be sticks of rock for his brother and sisters, and checked that in his trouser pocket he still had his present for tomorrow: a tiny brooch, wrapped for safe travelling in his handkerchief.

The policeman moved away to join his colleagues, who were trying to force apart the gangs of sweating, swearing, pebble-throwing, belt-belabouring teenagers. The fighting had taken an even more violent and hysterical turn and, hopelessly outnumbered, the police only hoped to contain the gangs to the beach and so limit the damage from flying bottles, stones and deck-chairs.

* * * *

Peter crossed the beach at the fringe of the fighting to reach the steps to the promenade to begin his journey home.

The pebble that hit him as he trod the first step was the size of a goose egg, but as anonymous as any other pebble on the beach. So, too, was the tangle-haired youth who aimed it with the utmost venom at another, though differently dressed, lad with STEVE in red letters on his white sweater. The pebble hit Peter on the back of the head with such force that he was flung against the sea-wall.

It was several minutes before he was noticed and an ambulance was called. It was delayed by the fighting that had now spread to the promenade. But nothing could have saved Peter. He was dead when they lifted him into the ambulance. He must have died almost instantly, for his little head was broken as though it were the shell of an egg.

It was nearly midnight before he was identified: before the name tag on his jersey became the boy reported missing by a distraught widow in a village 20-odd miles away. Not far, those miles, for a police car to cover, but a great divide for Peter.

Photo by Alex Bareham

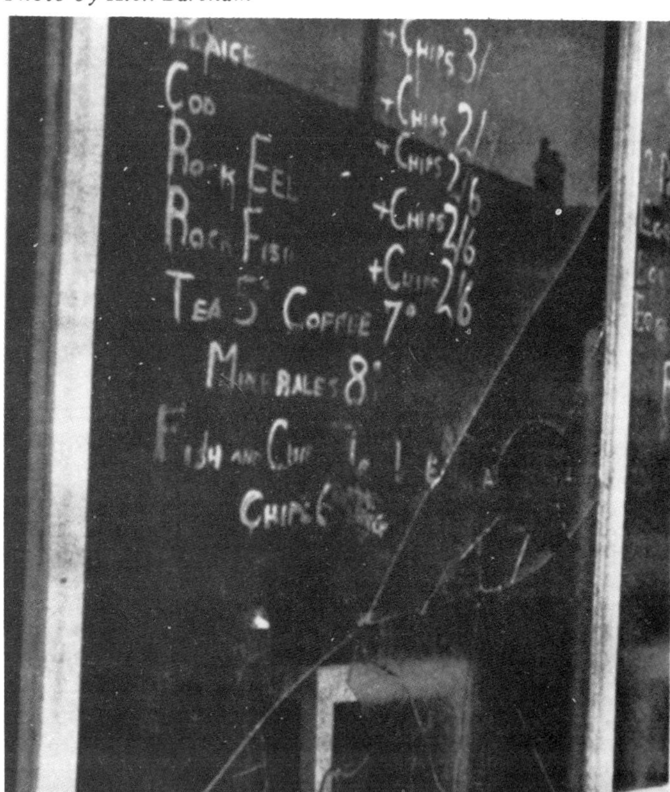

Some Colchester Characters

by PETER SHERRY

Marmalade Emma and Teddy Grimes.

THE OXFORD DICTIONARY defines an eccentric as, 'an odd whimsical person'; and if this is so, Colchester certainly had its share of eccentrics in late Victorian and Edwardian times.

One man was named 'Obadiah', possibly because a music hall song was quoted, 'said the old Obadiah to the young Obadiah', when he addressed a little crowd of youngsters after he had walked along a road, and quickened his pace to speak at a street corner.

'Obadiah' was a harmless person who believed he had a gift of prophecy by which he would reveal scientific wonders of the future. He usually started: 'The telephone, the microphone, the phonograph and electricity, and if you don't believe me now you will eventually.'

'Obadiah' said little more and an expression of relief would appear on his face after delivering such an inconsequential statement with an authoritative air.

'Obadiah's' hair was shoulder length. He wore a frock coat but scarcely ever any headwear.

Another character was thought to be a retired bandmaster and was known as 'The Minstrel'. He wore a faded 'undress' military jacket and beneath his arm he carried an old key bugle. He usually walked quickly with an air of importance.

From time to time 'The Ministrel' pulled himself up and attracted passers by with a few haunting notes on his musical instrument. His listeners would be disappointed for he did not continue playing. Instead he looked sad and mystified at his bugle.

There was also a lovelorn lady whose peculiarity was caused by a broken romance. She would roam

The Silly Annas.

about saying: 'Yes, Alfie but . . .'

Far better known are the 'Silly Hannahs' or Annas. These were two sisters who haunted the Colchester streets for many years. One walked before the other at a distance of about 18 feet. Because they never walked together they were called 'The princess and her attendant'.

The two Hannahs spoke in a high pitched voice, and for many years they lived in a cottage (long demolished) at the junction of Maldon Road and Alexandra Road.

They were given a charitable allowance by their friends, and they made a crude type of basket which they called 'cobs'.

The clothing of the two sisters has been described as 'a strange rag bag of ribbons and lace'. To keep in touch with the latest fashions there were new embellishments to their hats.

They loved their freedom too much to go into the Workhouse. However, after one sister died, the other agreed to make the infirmary her home.

'Marmalade Emma' and Grimes were something more than characters. These lovable tramps became immortalised in a novel by Eden Philpotts. These wanderers were well known figures of the Colchester and district scene. Like the two Hannahs they were featured in local postcards.

It is thought that Emma was nicknamed 'Marmalade' because one day she broke a jar of marmalade and began to scoop it up. She carried food wrapped in an unclean handkerchief, and was very much attached to her old handbag. It is believed that Emma was once a nurse.

Teddy Grimes was educated and came from a good family. He was also something of an artist and sometimes helped to paint the scenery of the Colchester Theatre Royal in the 1880's.

He had a childlike simplicity and at times Marmalade Emma's mission in life was to nurse the 'child' Grimes. They were devoted to each other, although at times Emma would be angry with Grimes and speak of desertion and disaster.

Both tramps smoked short, clay pipes. Emma's was much shorter and much blacker.

Teddy Grimes wore a long frock coat with a ragged tail. It is thought that he became nomadic due to a nervous breakdown.

Both he and Emma were taunted unjustly by the children of the Ragged School and by boys from the Grammar School. They were perfectly harmless and it is not surprising that Emma, full of righteous indignation, would run after the children, swearing and brandishing an umbrella.

She regarded Colchester as 'a parson ridden town'. Often Emma and Grimes would sleep in such places as the Lexden fields.

They appreciated any kindness shown to them, and any addition to their larder would be warmly welcomed.

In this age of conformity that threatens individuality, the breed of eccentrics seems largely to have disappeared. Without doubt there is something sad about these uncoventional people, but they gave life an extra dimension, a touch of colour in a bygone age.

BOOTS

by SPIKE MAYS

IN THE SECOND DECADE of this century, when I was a schoolboy and progressed to boot-boy, house-boy and farmhand, an Austin 20 was the only motor car in Bartlow Hamlet where I lived in a brick and stone cottage in the village of Ashdon, Essex. I used to marvel at its soft purrings and glidings as it took my first employer, Major Tansley Luddington, gentleman farmer and squire of Walton's Park, to little Audley End Junction or to Bartlow Station to catch the London or Cambridge train.

Apart from farmers, tradesmen and doctors who had gigs and pony-carts – and two tallymen who sometimes gave us rides in their covered vans – the remainder of our village community had to proceed to places on foot, or by Shank's pony, as it was called. The two railway stations, Ashdon Halt and Bartlow, were two miles distant. On weekdays we children walked a mile to school. On Sundays we walked two miles to church and Sunday school with two attendances at each. In spring and summer when the weather was fine we would short-cut across the field footpaths and meadowlands. In autumn and winter when the fields were morassed we walked the winding flint-capped roads and lanes.

When we had good boots we enjoyed it; and when we boys left school to work on the heavy soil of the farmlands our walkings and our boots took on a new importance. We were all desperately poor. In our life below minimum, two things were of paramount importance, bellies and boots. Often we had little to put into the former. Sometimes we lacked the latter. At school I had seen Mr. William Tuck, our kindly schoolmaster, weep and wince as he bathed the filthy feet and ugly chilblains of shoeless children with hot water from his cheap tin kettle; and had seen his tears fall as he peeled off strips of brown paper from the feet of children who were even poorer than us. But we never complained.

New clothes were a rarity. My bother Leslie and I often wore the cast off clothing of our farm labourer grandfather Reuben Ford who lived in the cottage next door. Knickerbockers were made from old corduroy trousers. Once a pair of jackets were made to a kind of Norfolk pattern from an old jacket thrown out by uncle Jasper Miller the gamekeeper. We were proud of those jackets. They were very thick and kept out the cold wind; but more important they had big gamekeeper's pockets – very handy for hiding snares and other poaching equipment. Mostly we wore thin jerseys, all topped up with white celluloid collars that would burst into flames when boys trained sunbeams on them through magnifying glasses; but our boots were always hob-nailed and heavy, even for the dancing classes, and used to scratch the polished floor of the Village Hall.

I knew what proper boots and shoes should be like, for I used to clean them in my Walton's Park cubby hole. The Major had fine brogues, with ornate perforations, even on the tongues. His wife's shoes were most elegant, as were the shoes of his daughter and her companion. The butler's boots were of soft calf leather, as were the shoes of the cook, house-maids, chambermaids and kitchenmaids, and I used to polish them all well. I used to envy the boys who went to Newport Grammar School. There was never a bit of mud on their nice brogues, and they used to make me feel ashamed – without complaining.

But when I went to work on the fields my clod-hoppers took on a new significance and extra weight. I shall always remember mine. They were ugly monstrosities of unyielding hide, tipped at heel and toe and encrusted with blakeys and hobnails. And in the fields when following the drill, harrow or roll, my feet became leadened; each step an effort of lifting the steel, hide and mud; to make my puny muscles protest with darts of pain before developing into that dull, mind-devouring ache which seemed to cancel me out as a human being. After walking all those miles in a 10-hour day across that heavy land I had to walk back to the farm with my horses and then to my home, with little spring in my step. It seemed that I was doomed by my big boots to be permanently anchored to the land; but I was not.

In 1924, at the age of 16, I enlisted into the Royal

Dragoons as a bandboy. It was then that boots became even more important to me than to anyone else in the British Army. For the first time in my life I had plenty of footwear. Two pairs of sturdy ammunition boots, which I boned and polished until I could see my face in them. One pair of soft calf leather Wellington Boots – with swan-necked spurs – to wear with my smart blue overalls with broad, yellow-ochred Dragoon stripes down their sides. I had plimsolls for P.T.

Later, when I became a remount rider and trained horses, I had a pair of riding boots with silvernickle spurs. Later still, in Egypt and India, I wore other riding boots; some brown, some black, of soft yielding leather made by skilled native craftsmen. They used to shine like the sun, were a joy to wear, and seemed to be part of me. Then in Hitler's War I was arrested in Le Mans as a spy by the military police. All because my black ammunition boots were undergoing repair at a French cobbler's in Cherbourg; where I had bought from Ratti's store – from my own money – a pair of brown boots to go off to Le Mans with my comrades. For once the Army had run out of boots.

Boots have always fascinated me. My Uncle Will, who used to be Ashdon's cobbler, used to tell me about boots . . .

'Yew can tell a man's character by his boots. Look at the heels. If they are down, he ain't up to much, boy. If he wears his soles smack in the middle, yew can trust him. If he don't clean under the insteps and the backs he won't get on in life.' And so on.

Because my boots were always highly polished throughout my time as a professional soldier – from 1924 until 1936 – my comrades used to borrow them for guard mounting parades. The smartest one of the guard was excused the actual guard duty of two hours on and four off, and used to deliver messages from squadron to squadron. My boots have got many a man off guard duty.

But there was more to it than being spick and span. My obsession stemmed from the ordeal of my sister Poppy, one that I shall never forget.

Poppy was a schoolgirl at Ashdon Elementary School in those hard times immediately after the 1914-1918 war. All girls wore boots then; but hers had worn out. The soles had gone, so too had the welts. She protested at having to go to school with the shreds and remnants, but my mother was adamant.

'Schooling comes afore boots, m'gal, and to school you will go. Jest you wait a minute.'

Mother went next door to Granny Ford's cottage. In about five seconds flat she emerged with a pair of Granny's knee boots. They were of leather bottoms and soles, but of rubber from ankle to knee and buttoned. She gave them to Poppy.

'Put them on this minute, and off you go to school.'

Granny's legs were short and plump. Poppy's were like pipe-stems. The toes of the boots extended a good six inches beyond Poppy's great toes, not unlike the comic boots of comedian Little Tich. Her skinny legs were lost in the vast tops, so mother padded them with newspapers and packed Poppy off to school. She cried all the way.

'Coo! Looket Pop Mays's owd boots. Jist loike an' owd gamekeeper's.'

The toes flapped like webbed feet of modern divers, and hit the ground twice at each step with a resounding slap. Her colleagues roared with laughter. At playtime Poppy hid in the porch and the lavatory, but the children dug her out and subjected her to ridicule. She did not eat her sandwich for lunch. Dehumanized by her ugly boots and the ugliness of poverty, she hid somewhere in the village until the hour of eating was over, misery incarnate.

But in the late afternoon there came a knocking at the class-room door. Schoolmaster William Tuck opened the door to my mother,who carried a parcel and was soaked with the rain.

'Send out my Poppy,' she demanded.

Poppy walked in front of the jeering class to the porch, and to our mother.

'Take off those old boots, m'gal, and put these on.'

They were buttoned boots. The latest style with sturdy flat heels. They fitted perfectly; and Poppy cried again, with happiness.

Mother had walked to Saffron Walden. In the pouring rain. Five miles there and five miles back. To get a pair of boots – on the strap! – for her daughter.

CROMER'S GREATEST SON

by DORIS M. CROSS

A memorable rescue in 1933. The barge 'Sepoy' was wrecked off Cromer. Two men could be seen clinging to the rigging, Henry Blogg drove his boat over the wreck to enable the sailors to drop into the lifeboat.

MY FIRST memories of Coxswain Henry Blogg are not of 'Cromer's Greatest Son', as he has been called, although I now have no doubt that he was that and more.

In fact, it is not easy to sort out impressions and recall exact dates; but what is certain is that he is ineradicably part of my childhood's dearest memories; and my first sight of the sea, although I was only about 18 months old, was also my first sight of him. This seems exactly right to me, as he gave so very much of his life to the sea.

We were on holiday in Cromer at the time and, according to my mother, I promptly squealed with delight and ran straight into the water, fully clothed. Nothing she could do would keep me from it and, apart from when I was safely strapped into my pram, spent two weeks in a succession of bathing suits. Owing to the fact that this was some little time ago, and to the rather voluminous nature of the material and lack of quick-drying facilities, mother was forced to buy six of these ungainly outfits, to the vast amusement of some of the local fishermen. My favourite was Captain Blogg, the famous Lifeboat G.C.

I am told he was particularly taken with my obvious delight in the sea and, when my long-suffering mother got annoyed with me, begged her to forgive me, as 'anyone who loves the sea that way, just can't keep away from it'.

I remember we lodged with his sister, Mrs. Kimm, and during many later holidays at Cromer I was to get to know him very well indeed.

It is difficult to say when my conscious memories of him began, although I know from the very first I looked on him as a friend and ally. In those early days, of course, it was the personality of the man that I remember. In fact I called him 'Man' for a long time, much to his amusement, and never thought of him as anything else – I did not realise until years later just how apt the title was.

I shall never forget Henry Blogg's patience with me as a child. He called me 'His girl', his very blue eyes twinkling, and said he'd 'Wait for me to grow up'. As I grew through childhood I would spend days at the Cromer slipway, and in or around the lifeboat station, which fascinated me. I remember mother buying fish at the stall at the top of the slipway and taking it back for Mrs. Kimm to cook for breakfast – never has fish tasted better. Apart from anything else, more often than not, I had seen it landed, and my friends

1934: Coxn. Henry Blogg, Cromer; Sec. Coxn. Geo. Balls, Cromer; Ex. Coxn. Wm. Fleming, Gt. Yarmouth and Gorleston.

Coxswain Blogg, G.C., B.E.M.
(All photographs by courtesy of the R.N.L.I.)

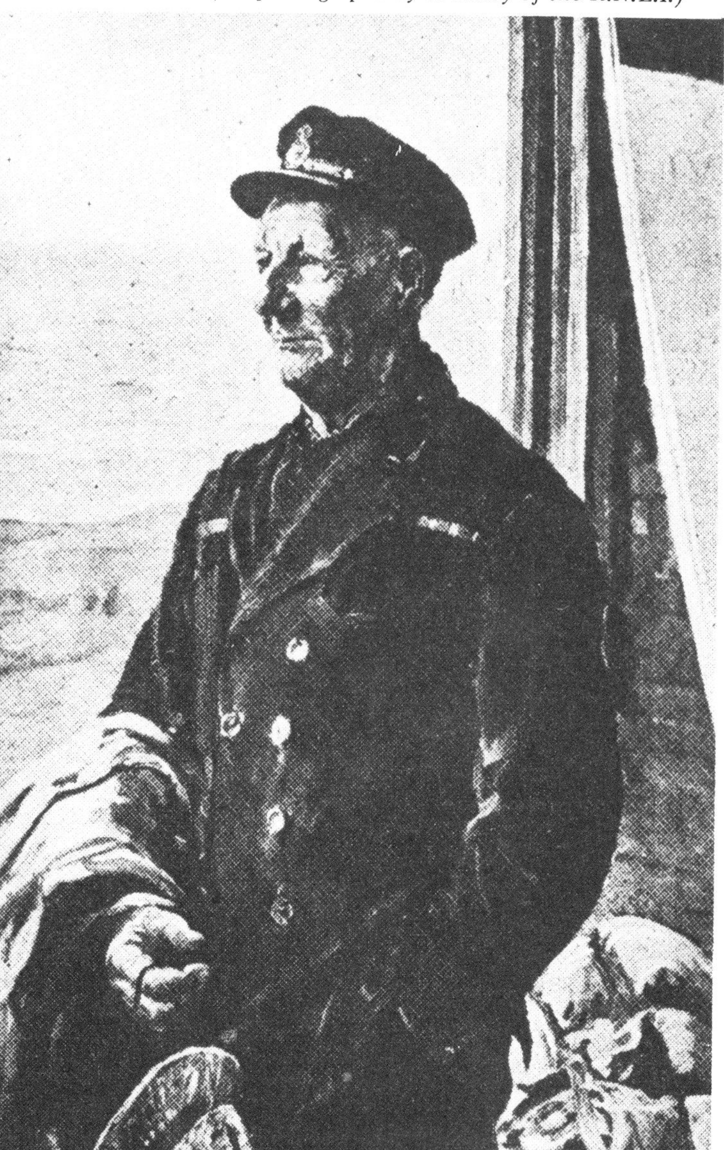

had caught it. This was wonderful to me.

I was shown every inch of the lifeboat station and, as I grew older, I read everything I could find about the Institution, and about the Cromer boat in particular. As time went on I realised more and more how inextricably was Coxswain Henry Blogg's name tied up with its history. He made so much of that history his own. My knowledge of him then was a combination of my own deep feelings for him, my mother's stories of his exploits, those of his men, and all I read of him, before, during, and after the war.

His service totalled 53 years, during which he put to sea on 'active service' 387 times, and personally assisted at the rescue of 873 human lives, not forgetting one dog. Three times he won the Institution's Gold Medal, which ranks with the Victoria Cross. He won the Silver Medal four times, the George Cross and the B.E.M. and even the Canine Defence League silver medal; and for 38 of the 53 years he served he was coxswain of the Cromer lifeboat.

As can be imagined, the story of the saving of 873 lives could fill a small library, although some of his exploits are now well known, showing as they do all the finest qualities of the man.

As early as 1917, in a 'pulling and sailing' lifeboat, he and his men went out in appalling conditions and took off the crew of 16 from the Greek ship *Pyrin*. As they returned to the shore, another ship, the *Fernebo*, exploded and broke in two. Although exhausted, Blogg and his crew made repeated attempts to reach the ship.

The lifeboat was under oars at this time and at times completely lost to sight in the enormous waves. At the third attempt, however, Blogg and his men succeeded, and the 11 men on board were taken safely off. This was one of the occasions on which he was awarded the Gold Medal.

After so many hard years in the service, normally, in 1941, when Henry Blogg was 65, most men would have been retired; but such was the shortage of men and the high quality and record of this particular man, that Henry Blogg worked on.

At this time a convoy of six ships were stranded on Haisborough Sands which lie to the east of the Norfolk Coast. A gale was blowing and an emergency call was put out. Four lifeboats were available – Lowestoft, Gorleston, Sheringham and Cromer – and they all turned out. 119 men were rescued. 88 of these survivors were brought ashore by Cromer's number one boat, coxswain, Henry Blogg.

Perhaps his most incredible exploit took place in the same year, in October, when *s.s. English Trader* ran aground on a sandbank about 22 miles off the coast of Cromer.

In mountainous seas, added to squalls of rain, sleet and hail, Coxswain Blogg and his men reached the *English Trader* in 3½ hours. The seas were so high only her masts were visible – the sea was littered with cargo and wreckage and in the middle of this chaos 44 men were huddled in the chartroom. Five had already been swept overboard.

After many abortive attempts to come alongside, the lifeboat heeled over under a huge wall of water. Many of the crew, including Blogg, were swept into the sea – although not a self-righting lifeboat, by some miracle she righted herself. One by one the men, encumbered by lifejackets and heavy with water, were dragged aboard. One man died – the first time Blogg had lost a man – and it was a bitter blow to them all, and to Blogg in particular.

It was war-time and no lights could be shown; other lifeboats tried to help, but without success. Finally the engines of the Cromer boat stalled, and they were forced to return to Yarmouth at reduced speed.

The lifeboat crew were so exhausted they had to be helped ashore and given hot baths, food and dry clothes. But not for Henry Blogg; he rang Cromer, and saw to the refuelling of the boat and repairs completed.

During the war a boom was raised across the entrance to Yarmouth harbour for defence purposes, and the admiral in charge had ordered that in view of the bad weather no vessel was to be allowed out.

Undeterred, Blogg rang the duty officer, and persuaded him to lower the boom against the admiral's orders . . . what might be called the 'Nelson touch'.

At 4 o'clock in the morning, in complete darkness, Blogg had to use all his vast knowledge and instinct to battle his way past sandbanks and against the full fury of the gale. At 8 a.m. they reached the *English Trader* once more. The seas by this time had gone down a little, and Coxswain Blogg brought the lifeboat alongside. In half an hour the crew of 44 were taken off. The weather was still too bad to take the boat into Cromer, and the survivors were therefore landed at Yarmouth. Twenty-seven hours with no rest, and at 65 years of age, Captain Henry Blogg can truly be said to have been the greatest of them all.

I last saw him in 1949, when he met my three oldest children, aged 7, 5 and 2. We found him sitting on an old breakwater gazing out to sea, as he often did. At first he greeted me as though I had never been away. Then as he turned to the children, still with that lovable twinkle in his eyes, reminded me that he'd waited for me, though I obviously hadn't waited for him. . .

Five years later, in 1954, I read of his death with sadness and nostalgia. Thousands of people turned out in the pouring rain to show their deep and abiding affection and respect for this wonderful man.

East Anglia

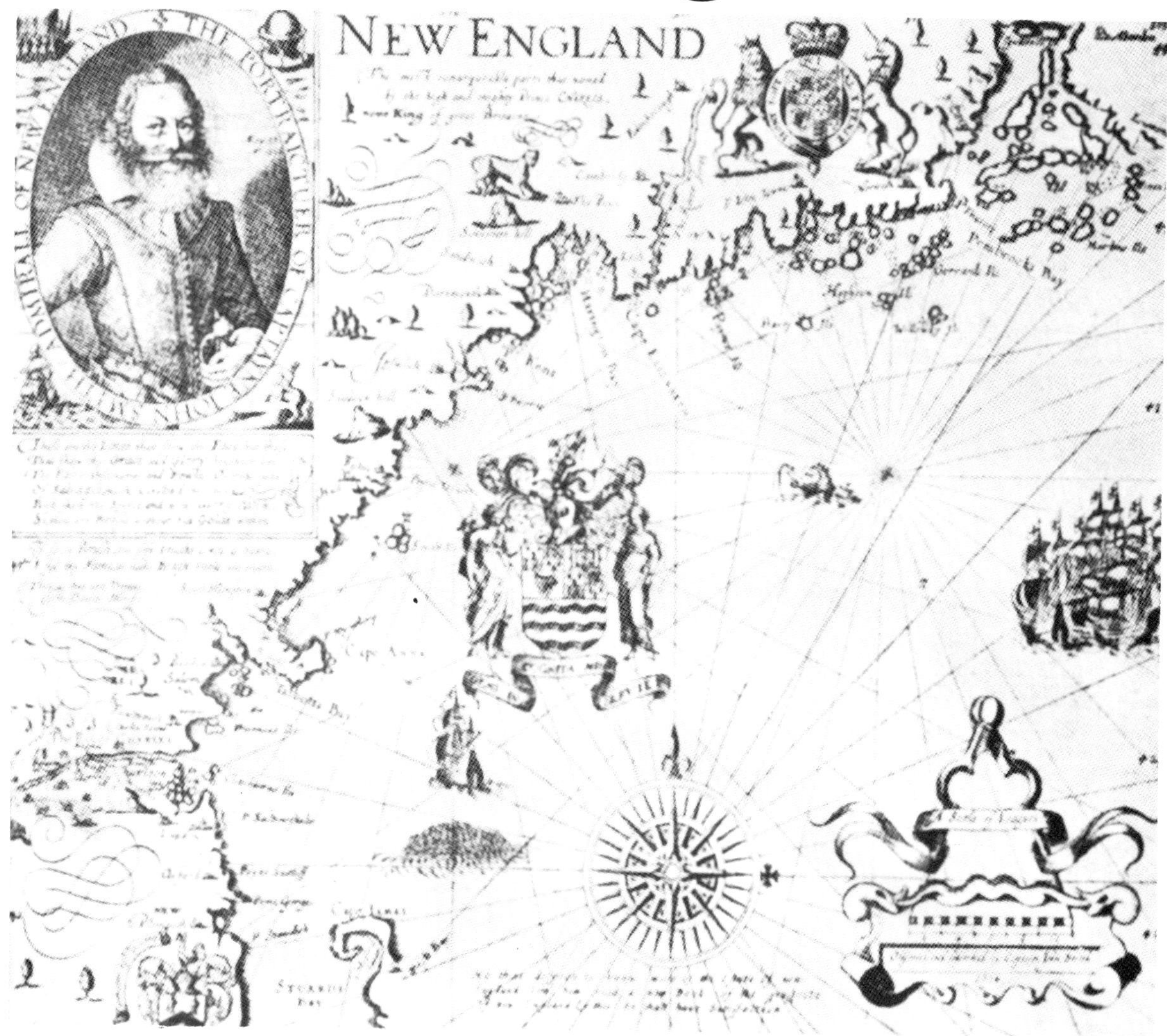

Captain Smith's map of New England 1614. (Courtesy the University of Michigan)

Salutes America

by JOHN RYDEN HARRIS

'For support of this declaration, we mutually pledge each other our lives, our fortunes, and our sacred honour.'

— *Declaration of Independence, 1776*

WHO WERE those American colonists who, in 1776, declared their independence of Great Britain? Far-spread in 13 colonies, in total they formed a mixed bag of saints, scholars, opportunists and scallywags. In short, they were vigorously representative of the English stock from which they chiefly sprang. As such, they likewise nourished a stern sense of their inalienable right to go through every kind of purgatory in pursuit of that dream of heavenly grace called happiness. For those reasons alone, present-day Britain has an inherent right to share in the celebrations of the 200th birthday of the United States.

Nowhere does this hold more true than in East Anglia and its neighbouring eastern counties with which so much of the early American story is closely linked. As some illustration of those innumerable links, I wrote a book. Here I can cite only a few instances of the prominent contribution made by East Anglians to the conception and birth of the American nation.

By the close of the 16th century, disastrous attempts to plant an English colony in America had induced a mood of pessimism. In 1602, upon his return from charting the east coast of North America, that mood was powerfully challenged by Captain Bartholomew Gosnold of Grundisburgh, Suffolk. Young, energetic and far-sighted, Gosnold's enthusiastic advocacy of a further colonial venture won the instant support of Captain John Smith.

Resulting from their mutual endeavours, in 1606, three vessels sailed for Virginia, two of them commanded by Gosnold and Ratcliffe, both Suffolk men, the third being commanded by Christopher Newport, said to be of Essex. A high proportion of the 105 passengers were likewise East Anglians. The first haven they found after their voyage was a natural harbour which they called Norfolk, today marked by the City of Norfolk, Virginia. Soon, numerous other people joined the infant settlement at Jamestown, a significant number of them hailing from East Anglia, including John Rolfe of Heacham. Gosnold meanwhile, succumbing to fever, did not live to see his colonial aspirations realised.

In 1620 sailed the *Mayflower*. Her master, most of her crew and an estimated two-thirds of her passengers were of East Anglian orgin. So was blazed the trail for a mass emigration which began 10 years later, led by John Winthrop of Groton, Suffolk. Three impressionable years at Cambridge, the hot-bed of religious discontent, had caused Winthrop to develop a conscience which imparted to his inherently strong character an austere and rigid aspect. He was, nevertheless, a robust and virile man. Four times married, he begot 16 children. In all, he was the ideal man to lead the 700 men, women and children who founded the colony of Massachusetts in 1630. As others followed, those hundreds swelled into thousands. As one outcome, the place names of East Anglia began to spread in profusion upon the terrain of New England. Only the English Civil War, bringing disaffection to a head, aligned East Anglia on the side of Parliament and stemmed the flow of that vast tide of emigrants.

The Lincoln story shows how, in those years before the Civil War, whole families and their kindred came to see America as the promised land. In that time, at least six male Lincolns sailed there, all of them assumed to have left Hingham, Norfolk, though this is questionable. That they all settled at Hingham, Massachusetts, however, is true, and is indicative of their kinship with those who founded that settlement, having followed Robert Peck, the dissident minister of Hingham, Norfolk. That all those Lincolns were kinsmen is equally clear. At that time a veritable clan of them dwelt in mid-Norfolk, some of them at Hingham. Among those latter was Richard Lincoln, a substantial yeoman.

John Winthrop was born at Groton Manor.

John Winthrop. (Courtesy of the Moss Historical Society).

Sometime about 1599, Richard Lincoln acquired a small estate at Swanton Morley where, in 1610, he erected what he called his 'new mansion'. Brick-built, crowned with ornamental chimneys, it signalled him as a man of solid substance. Four times married, by his first wife he had a son, Edward. By his fourth wife – a sister-in-law of Robert Kett's grandson, John – he had another son, Henry.

On a day in 1615, Richard Lincoln sat down in his 'new mansion' at Swanton Morley to make his will. When proved in 1620, that will disclosed that he had disinherited his eldest son, leaving his estate to Henry. All Edward had, it is said, beside a largish family, was a 'cottage and two acres at Hingham'. His unsuccessful attempt to contest the will in Chancery did not improve his circumstances. They were such, it appears, as to compel his son, Samuel, to enter the service of Francis Lawes, a Norwich weaver. Claims that Samuel was an apprentice weaver are not supported by the records of Norwich Apprentices nor by the Yarmouth Passenger List for 1637 (both records published by the Norfolk Record Society). In the latter, SAMUEL LINCORNE is described as one of 'two sarvants' Lawes took with him to New England, where the entire party settled at Hingham. Samuel became the ancestor of President Abraham Lincoln. The distinguished contributions made to American history by many other Lincolns, one of whom was a general during the War of Independance, is another story.

Discontent leading up to that war was crystallized by the Stamp Tax imposed in 1765 by Charles Townshend, member of one of East Anglia's most distinguished families. The Townshends of Raynham had consistently exhibited an independence of character, plus what might be described as an unorthodox liberality of outlook. In religion they were Calvinists. One was buried close by Calvin's grave. Another had gone to New England, there to build his own Raynham Hall. Yet another had served with Cromwell, whilst young Horatio Townshend had represented his family on the commission of the Eastern Association, during the Civil War.

A pilgrim family fleeing England.

With that background, Charles Townshend was hardly the inane, authoritarian fop he is sometimes thought to have been. Sir Lewis Namier depicts him as a man of robust build with a good brain, a devastating wit, a golden tongue, a liking for cricket, and as the long-standing friend of the rebellious John Wilkes. There was much of the rebel in Townshend himself; clearly evident in his attitude to paternalistic authority, when he was disposed to go his own way and damn the consequences. In just such a rash moment, he imposed the Stamp Tax. Yet in spite of this, and had he lived to do so, in the last resort he might well have supported the rebel colonies, on which he was the accepted authority, and for which he had a warm regard. Not for nothing was he called Weathercock.

One who unhesitatingly allied himself to the cause of those rebellious colonists was the man born a mere 25 miles south of Raynham – Thomas Paine. American-East Anglian links are as real as they are innumerable. Paine is the bright symbol of them all. With the passage of time his true stature has become increasingly recognised. He is surely one of East Anglia's greatest sons – and none the less so because he regarded himself as a citizen of the world. Yet only recently in Thetford, I heard him declared a 'bloody traitor'. But had it been Paine standing on the plinth and not his statue, he would have been the first to assure his critic of her right to express her own opinion. Throughout the English-speaking world we enjoy such rights because of men like Paine. His vision, many of his views, his generosity of mind, are as relevant to our times as they were to his own – if only because we seem to stand in such desperate need of them.

In the light of its history and character, it would seem that only East Anglia could have produced Thomas Paine. His own character and achievements seem, in some ways, to reflect that traditional East Anglian 'du difference' which, though it can sometimes lead to errors of judgement, often begets a new and challenging angle on things hitherto taken for granted. Given his innate character, the young Paine benefited from an early environment where no mountains obstructed his view of broad horizons. Virtually from his front door rolled the open expanse of what we now call Breckland where there was freedom of air and movement and a vast wealth of sky. These, in their own way, went to mould the intrinsic character of the man who, for all we yet know to the contrary, may have been a kinsman of that 17th century dissident pamphleteer of Norwich who bore the same name – Thomas Paine.

All this, the total sum of a man armed with talent and vision, was supremely challenged on the day Paine sat down to write the words designed to inspire an army of battle-weary American colonists with renewed determination and vigour. His own declaration of faith he made in these words:

> 'I believe in one God and no more. I hope for happiness beyond this life. I believe in the equality of men, and I believe that religious duties consist in doing justice, love and mercy, and in endeavouring to make our fellow-creatures happy.'

Those convictions, and even the style of Paine's phraseology, warmly inform the Declaration of American Independence.

That independence was inevitable. Alternatively it would, I believe, have become necessary, at some time, for Britain to declare her independence of those colonies. For the motherland had bred a vigorous child destined to become a giant. Yet, in a host of ways, the two nations have remained mutually dependent over the past two centuries. May it long continue to be so. Paine, the East Anglian American, would have wished it so.

Richard Lincoln's house at Swanton Morley, a photograph taken between the two World Wars.

One of the pictorial menus executed by Sir W. Gurney Benham, by whose kind permission it is published.

St. Mary's Square. (Photos John Ayliffe, Bury Free Press).

BURY ST. my love

ONE EXCELLENT TEST of love is the response to the beloved's name. Let the name of my beloved be included in the largest page of the smallest print and it leaps to the eye. Any mutilation is an offence — people who write to me at *Bury St. Ed's* do not receive answers. During my first exile — two years in Norwich, that fine city, I used to make a point of being in a certain place at a certain time in order to see a brewer's delivery truck, bearing the magic name. I would stand there, homesick tears in my eyes, thinking — Oh lucky driver who will sleep, oh, fortunate truck, which will be garaged, in Bury St. Edmunds this night!

By one of those quirks of fate, so odd, so ironic that in a book nobody would believe it, that very same firm of brewers was directly responsible for my second exile 20 years later. The birth of a son, the mounting of books and papers made it absolutely necessary that we should find a house with a bit more space. We found it; my husband went to bid at the auction. Somebody in the know whispered: 'You might as well go home; the Brewery wants it.' Unequipped to compete at this level, we bought a house in another place, a place, to be honest, far more favoured in the eyes of the world.

Almost my last words to my mother were, 'Send me the *Bury Free Press* every week,' and she most faithfully did so. I suffered jibes and jeers, such as 'Well, and what's the news from the great metropolis?'. How would I know? I was looking for Houses for Sale. And I found one and was back home in less than two years.

All this taught me a valuable lesson. I have a trade I can ply anywhere, I could dodge taxation and enjoy a more clement climate were I to emigrate; but a person who can be homesick in Norwich, in Frinton-on-Sea, isn't likely to be happy in Mexico.

In one of his immensely shrewd comments on life — disguised as Sonnets — Shakespeare said 'Love is not love which alters when it alteration finds.' My love has withstood this test. When I first came to live here, in 1913, Bury St. Edmunds was the perfect, small-but-not-too-small market town from the centre

A corner of St. Mary's Square.

Entrance to Norah Loft's house in Northgate Street.

EDMUNDS

by NORAH LOFTS

of which, in any direction, five minutes, at the most 10 minutes, walking took one into flowery lanes. One of them we called in our innocence 'Midsummer Night Lane', we gathered scabious and knapweed, hips and haws, sloes and crab-apples there; and the cuckoo, in her season, called. Eastern Industrial Estate! Who hears the cuckoo now?

The market has changed too. Once it was a natural growth, the produce of the country brought in to feed the town. Now, every week more and more given over to the city slicker, out to make a quick buck with brassware, purporting to be of Oriental origin, but smacking of the Midlands. And the good earthy scent of carrots and onions and beans and cabbages, and flowers, swamped out by an alien odour, onions not about to be cooked, but cooked. Hot dogs!

So, who cares? Do you love a person less because he or she grows older, grows grey, fat or thin, and tries, poor foolish creature to keep up with the times? Of course not. Seeing the loved one exploited, misguided, has exactly the opposite effect.

I have very seldom — in fact I think once only — used Bury St. Edmunds as a background for a book. Too risky. I knew that if in a book I mentioned cobbles in 1749 it was only too likely that somebody, better informed, would pop up and say: 'But all the cobble stones in Bury St. Edmunds were removed in November 1748.' So I invented — or so I thought — a town called Baildon, which had an abbey and a market, my beloved under another name. And this also is an irony. In the third book of my trilogy about a house in Baildon I invented, I mentioned, unfavourably, something called *Baildon Properties Ltd.* My publisher — and publishers must be very careful — found that there was a town actually called Baildon and that it had within it, naturally, a company or two. But they dealt, thank Heaven, not in property, so we were clear.

However, though I have, in the main, restricted any reference to Bury St. Edmunds to the Grammar School, once a vibrant, potent thing, and now to be no more, I have no doubt that I owe Bury St.

Rear view of Norah Loft's home, elegant even in winter.

Southgate Street.

Edmunds, its historic past, its market, its squares, its Tudor, Georgian, and even its Victorian houses, a certain debt; I breathed its air; I absorbed, unconsciously, its atmosphere.

And when one's love dies? What then?

Well, almost within arm's reach of me at this moment, there is a lane – not a country lane. It was narrow, bordered on both sides by high walls over which Virginia creeper and wistaria tumbled. and it had a name which linked it directly with the past. It was dear to me; and once, during my first exile, I wrote about it, a description as near poetry as I was capable of producing.

Oddly enough it never struck anybody, not one of the high-powered well-paid blockheads in Whitehall, nor one of the unpaid, well-meaning blockheads on the spot, that widening a few feet of lane by a few feet would not cure a traffic congestion which could only be relieved by a by-pass. So now, down with the wall – a lot of the old Abbey stone in it; down with the wistaria, the trees behind that have taken a hundred years to grow. Going, going, gone! But I remember. I grieve a bit for the children who will never walk up Looms Lane and correlate its name with history – the weavers – or venture further, gather flowers, hear the cuckoo. I tell myself that they will, with any luck, be able to resort to a heated swimming pool.

And that is the point about my love; it is a tough town. Here assertive, here yielding, it has outlived both friends and enemies. It will outlive me – and what could anyone ask more of a loved one?

Frederick Vining.
(courtesy Norfolk County Libraries)

The BATTLE of the PENS

BY ELIZABETH GRICE

'FOR MY own part, I hold it villainous and cowardly to publish a censure of any man's actions anonymously. It is a king of Literary Assassinship, a sort of Stabbing in the Dark.' Benjamin Plim Bellamy, the Norwich actor who addressed this protest to the editor of the *Suffolk Chronicle* in 1813, had good reason to feel aggrieved. He and some of his fellow actors had been the subject of a series of what would today be called 'vitriolic attacks' by the drama critic who served the Ipswich and Bury St. Edmunds newspapers. And they did not know who to blame.

They were no ordinary attacks. These, after all, were the days when, if the provincial press had nothing good to say about a performance, they said nothing at all. Dramatic criticism hardly existed out of London, it being the custom for theatre managers to write their own puff pieces before a play and sometimes even pay to write their own 'notices' after it. Up to 1810, when the *Suffolk Chronicle* hired a corrosive new critic, the Norwich Company of Comedians had been used to receiving the press they wanted. There were of course grouses to the editor, spirited replies, more grouses; but there had been nothing like the systematic criticism which was now unleashed on the unsuspecting and probably rather complacent actors of the Norwich Circuit.

The trouble started during the summer season at Ipswich in 1810. *She Stoops to Conquer* by Oliver Goldsmith had been going down well for a few days with Frederick Vining, darling of the Suffolk audiences, in one of the major roles. Without warning, the *Suffolk Chronicle's* new pen began its devastation. 'The performance,' it reported, 'possessed all the worst defects of a provincial exhibition and the few occasional touches of excellence which appeared were insufficient to dispel the langour which the prevailing dullness was so calculated to produce.' Fred Vining was rapped for his 'schoolboy recitation' and the managers were accused of having dredged up a miserable orchestra.

Worse was to come. The *Chronicle* sent its reviewer to every play that week. Cobb's opera *The Seige of Belgrade*, performed, he noted in passing, 'under the grandeur of three violins and a horn', was defective in its dialogue, the William Dimond play, *Foundling of the Forest* was dismissed as 'one of those monstrous compositions of the present day' and poor old Greffulhe's farce *Budget of Blunders* was considered more than aptly named.

The faceless critic cemented his unpopularity by compiling a sort of top 10 among the Norwich Company, with Bellamy, Bennett and Fitzgerald

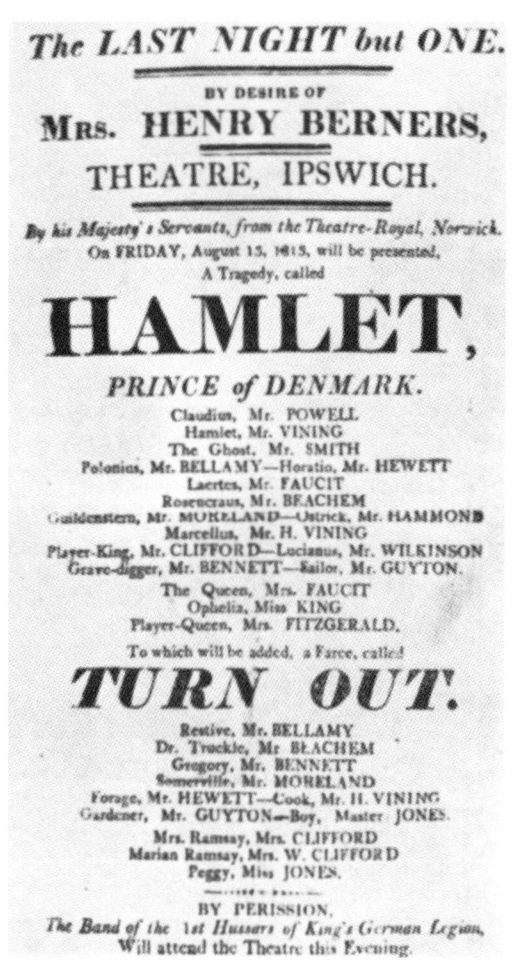

The LAST NIGHT but ONE.

BY DESIRE OF

MRS. HENRY BERNERS,

THEATRE, IPSWICH.

By his Majesty's Servants, from the Theatre-Royal, Norwich.
On FRIDAY, August 13, 1813, will be presented,
A Tragedy, called

HAMLET,

PRINCE of DENMARK.

Claudius, Mr. POWELL
Hamlet, Mr. VINING
The Ghost, Mr. SMITH
Polonius, Mr. BELLAMY—Horatio, Mr. HEWETT
Laertes, Mr. FAUCIT
Rosencraus, Mr. BEACHEM
Guildenstern, Mr. MORELAND—Ostrick, Mr. HAMMOND
Marcellus, Mr. H. VINING
Player-King, Mr. CLIFFORD—Lucianus, Mr. WILKINSON
Grave-digger, Mr. BENNETT—Sailor, Mr. GUYTON.
The Queen, Mrs. FAUCIT
Ophelia, Miss KING
Player-Queen, Mrs. FITZGERALD.

To which will be added, a Farce, called

TURN OUT.

Restive, Mr. BELLAMY
Dr. Truckle, Mr BEACHEM
Gregory, Mr. BENNETT
Somerville, Mr. MORELAND
Forage, Mr. HEWETT—Cook, Mr. H. VINING
Gardener, Mr. GUYTON—Boy, Master JONES.
Mrs. Ramsay, Mrs. CLIFFORD
Marian Ramsay, Mrs. W. CLIFFORD
Peggy, Miss JONES.

BY PERISSION,
The Band of the 1st Hussars of King's German Legion,
Will attend the Theatre this Evening.

Ipswich Playbill. (courtesy Suffolk Record Office)

Benjamin Bellamy.
(Courtesy Norfolk County Libraries)

heading the list and Vining somewhere below the middle. But most of the shame fell on the hapless manager, John Clayton Hindes, a man not noted for his popularity or talents.

There was an uneasy truce during the Norwich Company's next two visits to Ipswich; but hostilities opened up again during the July performance of *Hamlet* in 1813. Ben Bellamy, a promising young actor, was playing Polonius to Fred Vining's Hamlet. When he saw what the *Chronicle's* man printed of him — 'We never saw a viler Polonius than Bellamy's' — he claimed he had been slandered. He had played Polonius too tragically, the notice went on, his accent was bad, he was miscast. Bellamy had enjoyed seven popular seasons at Ipswich and he was not going to have his reputation ruined by 'an obscure provincial paper'. He retaliated with a tract headed *A Letter to the Dramatic Censor of the Suffolk Chronicle by B.P. Bellamy, of the Theatre Royal, Norwich.*

Bellamy accused his still unknown opponent of being 'a hireling, paid to traduce the Norwich Company' in order to promote the sale of the paper. His long diatribe was largely wasted on the *Chronicle*, which far from retracting, added insult to injury. On 21st August, 1813, the critic took up his best provocative pose:

'Whether we shall pay "His Majesty's Servants" from the Theatre Royal, Norwich, so much attention when they next honour the town of Ipswich with a visit as we have recently paid them, is doubtful. We have found it a serious sacrifice of time, which might have been far more advantageously and far more pleasantly employed. Instead of wasting our powder and shot upon crows, we might have been shooting at nobler game.'

The following week, instead of belabouring the players, he turned his attentions to the plays they were serving up — and found them equally wanting. The week after, he was back to the players again, declaring Fitzgerald incompetent for the parts he was given, Vining too young and too slight for tragedy, and Bellamy the only one who had nothing to fear from criticism.

The 1814 summer season at Ipswich brought a further deterioration in relations. Frederick Vining was at the time playing at Covent Garden and the critic remarked that his place had been 'more than supplied by the accession of Bromley'. Bromley's face evidently fitted. Meanwhile, Vining's brother, Henry, became the heir to abuse. 'That miserable stick,' the *Chronicle* called him, 'he would disgrace the lowest booth at a country fair'; the ultimate insult.

Before the season was over, there was 'a brutal violation of the peace'. At the close of the second act of Isaac Bickerstaffe's play, *The Maid of the Mill*, the critic assumed his seat in the lower circle. He was by now known to most audiences by sight; and his name, which he was soon to declare in public for the first time, was Thomas Harral. Henry Vining, a good mimic, had been diverting attention in an adjoining box. He stationed himself with his hat on by the side

Interior of Theatre Royal, Ipswich. (courtesy Suffolk Record Office)

of the critic, primed for a confrontation. Seeing the actor on the wrong side of the footlights, the audience rose indignantly and bedlam broke out. Struggling from backstage, the manager hauled Vining out of the box.

Hewett, who had been billed to sing a ditty, refused to be done out of his turn. Dressed like a ballad-singer, he went on stage and began his piece. In the renewed uproar he protested that he was the victim of a plot to prevent his act and pointed to a figure in the pit. The accused character fled from pit to boxes and from the boxes into the street, losing his hat in the getaway. Before long the stage was filled with a pandemonium of actors and audience.

Once a measure of calm had been re-established, the players attempted their afterpiece; but one of their number, Richard Jones, broke up the evening with another anti-critic speech. The show was over. As the house thinned, Harral, who had kept his seat throughout with remarkable aplomb, heard that 'a band of desperadoes', supporters of the actors, had stationed themselves outside the theatre to waylay him. Enlisting the protection of a few sympathetic members of the audience, Harral retreated. But Vining was lying in wait for him in Tankard Street shouting 'Let him come out! Let him come out!' The critic took some bad knocks, had his coat ripped from his back and narrowly escaped a ducking. An inglorious season was at an end and the company returned to Norwich with as much dignity as they could muster.

The battle rattled on for another two seasons on much the same lines until finally Harral was stung into abandoning his anonymity in the public prints. In an open letter to the proprietor of the *Suffolk Chronicle* he defended his high motives, his pursuit of the pure, honest and liberal viewpoint. It seemed as though he genuinely felt that since the summer of 1813 the Norwich players had degenerated and that it was his job to save them from themselves.

But his critical spleen had discouraged and unsettled some of the leading actors. In May 1815, Vining left for Covent Garden and Bellamy soon followed him. The year before, Fitzgerald had delivered a farewell address and left to take charge of the theatres at Hull and York. The company began to look anaemic and in need of a transfusion of new blood. Their answer was to invite London stars to the local boards for one, two or three night stands – a process which gradually impoverished the Norwich troupe, despite the immediately healthy look of the box office. As for Harral the Fearless, he was seldom seen in print again; blander, safer reports began to appear, and while they may have delighted the players they make, by comparison, uncommonly dull reading.

SUFFOLK HOUSES
A Study of Domestic Architecture

BY ERIC SANDON

THE EDITOR has invited me to say how this book came to be written. It is never easy to trace an idea back to its source but I would guess that the genesis of *Suffolk Houses* goes back to about 1935. In the summer of that year, Archie Rose – who had lately acquired The Moat Farm, Badingham – showed me his copy of Basil Oliver's *Old Houses and Village Buildings in East Anglia.* With ancestral roots in Suffolk, and as the new owner of a solidly built timber-framed farmhouse, he was intensely interested in local architecture. I can recollect his enthusiasm for Oliver's book, published by Batsford in 1912 and then out of print. With his flair for the esoteric, he introduced it to me as something unique – as indeed, at that time, it was. Still looking for seminal sources, I could add two more; Julian Tennyson's *Suffolk Scene,* which appeared in the fateful year 1939, and Vita Sackville-West's poem *The Land.* I owed both to Archie Rose. As patron and friend, he and I worked together on adding a porch to the Moat Farm and designing the pargetted decoration when the house was re-plastered. These may seem slender roots but from them was to grow respect and affection for Suffolk and some knowledge of the traditional ways of building.

Oliver began his book about old East Anglian houses on a slightly apologetic note: 'Collectively these cottages, farmhouses, and kindred buildings play an essential part in the history of our national architecture, though individually they are not of much importance.' (It has taken two World Wars for the pendulum to swing to the opposite extreme. Most buildings considered to be of historic and architectural interest are now protected by statutory listing; and it is an offence to alter or demolish them without permission. Already in his day some of these lightly regarded old dwellings had been destroyed since his photographs appeared.) The work, which

West Stow Hall *drawing by John Western*

Top: Great Saxham Hall.

Below: Framlingham, Regency House. (photographs from 'Suffolk Houses' by Eric Sandon)

Read Hall (drawing by John LeComber).

covered Norfolk, Suffolk and 'the rural parts of Essex', was published in order to show a collection of delightful 'finds' in book form. It never achieved more than a single and, I suspect, fairly small edition and had certainly not penetrated schools of architecture.

Vernacular studies would have seemed mildly eccentric in the curriculum of the Architectural Association when I was there during the late 30's. It was during these years, however, that the smaller house and cottage was being looked at in its own right and not merely — as had been the case in the early 19th century — as a model for 'picturesque' reproduction. An antiquarian movement started later in that same century was led by the local Archaelogical Societies. The Reverend Edmund Farrer, F.S.A., described 385 old Suffolk houses, and his articles are bound in six volumes, held by the Suffolk Record Office. During the same period *Country Life* published nine volumes on *English Homes*, by Avray Tipping; including some in Suffolk. Still nothing comparable to Munro Cautley's work on the churches had appeared, when Professor Pevsner published his *Suffolk* in 'The Buildings of England' series (Penquin : 1961). Under 'Further Reading' he commented that when it comes to houses . . . one has to search'. That was still the state of affairs early in 1971, when a friend cast me, somewhat rashly, in the role of author of a new book on Suffolk houses.

They do say that, if you are not born and bred in Suffolk, you remain indefinitely 'a furriner'; but perhaps this makes for a certain objectivity. Thus when it came to writing about the domestic architecture of Suffolk, it was possible to see it, instinctively, from outside. The long history of house building could be seen as a panorama, in which Suffolk occupied an important place in East Anglia, and that region in turn looked across the North Sea to Flanders and the Netherlands. Those coastal European neighbours received through France and Germany ideas travelling east from Italy. Thus it seemed natural to discuss comparable buildings and the dating of timbers with authorities in Germany, and questions of style in brick gable design with historians in Holland. Then there was the tantalising, if unresolved, question of possible connections between the old timber buildings of Normandy and those of Suffolk.

Suffolk Houses does not attempt to answer all questions. Its character is that of an introduction to an immense subject. As with a person, an introduction is what you make of it. If already familiar, or of little interest, the acquaintance is not pursued. On the other hand it may lead to new discoveries and the wish to explore the subject in greater depth. Take, as an example, the wool staple and cloth trade. It is well known that Suffolk was one of the most prosperous industrial counties of England in the middle and late medieval periods. What is little known is the way these trades influenced — or rather dictated — the form of houses. Much more correlation is required between the processes of cloth-making and dyeing and the planning of houses, with their yards and entrances and proximity to streams, rivers and roads. Then there are the intricate links between hamlets and agriculture mentioned in the section of the *Siting of Houses:* these need the study of movement-patterns, not only within the house and its immediate surroundings, but also those wider communications between parishes. A whole class of Halls and Manor Houses lie off the beaten track, sometimes attached to isolated churches. These have been listed in separate appendices, together with another phenomenon of the county — the extraordinarily large number of moated sites. Some of these moats contain houses, but many do not: few have been accurately dated.

Architecture does not usually make for easy reading matter. It was one of the conditions of a new book on Suffolk houses that it should attract a fairly wide range of prospective readers. This would include not only the specialist, but also visitors and local people who want to know more about the area and the type of houses they can find, and the prospective buyers of houses. The subject has four aspects of general interest that can be summarised quite simply: (1) whereabouts (i.e. the site), (2) planning, (3) construction and (4) design. As it happens, the last three belong to the classic formula of 'well-building' propounded by Sir Henry Wooton in 1624 — Commoditie, Firmenes and Delight. To adopt this formula was thus to proportion the subject-matter into manageable parts. (An incidental advantage was to give the casual reader the chance of isolating the aspect in which he was chiefly interested.) In this way the book came to have a structure of its own similar to that of the houses about which it was written. My hope is that this book will contribute to the appreciation of one of Suffolk's great qualitites — a tradition of fine house-building.

When *Suffolk Houses* was published in 1977, it caused widespread interest. I have included these notes by the author as a reminder of the book's merit — M.W.

Otley Hall.

Typical of the ships of Hakluyt's time, Lord Howard Effingham's flagship the Ark Royal. (by courtesy British Museum)

A BORN LISTENER

by MAUREEN TWEEDY

SINCE THE DAYS of Pliny many returned travellers have felt the urge to record all they have seen and heard in foreign parts either for posterity, for their friends, or merely a desire to relive, often during the dark winter months, the new experiences and scenes they have enjoyed.

The exception to this generalisation was one of the greatest travel writers of all time; a stay-at-home who listened tirelessly to intrepid voyagers, then wrote out all he had heard. He was Richard Hakluyt, a retiring modest man by all accounts who preferred a tiny country living to all the important preferments showered upon him. Country lovers who have visited the small Suffolk village of Wetheringsett will easily understand how a scholar preferred its tranquillity to the intrigue and bustle of the court of Elizabeth the First.

The village is enchanting and, at first sight, appears quite unconnected with the nearby housing estate sprouting like a new shoot on an old tree. The village street is lined with pink, cream and white thatched cottages and bordered by a stream, a humble tributary of the river Dove. The stream meanders under a curved brick bridge on which sits a picture book cottage. The post office operates from a minute bow-fronted shop reminding one of the illustrations in a Kate Greenaway book. The old grey 14th century church of All Saints faces the rectory, surrounded by magnificent trees, and it is to this remote corner that some of the boldest circumnavigators of that adventurous swashbuckling age came to tell Richard Hakluyt of their daring ventures.

He was a man of considerable foresight and therefore quick to appreciate the great potential of the newly discovered continent of America. In 1582 he published his *Divers Voyages touching the Discoverie of America*, a work which brought him to the notice of Lord Howard of Effingham who saw to it that the author should be made acquainted with 'the chieftest captaines at sea, the greatest merchants and the best mariners of the nation'. What tales these men could unfold and what a champion they had in Richard Hakluyt.

To ensure he obtained the utmost information from these sea rovers he added the French, Italian, Spanish and Portuguese languages to his already acquired Latin and Greek. At that time England was only on the threshold of her emergence as one of the paramount sea-faring nations and Richard Hakluyt was appalled to find our sailors lacked scientific

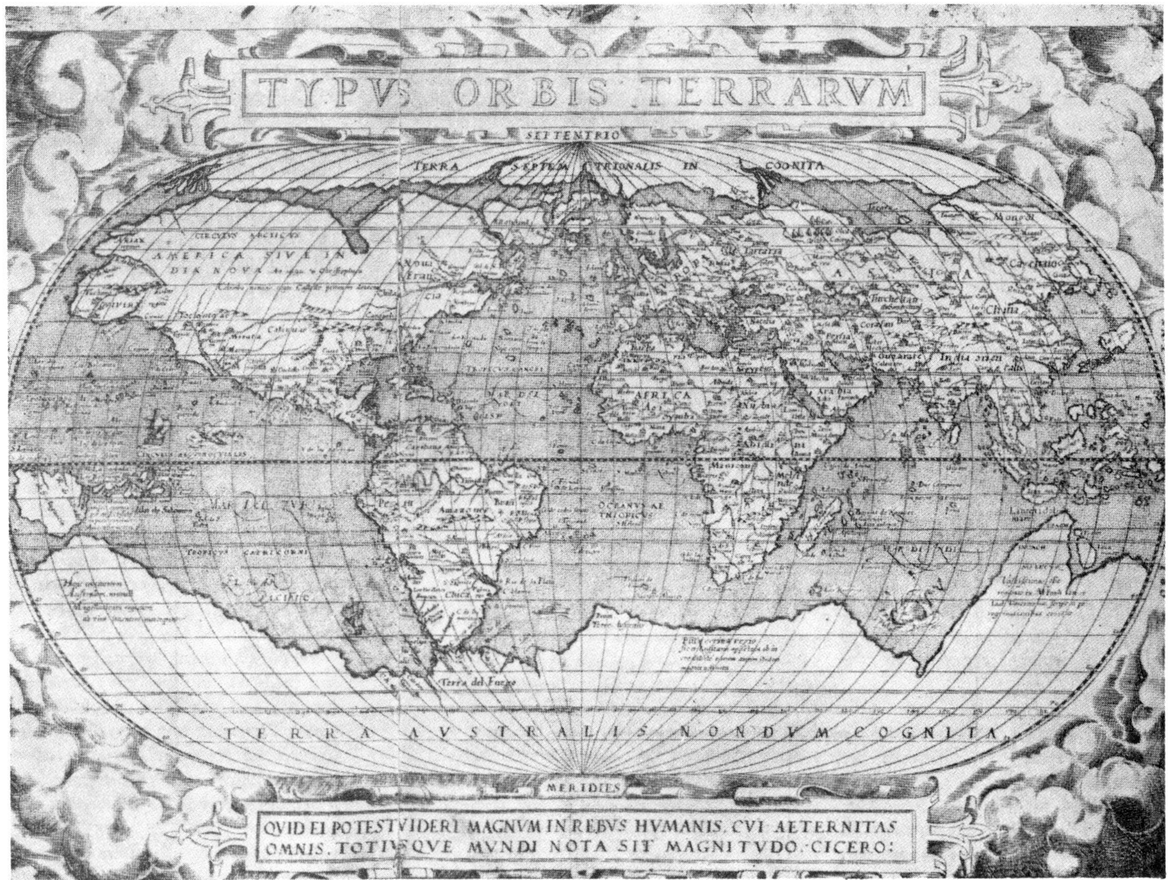

A map of the world that was inserted in the first edition of 'The Principal Navigations 1589' by Hakluyt. (by courtesy British Museum)

instruments and that, through lack of any written accounts, the tremendous voyages undertaken and so fraught with peril of all kinds should remain in oblivion. It was to be his life's work to remedy this deplorable situation and give his knowledge to the world.

When Sir Edward Stafford, brother-in-law of the Lord Howard of Effingham, was appointed British Ambassador to Paris he took Richard Hakluyt with him as his chaplain. Here he worked hard to promote the colonisation of the unsettled Western Hemisphere, notably Virginia, by the English race and, on his return to England in 1588, he gave a copy of this work to Queen Elizabeth the First. This was to be his only venture across the sea, efforts to sail with Sir Humphrey Gilbert on his ill-fated expedition having come to nothing.

Being that rare personality, the born listener, Hakluyt soon became the friend of many famous men of the day; Sir Philip Sidney, Sir John Hawkins, Sir Walter Raleigh and Sir Robert Cecil. He was willingly eclipsed by the brilliant company, in which he found himself being perfectly content to observe, to listen and to record. The East India Company sought his advice on maps and markets for the East and the great Cecil was not too proud to ask his opinion about the wisdom of colonising the Guianas. In 1606 he was one of the chief promoters of the petition to King James I for the colonisation of Virginia.

All this fame came to Hakluyt after the publication of his great work in 1589; this was the *Principall Navigations, Voiages and Discoveries of the English Nation*. Typical of this self-effacing man, he had his name omitted from the title page. A greatly enlarged edition of this famous work came out in 1600.

In recognition of his achievements preferments were freely offered: the arch-deaconary of Westminster, Chaplaincy of the Savoy, prospective living of Jamestown, Virginia, rectory of Gidney in Lincolnshire and the rectory of Wetheringsett in Suffolk. He chose to live the last 16 years of his life in this comparatively humble living and there he moved in 1590.

By no means all the illustrious sea dogs of that splendid era came from Devon. Two men who found their way along the winding Suffolk lanes to the book lined study of their chronicler were East Anglians.

John Eldred, Norfolk born, who became an Alderman of the City of London; and Thomas Cavendish of Trimley near Felixstowe. The former had travelled widely in the Middle East and, after five years absence, returned with 'the richest ship of merchant goods that ever came into this realm'. He built himself a house at Great Saxham in Suffolk and called it 'Nutmeg Hall' because he was the first man to bring this spice to England. He died there at the age of 80 in 1632. The house was burned down in the 19th century and the replacement bears the unimaginative name of Saxham Hall.

Thomas Cavendish, the third Englishman to circumnavigate the globe and the first to make contact with the Patagonians, made his first voyage in 1586. He was fortunate in that a member of his crew, Francis Pretty of Eye (Suffolk) wrote an account of the voyage and the Master, Thomas Fuller of Ipswich, kept a log. After two years they returned so laden with spoils that the ship's sails were of damask, her topmast covered with cloth of gold and her sailors dressed in silk. Cavendish went back to his Suffolk home, Grimston Hall, and ran through his fortune so quickly that he set out again in 1591 to recoup matters. It was a disastrous and fatal voyage with the crew falling ill 'from a most strange and noisome kind of worme bred of unsalted penguins'. Cavendish became ill in the Strait of Magellan and died when the ship was off Ascension Island and buried at sea. The Master sailed for home and arrived with only 15 crew left out of a complement of 76.

A description of these two epic voyages appear in Hakluyt's great work. Characteristically he was so occupied keeping alive all the exploits deemed worthy of adding to his country's glory that he had neither time nor inclination to write about himself. We know he married and his wife died at Wetheringsett: he had one son. On coming into his inheritance he proved himself unworthy of so fine a father and squandered everything bequeathed to him.

In his search for elusive mariners Hakluyt once rode 200 miles to listen to first hand knowledge of Newfoundland from a man who had recently come back.

In the little porch of Wetheringsett church is a short account of Hakluyt's life, placed there by the rector of our time, or there was when the writer paid a visit there.

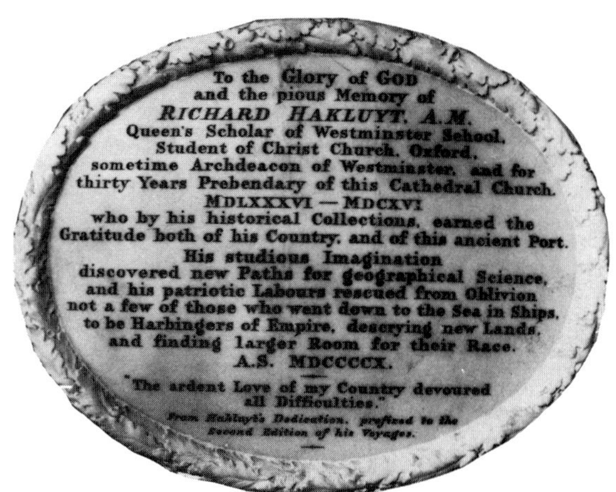

A memorial plaque to Richard Hakluyt in Bristol Cathedral.

On 23 November 1616, this great geographer and compiler of other men's travel tales died at Wetheringsett. Three days later he was buried in Westminster Abbey.

In 1846 the Hakluyt Society was founded with the object of printing rare and unpublished voyages and travels.

Eleventh Century Pep-Talk

Letter from Bishop Losinga to the monks building Norwich Cathedral.

"I love you, and I am striving to deliver you, slow and indolent as you are, out of the hands of the divine severity. Often have I stirred you up in person by reminding you both privately and publicly of your duty in this respect, to apply yourselves fervently and diligently to the work of your church and to show carefulness in that work, as done under the inspection of God's own eyes. I was wont to entreat and to persuade you and would that I had succeeded in convincing your minds how great is the sincerity with which God must be served. But alas! The work drags on, and in providing materials you show no enthusiasm. Behold the servants of the King and mine own are really earnest in the works allotted to them. They gather stones, carry them to the spot and fill with them fields and ways, houses and courts. You meanwhile are asleep with folded hands, numbed, as it were, and frost-bitten by a winter of negligence, shuffling and failing in your duty through a paltry love of ease."

John Crome by John Opie, R.A.

by Sybil Edmondson

HE WAS CALLED 'Old Crome' to differentiate between himself and his son, 'Young Crome', both with the Christian name of John; both well-known Norwich men; both celebrated landscape artists, and both exhibitors at London's Royal Academy.

'Old Crome's' start in life was humble, his father being a journeyman weaver in poor circumstances, and the boy therefore having to begin his working life at the age of 12. His first job was in the employment of a doctor as errand-boy. The doctor liked him, put up with his boyish pranks and, because he was convinced that, given encouragement and training the boy would get on in the world, enabled him two years later to apprentice himself to a 'house, coach and sign painter' named Whisler, where Crome remained for the full term of seven years, and stayed on afterwards in Whisler's employment as a journeyman. Here Crome had his first introduction to 'paint' for one of his principal jobs was to grind the colours and mix them for Whisler.

Born on 22nd December 1768, exactly 200 years ago, Crome's early up-bringing in a home where hard work was the order of the day meant that he was never afraid of it; and Whisler, quick to notice this, soon allowed him, in addition to his ordinary work, to paint signs, at which Crome was obviously good. He was, it is said, the first man to introduce 'graining', painting in imitation of the grain-markings in wood, and both these occupations took him out and about, meeting people in all walks of life, some of whom were to prove extremely useful to him in his first struggling years as an artist.

During his apprenticeship he became friendly with another lad in like circumstances and with the same ambitions – Robert Ladbrooke, who was apprenticed to a printer. The two lads took a garret together in Norwich, continued in their respective jobs, and went out into the countryside and sketched in every minute of their spare time. By pooling their wages they lived a hand-to-mouth existence for two years, meantime occasionally scraping up enough money between them to buy a print for the purpose of learning by copying, since they could not afford to take painting lessons.

Ladbrooke had soon achieved a good enough standard to be able to do portrait heads for 5s. each; and Crome sold his landscapes whenever he could for –at the most – 30s. Eventually Ladbrooke was able to take proper painting lessons; but Crome continued to live on in the garret. However, his persistence and determination to get on in the painting of landscapes attracted the attention of Mr. Thomas Harvey of Catton who, being an artist himself, and in far better circumstances than Crome, encouraged him and gave him access to his collection of pictures –some Gainsboroughs and many of the Dutch and Flemish schools–and by copying them at first, then going out and painting landscapes in a more or less similar style, Crome improved his painting enormously. One of the friends he made through Harvey was Sir William Beechey, R.A., who, having begun his own working life as a housepainter, had a great deal of sympathy for Crome and gave him painting lessons.

After a while both Harvey and Beechey urged Crome to take up a career as art teacher and, through them, he was introduced to people in good society, who could pay well for their drawing and painting lessons. Crome took his pupils outside where he taught them to paint from nature, rather than pursue the ordinary art-lesson routine of staying in and copying other people's pictures. Now, as he was earning a respectable income, he decided to get married. He and Ladbrooke married two sisters, the Misses Berney; and Crome's eldest son– who later became as well-known as a landscape painter as his father– was born in 1794. Crome himself then being 26.

'Old Crome' had eight children and, although several others besides 'Young Crome' became artists, none achieved the fame of their father and brother. John Berney, the eldest, was brilliant and, besides exhibiting at the Royal Academy, travelled far and wide throughout Europe to paint his pictures.

'Old Crome' himself remained always in Norwich and continued giving art lessons, earning enough to

Mousehold Heath by John Crome. (Reproduced by courtesy of the Victoria & Albert Museum)

send some of his children to the Grammar School and residing with his family in a good-sized house in Gildersgate Street, Colegate, where they lived in comfort. He also owned two horses, for he had long journeys to take to some of his pupils. He had little leisure-time, most of his pictures being painted on Sundays and Bank Holidays, his first to be exhibited at the Royal Academy in 1806, when he was 38.

He excelled in his painting of trees and sky effects, and his landscapes were beautiful and realistic. Some of his tree pictures now give rather an impression of browny-yellowish colouring; but it must be remembered that in Crome's day blue was a fugitive colour, apt to separate over the years from the greens of the original colouring, and thus leaving a shade where ochre seems to predominate.

It was 'Old Crome' who thought of founding the 'Norwich School' and assembled 'artists, amateurs and pupils' to help in instituting something that was then unique — a provincial school of painting. The first meeting took place in February 1803, and of this school was born a bevy of famous artists, among whom were two of Crome's pupils, Stark and Vincent, with Stannard, Thirtle and the Ladbrookes as other well-known members. Crome himself and John Sell Cotman were of course the two most celebrated of all.

This meeting took place in the not-very-salubrious quarter of 'Hole in the Wall' but the exhibitions, which continued to be held annually until 1833, were held in a large room in Sir Benjamin Wren's Court. This large room disappeared when other buildings in this district were demolished and the new 'Corn Hall' was built on its site; but many pictures painted by members of the 'Norwich School' are permanently on view in the drastically restored old castle keep.

The School met once a fortnight at seven p.m. to study books on art, engravings, etc. for one and a half hours after which time there was a discussion on some pre-arranged subject; and each member took it in turn to provide the bread-and-cheese supper and read a paper on art. The full title of the School was the 'Norwich Society for the purpose of an enquiry into the use, progress and present state of Painting, Architecture and Sculpture, with a view to point out the best methods of Study, and to attain to greater perfection in these Arts.'

Crome always said that one should be able to regard the whole picture at a glance, not dwelling too much on the detail— but, nevertheless, he did put a good deal of detail into his lovely landscapes. His advice to his son, John Berney Crome, is well-known: 'Paint for fame, and if your subject is only a pigsty, dignify it.'

Crome's subjects comprised many different types of landscape—all beautiful and all breathing of the 'great outdoors' which he could portray with such perfection; and some of the subjects we meet with are river views, views of leafy lanes around his own countryside, heathland views—his 'Mousehold Heath' hanging permanently in London's National Gallery—charming sunny views of Yarmouth shore and jetty and the red-brown sailed barges sailing through the Norfolk 'flats'. Although he did sometimes paint in water-colours he preferred oils.

He died at his home in Gildersgate Street on 22nd April 1821, after an illness of only seven days. In his 53rd year, his painting was now at its very best; and it is said that, on the morning when he was taken ill, he sketched in a canvas six feet long the finished picture of which he had intended to be his masterpiece. The sketch shows a scene of a water frolic on Wroxham Broad.

Poringland oak by John Crome. (Courtesy of the National Gallery).

The cottage at about the turn of the century.

Willie Lott and his 'Cottage'

by HARRY C. LOTT

I HAVE BEEN RE-READING the account book and journal of my great-great-grandfather John Lott of Flatford, Wix and Layham. John Lott was the grandson of English Lott, who came in 1712 from Washbrook to Flatford. The 'Valley Farm' – opposite Flatford Mill – was the home of the Lott family till 1890.

In 1810 John Lott bought his 100½ acre farm from Sir Richard Hughes, Bart, of East Bergholt for £2000. They seem to have been doing rather one-sided business together for some time before the purchase. There is a note on 30th October 1809:

'Sir Richard Hughes received of me for 14 days £40. I have in all against Sir Richard £240.'

Sir Richard was clearly in deep waters for, though there is a note in January 1810 'Sir Richard gave a draft for the £40 had on the 30th Oct' (rather a long 14 days), we read in February 1810: 'I have against Sir Richard £240 . . . due £2 10s. 0d. Sir Richard received on a note till I settle for the farm £300, total £540.' Finally, 20th February 1810:

'I bought a moiety of this farm for £2000 to be paid for on the 6th day of April next, Sir Richard to make a good title and pay for the abstracts.'

John Lott had a younger brother William who, being a semi-invalid, left all his accounts to John. William owned the farm adjoining the Valley Farm, and the small farmhouse (eight rooms and two attics) now better known as 'Willie Lott's Cottage'. Willie Lott, although delicate, lived 88 years – without leaving the house or going away to school. (Incidentally, the 'hay wain' – of Constable's painting – was undoubtedly Willie Lott's wagon going to the meadows across the river, using the (Flat-ford).

John Lott's perceptive eye can be seen in this extract from his journal, slightly edited to modernise the spelling:

'The following is the account of the Festivity, according to Dr. Rhudde of which the following is a copy.

'Be it remembered that on Saturday the 9th of July 1814, the Inhabitants of this Parish (East Bergholt) entertained the Poor of it, Men, Women and Children to the number of nearly 800 with a Dinner of Plum Pudding and Roast Beef with a Sufficient Quantity of Strong Beer at an Expense of £113-13-1, which sum was raised by Principal Inhabitants in order that the Poor might Commemorate the Blessings of a General Peace, for which they had thanked God, by Religious Services on the Thursday preceding.

'The Festivity concluded by Musick and Fire Works and the several Parties for whom the Entertainment was prepared, appeared pleased and happy and conducted themselves upon the occasion with the utmost Propriety and Decorum.

'N.B. The Dinner was cooked at the Houses of the Principal Families and Served on Tables, Erected on the Green where the Fair is usually held.'

John Lott adds the following comment in very small but perfectly clear handwriting:

'Mishaps, one of the Bells was out of repair and would not ring. And the Band did not arrive until after Dinner having lost their way and there was too much Bread and too little meat.'

The Benefactors to the Parish Dinner are listed, including:

The Revd. Dr. Rhudde, Rector	£13 6 6
Peter Godfrey Esq, Lord of the Manor	£13 6 1
G. Constable Esq.	£6 0 0
Miss Tayler A lady that keeps a boarding school in the Street	£5 0 0
and	
J. Lott and William Lott Farmers	£2 0 0

In 1815 John Lott, as one of the two churchwardens of East Bergholt Church, was instrumental in arranging for Mrs. Daniels, sister of Sir Richard Hughes, who had lately died, to have 'the first Pew on the right side of the South aisle of the Church . . . so long as she continues to reside in the house she now occupies, but no longer'. If she quitted her house, she had to undertake 'to leave all such materials as may be used in fitting up the said Pew attached to the same, Curtains Cushions Mats and Hassocks only excepted'.

He clearly delighted in the quirky, for he records in his journal the following from the Ipswich Chronicle of 20th April 1822:

'Married in London Mr. Henry Hicks widower of Stratford St. Mary in Suffolk to Ann, daughter of Mr. Wm. Hicks of Wherstead and of Mr. Henry Hicks' former wife's sister. The bride is now wife to her unkel, mother to her two cousins by Mr. Henry Hicks' former wife, sister to her father and mother, sister to 22 unkels and aunts and to about 10 brothers and sisters, aunt to a great number of her first cousins and daughter to her grandmother.'

My father, John G. Lott, as trustee for a cousin, sold 'Gibbons Gate' ('Willie Lott's House' and 36½ acres) in 1902 for £1000 to William Frost (another cousin), who allowed the house to become derelict. Then Mr. Parkington of Ipswich bought it in January 1927 and restored the building before presenting it to the nation.

The cottage as it was in 1974.

Downfall of a 'sporting gent'

by James Wentworth Day

illustration by Peter Kemplay

HE WAS PINK and in 'The Tins'. His little ginger moustache bristled with infant ferocity. His blue eyes flashed as though on parade. He smelt strongly of new leather. He arrived importantly in a little, low, red, smelly car. It snorted to a stop outside the Nelson's Eye.

Leather, brand-new and shining, was decanted. Bright brown gun-case. Bright brown boots. Bright brown cartridge bag and bright brown binocular case. His luggage, three suitcases of it, was also bright brown. So, for that matter, was the rest of his face, apart from the pink facade.

The elect regarded him cautiously through the fly-glazed panes of the Captain's Bar. They were all there: yacht skippers, smacksman, oyster-dredgers, winklers, with their faint eternal reek of the mud, wildfowlers and the rest of the long-shore community, including, of course, The Councillor. His is the smoothest tongue and slyest eye among all that company of guile.

'Young orficer,' remarked Titus the Gunner, thoughtfully. 'Come a-gunnin', no doubt. 'Haps he'll need a hand to larn him where to goo.'

'Reckon he'll need a punt to get there in,' said the Admiral, who builds them.

'Dessay he'll need a big gun to goo in it,' added Owd Swan. 'I've got a tidy piece what'd suit he right well.' Shocked eyes were turned upon the old man. Extreme age and a failing mind alone could excuse the fact that he had spoken aloud the predatory thoughts common to all.

Moreover, it was common knowledge that Owd Swan's tidy piece, of uncounted age, with a barrel seven feet long, had a hole half-way up the right-hand side of the barrel 'big enow for a worsp to crawl through'.

'Every time Owd Swan shoot the owd gal off,' The Councillor acidly remarked, 'there's a puff o' smoke come out on her half way up the barrel, like a train a-goin' through a tunnel. She's death at both ends, that owd gal, and right perilous in the middle. I reckon she's only good for a rent-day gun, one of them what shute round corners when the baliff's a-comin'.'

Owd Swan glared at him stonily. 'Don't you talk, mate. I once took harf a dollar oft o' you, long o' that owl gal.'

'Ah! That he did,' The Councillor admitted. 'That wore the winter o' tharty-sivin. The creeks were full o' ice. The snow laid on the marsh a yard deep and 10 foot deep in the drifts. I wore a-goin' down the sea-wall for the mornin' flight when I meets Bungo a-comin' back.

' "Anybody down the wall, Bungo?" I asks.

' "Nit nobody," says Bungo, " 'cept Owd Swan and his Owd Bitch."

‘ ‘Owd Bitch!” I says. “He ain’t got no dawg and he aint’ go no missus. How do you mean his Owd Bitch then?”

‘ “That’s his owd gun,” Bungo says. “The owd muck hev clinked him under the lug or clouted him on the snout so many times that he allus calls her the Owd Bitch.” Thass a true piece, ain’t it, Uncle Swan?’ The Councillor remarked, turning to that patriarch of the mudflats. The ancient nodded distantly.

‘I still took harf a dollar off o’ you,’ he grunted coldly.

‘That he did an’ all,’ The Councillor pursued. ‘I goos off down under the wall, up to me fetlocks in snow, and there I find Uncle Swan a-layin’ under the wall, wi’ his owd gun. The fore-end was lashed on with a bit o’ tar-band. The britch was lashed round with copper wire and he’d nailed a bit o’brass down the stock where that was cracked.

‘ “Is she loaden, Swan?” I asked.

‘ Double loaden,” the owd man says. “You can load the owd gal up till she twizzles ye round.”

‘ “I wouldn’t shute her orf for tew golden suvverins,” I says. “She kill at buth ends.” Then I sees a pair of tukies (red-shanks) a-walkin’ about on the mud. About 50 year out.

‘ “I’ll gi’e you harf a dollar if your Owd Bitch’ll kill them two little tukies, stone dead,” I says.

‘ “Done, mate!” says Owd Swan.

‘He pokes the snout of his owd gun through the grass on the top o’ the hill, tucks the butt into his showder, squints down the barrel and says: “Now you little- - -. It’s either you or me.”

‘Then he pulls the trigger. Off she goes, with a roar like a row o’ housen fallin’ down. The stock clouted Owd Swan on the snout. The barrel flew off the stock and clinked him on the skull. The smoke hung that thick I couldn’t rightly see what happened.

‘Owd Swan sent nip-over-tuck, down the wall, fell flat on his back in the snow – an’ laid there. Uncomscious. Blood a’runnin’ out of his eyes, ears an’ mouth. Right blanched, he was. I thought the owd boy was a dead ’un. I gits down and listens to his owd heart. That was a‘knockin’, all right. So I puts me knee in his owd stomach and work his arms back’ards and for’ards till he came round. He snorts like an owd dog, blows a gust of blood out of his snout, sets up, rubs his owd optics and glouts at me.

‘ “Where am I, mate?” he grunts.

‘ “Jist under the sea-wall, half alive,” I says.

‘ “Did I kill them little owd tukies?”

‘ “Kill ’em? Yew blowed ’em to bits and damned nearly half kilt yerself.”

‘ “Ha,” says he, his owd optics a ‘glintin’. Where’s me harf dollar? Come on, mate Piy up.”

‘ “You ungrateful owd muck,” I says. “Here I’ve bin and drawed you out o’ the Valley o’ the Shadder o’ Death and all you can think of is yer miserable harf dollar. Why, the owd gun damned nearly kilt yer.”

‘ “How long did she onsense me?” he asks.

‘ “Tew whole minutes,” I says. “There was me, a’prayin’ to the good Gawd to have marcy on your ungodly owd soul – and all you can think of is money.”

‘ “Tew minutes,” he says, scornful-like. “Don’t talk like a dam school-missus. The Owd Bitch has onsensed me for foive minutes afore now. Gimme that harf dollar and howd yer clapper.” ’

Meanwhile the ‘young orficer’, whose arrival had provoked this Odyssey, had retired to his inn bedroom, unpacked his bright brown bags, put out his monogrammed hairbrushes, stowed his bright brown gun-case under the bed and was now poring over a brand-new map, abstracted from its bright brown map-case. It depicted faithfully the estuaries, creeks, rills, gutters, mudflats, saltings, mud-horses, sandbanks, Red-Hills, sea-walls, dykes, deeps, swatchways, shoals and seaways which compose that sea-picture of which the Island is the bright jewel. The only thing it does not tell is how the tides run and where the birds feed.

Presently, satisfied, the young man folded the map, stuffed it into his pocket and fingered lovingly the bright pages of one of those large and glossy volumes which, illustrated in the best Bond Street mode of wild-fowling, paint for the would-be gunner Elysian visions of opalescent dawns of countless wild-fowl. It is a picture which never fails to charm, either in water colour or under the more arduous conditions of watching it on television, the screen which cannot lie.

Reassured by this best-seller, the young man paused before the looking-glass and gave the little ginger moustache a confident, upward quirk. Then he strode downstairs towards the bar, where, as all the best wild-fowling writers would assure you, the wit and wisdom of the foreshore awaited him. He entered.

A blue haze of niggerhead and a stale smell of slops momentarily stunned both nose and eye. A ginger-brown mongrel tried to trip him up. A chorus of hearty voices greeted him with simple rustic welcome.

‘Don’t you mind the little owd dorg, Sir. He ’on’t hut ye.’

‘Thass only me little owd Napoleon, Sir. Do ye give him the toe o’yar boot.’

‘Come in, Sir, come in – that does me right good to see a sportin’ gentleman walk in among us pore simple owd fellers.’ This from The Councillor, who is never backward in the drive for trade. ‘I can see you’re a gunner, Sir. Plenty o’fowl about. Plenty o’ fowl about, Sir.’

Thus encouraged, Pink Face advanced to the bar. A score of eyes followed the production of his wallet.

‘What’ll it be, Sir?’ asked Bungo Blow, the landlord, sweeping his eyes round the poor simple old fellows, with a compelling glance. Pink Face capitulated. Stronger men than he had fallen for the embracing order.

‘Er, what’ll these gentlemen have?’ he asked with a parade ground voice that had barely broken.

‘Drop o’ Nelson’s Blood, Sir. Hope they flies your way, Sir.’

‘Mine’s a double rum, Sir. Bes’ respex to you, Sir.’

‘Pint o’ mild and bitter – best make it a quart Bungo.’

‘Dog’s nose wi’ a double gin in it, Sir, bein’ as I’ve gotter cowd.’

The orders flew fast as snowflakes on a January gale. Little change was left from a pound.

‘I see you’re a proper wild-fowler, Sir,’ began The Councillor easily. ‘Dessay you can larn us chaps a thing or tew afore you’re done wi’us.’

‘Oh, I don’t know about that,’ Pink Face demurred. ‘I shall have to get to know the lie of the land first, you know. However, I’ve got my charts. Seems all plain enough. They tell me the Oyster

Fleet is a good place for wigeon and the Oaze End is the right place for geese.'

'Jesso, Jesso,' The Councillor agreed. 'Thass the place where tew gunners — *tew only*, mark you, Sir, — killed three ton o' geese in a season.'

'Three tons?' echoed Pink Face aghast.

'Well, thass what they said up in Parlyment,' The Councillor added, 'So it must be true, marn't it? There was gents, bird-watchers and sich, come down here and writ all about it. so that mus' be true.'

'Week-end gull-worriers,' grunted Owd Swan. Old age and a failing mind alone excuse his intolerances.

'I dessay you got a rare good punt, Sir; One of these here decked-over, double ones, what you gentlemen allus hev,' enquired the Admiral tenderly.

'Well, no, not exactly,' Pink Face confessed. 'I thought of looking round here for one — or, er, perhaps having one built specially,' he added lamely. The Admiral's blue limpid gaze has that effect. Snake-charmers have nothing on him.

'Happen I could build you a tidy little owd punt, Sir,' the Admiral agreed graciously. 'I've bin a-builden' on 'em 70 year or more and me dad and great-grandad and forever on us, hundreds of years back. We was a-buildin' ships when the fust owd Queen Lizzie was a-knockin' hell out o' them owd Spaniards.'

'What you want meanwhile, Sir, is a tidy little owd second-hand punt to be gittin' about in, round these here creeks, while the Admiral's a-builden' your new one,' chipped in The Councillor. He always has a punt or a pig, a dog or a crate of hens for sale, and will sell you a man-killer motor-car as soon as look at you.

'Happen you gotter a right good gun to goo w'it,' Owd Swan put in. He was squashed instantly.

'You don't wanter listen to he,' The Councillor interjected sternly. 'His owd gun 'ud only clout yer uncornscious. I gotter a gun now what I'll loan yer — fer a trifle, that is. She kills like a butcher. All yew gotter do is chuck yerself forrard when yew pulls the trigger an' then you'll cheat the owd muck. Don't, she'll clout yer.'

'Chuck myself — what?' Pink Face enquired blankly.

'Forrard, Sir. Forrard,' replied The Councillor. 'On'y you don't wanter do what owd Abraham d'Wit don or you'll be a goner.'

'What was that?' asked Pink Face faintly.

'Well, ye see, he was aboard the smack *Teaser*, wi' me owd gun, orf o' the Backsea Beacon, when they sailed right on to a rare pack o' wigeon. Sunned 'em up, y'know. They riz up like a swarm o' bees. Owd Abraham clapped the gun to his showder and fired. The owd gun clouted him on the jaw and oover he went, head-over-heels down the owd fish-hold and very near stove his blessed owd head in.'

' "Nex' time yew fires her, mate," I says, "chuck yarself forrard when yew pulls the trigger an' then you'll cheat the owd muck."

'presently we sail up to another big pack o' wigeon — all asleep on the tide. Owd Abraham gits right up in the bitts — in the bows, y'know, Sir — an' when they riz, packed that close ye could ha' hulled the kitchen carpet oover 'em, he claps the gun to his showder an' I sings out:

' "Chuck yarself forrard, mate. Chuck yarself forrard." '

'What happened?' enquired Pink Face, coughing slightly as a lethal gust of niggerhead got him by stealth.

'Oooh! He chucked hisself forrard awright,' said The Councillor with relish. 'On'y the owd gun misfired — an' he chucked hisself overboard. We sailed right over he.'

Thus warned, applauded, welcomed and financially bled, Pink Face retired to bed to dream of three tons of geese.

Within a week he had been sold a second-hand punt, its leaking seams carefully puttied the night before by The Councillor. He had placed an order for a new double one, which would make £100 look attenuated. He had been sold a muzzle-loading punt gun, which had done honourable duty as a garden fence post for uncounted years before being resuscitated, sand-papered, painted and oiled. He spent a week afloat with Titus at five shillings an hour, plus a pound for every bird killed. A day or two aboard Bungo's smack taught him the depth of the channels and the shallowness of a £10 note. Everyone was happy — except Uncle Swan. His Owd Bitch remained unsold. The others had seen to that.

Then came the night when Pink Face resolved to take to the tideways alone. Under the moon, the dark and sliding shape of his punt glided down the immemorial sea-way of the Danes. Somewhere ahead in the moon-haze the geese 'cronked'. On the Shore Ends wigeon mewed and purred like cats. The bubbling whistle of the curlew came from misty flats.

On just such a night, 40 years before, Owd Swan sitting on the mud with his shoulder-gun, his yard of white beard shining in the moon, had been shot at by his 'nevvy' Art in mistake for a wild swan. And, as Art will tell you: 'They shot still run about under his owd skin like a lot o' lice.'

We shall never know precisely what befell Pink Face on that night of moon and bird calls. The voiceless tides and Uncle Swan alone know the truth. The latter is economical.

'There was me, a-sprittin' along in me little owd punt when all of a sudden, I sees a black patch on the water ahid on me — just like a bunch o' wigeon. Yew knows how they packs sometimes. So I sets up to 'em wi' me big gun, all loaden wi' half a pound o' shot, as big as backache pills. Eighty yard. Seventy yard. Now, me beauties, I thinks, I'll hev ye. An' I pulls.'

'What did you get, Swan?' I asked.

'Biggest bag o' me life,' he answers simply.

'How many?'

'Ha! That worn't the numbers. That wore the *weight* what made the bag,' he replied. 'That wore a *man*. That young orficer.'

'Seems like he couldn't rightly manage his punt. Got athort the tide. Was a-driftin' sideways. An' bein' a ammiture his backside was a-stickin' up. Real gunners allus lays flat, as you know.'

'Did you get him?' I asked.

'Git him? That I did Reglar riddled that owd punt what owd Councillor sold him. An' one o' me pellets ketched him right acrorst his backside — cut a furrow what you could lay a finger in.

'Pore young feller. I reckon he looked like a hot-cross bun for a month arterwards.

'No, Sir, He ain't bin back — and I doubt he will. There's many miss their free beer.'

The Owd Bitch was avenged. The three ton of geese are still alive and well.

The Cathedral of the Marshes

by FRANK R. COOKE

THE GREAT CHURCH of the Holy Trinity at Blythburgh has suffered not only the slow erosion of time, but many violent vicissitudes during the period of nearly 500 years during which it has dominated the countryside for miles around, rising majestically above the marshlands and the river.

Yet it has survived in its grandeur and beauty, with its aura of history and legend, an active parish church, a shrine for visitors from all over the world, a magnet for innumerable artists and, with its superb acoustics, a venue for festivals of great music.

Thus it is a heritage to be treasured, with an importance appreciated far beyond the confines of the small village of about 150 souls which is all that now remains of the once populous and flourishing port of Blythburgh.

It therefore seems certain that there will be a widespread and generous response to the appeal for sufficient money 'to preserve it and its contents for posterity', which has recently been launched by the distribution of a descriptive and illustrated brochure under the title of *The Cathedral of the Marshes*.

As the Bishop of St. Edmundsbury and Ipswich writes in a foreword to the brochure, 'The local people have done, and are doing, what they can to maintain this great fabric for the worship of God and for the delight of the many who come here. They have already raised about £6,000 themselves'. But at least another £20,000 will be needed.

There would not today be much to delight the many visitors, had it not been for the constant efforts of the present vicar, the Rev. John Stanton Jeans, his predecessors, the Friends of the Church and the contributions of the visitors themselves.

For it is only about 120 years ago that the Rev. Alfred Suckling, in his *History and Antiquities of the County of Suffolk*, wrote of Blythburgh Church: 'Unless a speedy and thorough restoration is here effected this stately fabric must shortly sink into irretrievable ruin.' Thirty years later, a newspaper reported the congregation as sheltering under umbrellas and shortly afterwards the church was closed.

In 1881, however, a Restoration Fund was set up. Under the auspices of Sir George Street, R.A., sufficient restoration work took place to allow the church to be re-opened in 1884. From those small beginnings, the work of making the church safe for

Photo by Norman Barker.

ever has continued and what is now being done and what remains to be done is set out in detail in the appeal brochure.

The crisis described by Suckling was, of course, only one of a series which afflicted the church almost from the time of its completion in 1492.

There had been a wooden church on the site, probably from about A.D. 620 and here, for a time, King Anna, the Christian king who, with his son, was killed at the battle of Bulcamp nearby, was buried. In 1130, Henry I founded an Augustine Priory in Blythburgh, a few remains of which still exist near the church. In 1412, the prior received a licence from Richard II to build a parish church and the resulting building was substantially in the form in which it stands today.

The first crushing blow of the many which the church was to endure came in 1538, when Cardinal Wolsey received a Papal Bull authorising him to suppress some of the smaller religious orders. The priory was stripped of its leaded roof, the community dispersed and its buildings and possessions handed over to the tender mercies of the Lord of the Manor. The buildings crumbled and decayed and the Catholic population and its church were exposed to the full violence of the Reformation.

The process of man's destruction was savagely renewed many years later under Oliver Cromwell. One of his lieutenants, William Dowsing – sad to say a Suffolk Man – was appointed Parliamentary Visitor to the Churches of Suffolk. His visits were missions of zealous destruction of 'superstitious pictures, ornaments and all such trumperies' and his work was so thorough that it is a wonder so much of the magnificence of Suffolk churches remains.

At Blythburgh he housed his troopers and their horses in the church and set about plundering it of its treasures, including brasses from the tombs, statues, stained glass from the windows and church plate. The glorious wooden angels in the roof were damaged by musket fire and, when Dowsing and his men rode away, they left a near-ruined church and evidence of their vandalism which remains today in bullet-holed doors and trampled brickwork of the flooring.

From that time until 1670, when a certain John Bull was appointed Perpetual Curate, the church was almost completely deserted and left to decay, though some religious worship, perhaps unauthorised, must have taken place at times. For in 1577, during a service, the elements joined with the neglect of man in damaging the fabric. A great storm shattered the door and brought the steeple crashing through the roof. Two parishioners were killed and many others declared they had been burnt by the Devil himself. Scorch marks can still be seen on the north door. The steeple was never replaced.

In some contemporary reports this catastrophe is associated with the legend of the dreaded Black Shuck, a creature which appears in one form or another all over Suffolk, sometimes as a hell hound whose howling foretells disaster, sometimes as an

The hammerbeam roof.

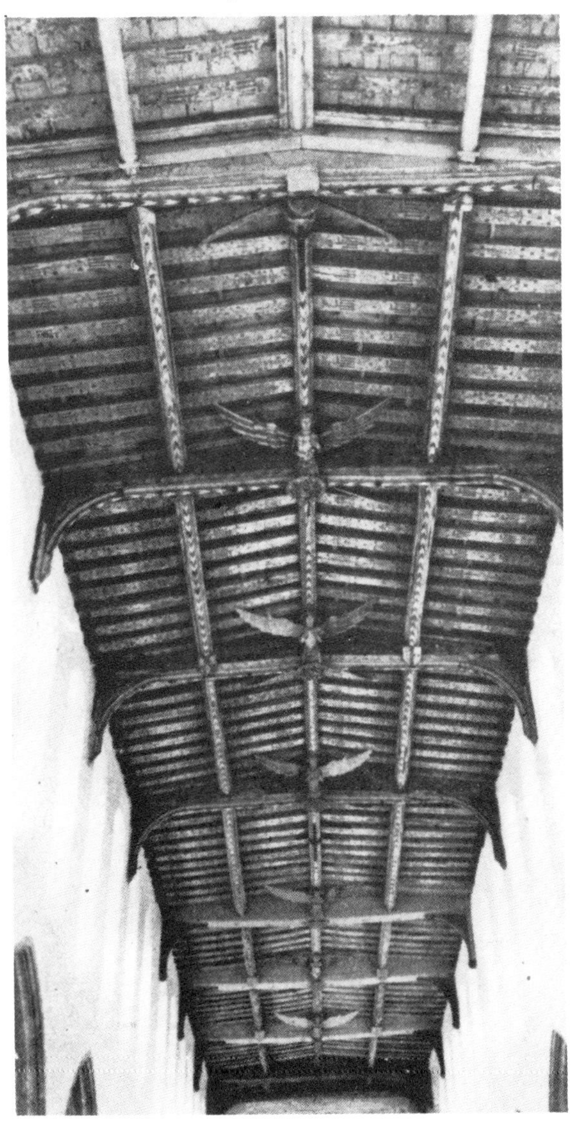

unidentifiable beast with flaming eyes.

The story of the damage to Holy Trinity continues into more recent times, with that caused by nearby enemy bombing during the two World Wars and the mysterious explosion in 1944 of an American aircraft piloted by Joseph Kennedy, elder brother of the late President of the United States of America. The blast from this is believed to have been responsible for severe damage to the clerestory windows, some of which are still unsafe and in a leaking condition.

A recent photograph of a bucket placed to catch rain water recalls that newspaper report of nearly a hundred years ago of the congregation sheltering under umbrellas.

Apart from the scars of history, which have their interest, the church, in spite of all its trials and tribulations, still contains many features and objects of historical, architectural and artistic importance. Some of these are described and illustrated in the appeal brochure.

These include the roof, a beautiful example of medieval craftsmanship. Its builders being without nails and iron bolts, relied for strength and stability on framing; morticing and tenoning the joints and finally fixing them with wooden pegs. The great span of Holy Trinity's roof is arch-braced and tie-beamed and so thorough was its construction that apart from work necessitated by the collapse of the spire in 1577 when it was struck by lightning and not permanently repaired until 1732, it required no major repairs until 1934 when the cross beams were strengthened and other minor work undertaken.

Throughout its length it has pairs of angels facing east and west, each pair being back to back and terminating at the hips in a large painted boss. Eleven of the twelve original angels still remain, each face being different in feature and having great wings carved and coloured. Six of the wings however, are unpainted, being replacements given by American benefactors in 1954. Between the angels the rafters are painted white with a floral motif in green and red.

Bench Ends. Lively and remarkable figures stand as finials to the bench ends. They are known to be of the fifteenth century and amongst them can be identified each of the Seven Deadly Sins, with Avarice sitting firmly on his money chest, Hypocrisy praying with open eyes, and Slander with a slit and protruding tongue being particularly obvious. Other figures representing the Seasons of the year are easily identified. In the head of each figure is a small hole where lighted tapers were placed.

Choir Benches. The carved figures of the choir-stalls are believed to have once formed the front parapet of a rood loft no longer in existence. The figures there represent Apostles and Saints and King Anna and his daughter Etheldreda.

Bookrests in the Choir. These were moved from the Hopton Chantry where a small village school was once held for the children of men who worked on the river dykes, and it is interesting to note that they are still pierced with the holes that held the inkwells and with rough carvings by one of the pupils. John Hopton was Lord of the Manor in the fifteenth century and was granted the right to build a chantry or chapel in the north-east corner of the church for the repose of the souls of those for whose benefit it was built. In the Reformation the chantries were suppressed and John Hopton's gift became the village school. It is a happy thought that it is now once again used as a chapel.

The Pulpit. Approximately of 1670, this is panelled and carved with floral patterns. Above it is an unusual crucifix of bogwood made by the boys of the local school in 1968. The figure is faceless, symbolising the catholicity of the Christian faith.

The Alms-Box. This is dated 1473 and is ironed and clasped with traceried sides and front. It is a fine example of its kind. The handcuffs securing the lock, however, were placed there recently for the better protection of the box after theft had been committed in 1965.

The Priest's Room. In the angle of the west and south walls, a narrow-stepped, circular stone stairway leads to the Priest's Room over the South Porch. It has recently been restored and is used as a Chapel and place of meditation. Its altar was made by the present vicar from timber from the flagship of Lord Nelson, H.M.S. *Victory*.

Other items of great interest will be found, including a lectern dating from the fifteenth century, and a First Edition of James I Bible – New Testament 1611, Old Testament 1613.

Finally, the Jack-o'-the-Clock, c.1682, is well worth seeing, being one of three remaining in England; one is at Southwold and the other at Minehead, Somerset. This is a painted wooden man in armour who originally struck the hours. His mechanism still works and is now used to announce the entry of the clergy at the beginning of Divine Service. A cord is pulled, and he turns his head sharply and strikes his hatchet on the bell.

Pride.

Gluttony.

Jack-o'-the-clock.

Mrs A. Woods

We have never met Mrs. Woods, who sent us a type-written manuscript with a pen-written note 'typing excuse I have only recently learned' but we think she must be one of the most delightful characters alive in East Anglia today. We reproduce extracts from her story exactly as it was sent to us, except that we have broken it up into paragraphs. – M.W.

BETTER Known as pat or murphy; age 82 years; my life began the twentysixth of juanary i889 as the clock chimed midnight the old woman that attended my mother to bring me into the world said she is dead; so i was laid out on the table as such; but i must have had different idears; so i was registered as marther ann ketteringham by john thomas egarr at terrington st clements in norfolk; and me born at midnight my mother said i should always be in trouble and quite true i always have been.

my mother was a very good living woman; she had therteen of us kids to bring up; my father was a clever man; but one fault drink; times were very hard thoes days; our cheefly food was bread and lard; throu fathers drinking habits we never stayed long in one house; mother hated the moving but us kids loved the novelity of it;

as far back as i can remember we lived in a big old house called the union we dident have such things as carpets we used to strinkle sawdust on our floor; now father decided to move to another house much smaller one; that was far to small for our famialy two weeks and we move againe to a bigger house called fourscors we did not stay there long we soon moved on to dawsmere bank this time there was no exitment for us kids we were scared; a man had cut his head off in the lavetory;

all to soon we moved to a house called the mill pad the old mill was very near our house and in the mill house mothers used to take there babies to have there tongues cut; from there we moved to a house in lutton marsh when the boss see family he soon put us in a big farm house; and the roof of the old house was full of honey; my we lived on honey for long enough;

mother used to say come on you wenches and go

to chapple on sundays never mind about being a bit raggy; our chapple was a kitchen at guys head the pulpit stood in the fire place and the pots and pans hung all around;

we only stayed there about two months; so off we go again; right into cambridgeshire a distance of fourty miles; throu wisbeach march and chattris untill we came to a little village called mepal the house we went in was so small we could hardly see it just like a heap of straw sticking out of a swamp; next day father had to take the doors off to get our things in; ten of us kids had the upstars leanto thatched roof; i well remember the night the roof blew off and us kids were bare to the sky;

mother and fathers bed room was downstars a room just big enough to put one bed in and that filled it; so father had his barrel of bear on the foot of the bed; he always sat on the side of the bed and had a tot when he went to bed; outside the dirty swamp wather splashed up the walls; but i never remember it getting in the house i expect it was built that way; we had to go to the toilet by boat;

i loved and longed to be a nurse i did get a nurses help job with nurse meekley at sutton bridge i was very happy then; now i was coming the age of twenty; truly all my life i had never been interested in the opperset sex but one day this charley woods came along and changed my life completly and i was married within the year; i loved him very dearly and hoped i should spend the rest of my life as his wife; and i did; we had eight babyes all my own feeding no bottles never and all perfect from them; we have twenty five grandchildren and twenty five great grandchildren; my kids are all around me and they are very good to me i also took a baby girl when its mother died at her birth;

we were married at long sutton registra; i had to buy my own wedding ring charley was to shy; and in my condition i got flustered and got the ring stuck on my finger and had to have help to get it off; i had three shillings left over from the golden soveren that father lent us to get married with; so i bought calico to make myself another shirt i onley had one; our best man was swinging a babies tete in front of uor faces and sure the next day we needed it;

off we go to charleys parents for our wedding dinner; no jolly fun no nothing; we just sat not to close; his mam was looking at us we stayed the night there; but earley next morning i relised i ought to be going to my own home where i lived so of me an and charley goes walking all the four miles to sutton bridge; i was then having the usual pains that a woman has at thoese times all the way; and charley held my arm every time i felt quer it took me a long time to get home; soon as we entered the door i remember my mother saying; come on i know whats the matter with you; she had so many she knew the signs; and in an hour i had a son;

at the end of may charley had a chance of a good horsemans job but we must live in large house that was once an hotel; our few things looked lost; i was very unhappy there i had neioubours that loved my charley; to much for my liking so we moved to lutton marsh where my seckond baby was born; in that house a man had bashed a womans head in only just before we moved in; that made me scared in that house too but the work i had to do seemed to forget the horror of it;

i had five lodgers and eleven paddies to look after and had time to help a poor woman that lived near she was horribly poor she layed on an old iron bed with only straw on and old coats; and a new born baby in her armes; i took her one of my beds and made her comfortable; altho i could ill afford it; she was very grateful to me, that is my nature i just carnt pass by a wanting being;

again charley move to a new job; he got more money being head horseman; our house stood in a forty acre field with little lakes dotted about and trees of every discription it was georgous; charley used to put me a swing on the big chesnut and swing me i was very happy then;

then my therd baby came along what a place to have a baby no proper road to the place only across fields; when the time came and i needed help charley went to an old gipsey camp; she dident stop to go across the field she went strait thro the river; when she got to me and my baby was being born the water was running out of her cloths; and a more horrible face i never did see; gipsey leach; lived in an old caravan with an old tin trunk as a lav; its true one half of the world dont know how the other half lives;

there were no pills those days; we had to have babies as they came; the night before my fifth baby was born the celing of my bedroom fell in and nearley smothered me; my mother dragged me out and then layed my bed on the floor of the other room; that same day my luciee was born; her black hair stood strait up she must have felt the shock as much as me the troubles i have been thro; and i have lived to be eighty;

after the war charley went back to work for his boss mr smith; charley used to say his horses knew he was home; his horses would on accasions break out of the field and come in front of our window and winney for him at four oclock in the morning; his brasses always hung shining on my wall;

charley got on well with the smiths at monks house and he stayed there the rest of his life; we were a very happy family by now the older kids were marring age; the clock of age one carnt stop and the grandchildren began to arrive and who better to have them home than mam so i piled the bits of furenture in the corner and a bed in and made a room for babies to be born with mam in attendance;

I had a large tea hurn which i kept shining, no use for it now; so charley as burried it under our concreat year to earth the wireless in this house where we live now;

illustrations by Jennifer Kent

Curiosities of East Anglia

By John C. Woodard

MR. R. G. BELCHER recently gave me two original cartoons by Reg. Carter. These are of a football match, which took place in 1905 between the Brewers and the Tailors of Southwold (Bung v. Snips), and I understand that the two players depicted are well-remembered characters.

I wonder how many interesting old photographs, prints and sketches are tucked away forgotten in boxrooms and attics. Many readers will know the amusing series of drawings (still obtainable as postcards) of the Southwold Railway.

These pictures by Reg. Carter can all be seen in the beautifully arranged small museum in the Dutch House (itself an historical building) in Southwold.

During the last war the German radio broadcast in the English news that heavy bombing had taken place along the East Coast and that the Southwold Railway was no longer running. This was to be expected, as the railway closed down in 1926, the rails had been taken up and were probably being used as tank traps on the beaches.

Another amusing news item was when the B.B.C. stated that during the night 'bombs had been dropped at random'. The German radio later in the day followed this by, 'the town of Random was heavily bombed during the night'.

Cartoons of a football match played at Southwold in 1905 *between the Brewers and the Tailors.*

THE NORFOLK WHERRIES

by STUART MITCHELL

The Albion, seen on the Norfolk Broads. Photo by kind permission of the Norfolk Wherry Trust, who now own her.

**Wherries at Coldam Hall taken in 1891. Photo by Payne Jennings.*

**Horning Lock No.1, North Walsham Canal, taken in 1901. Photo by P.C. Dewhurst.*

THERE IS NOTHING more Norfolk than a wherry under sail. Her low hollow-lined hull with the traditional white 'eye' on the bows, her blue, white and vermilion paintwork, the huge black sail tarred and dressed with herring oil, the fathom of blood-red bunting flying from the masthead all contrive to give an impression of barbaric splendour. This is hardly surprising because the ancestor of the Norfolk wherry was the Viking longship.

The Vikings came to Norfolk more than a thousand years ago, perhaps to plunder, but also in search of herring, a staple foodstuff which had suddenly disappeared from the Baltic. These barbaric adventurers found the Broadland district pleasant, married local girls and built settlements which survive today in place names such as Horsey, Winterton and Somerton.

Their longships provided a ready made means of transport along the rivers and estuaries. These craft were clinker built, sweet lined and double ended. Amidships was stepped a single mast which carried a square-sail. The specifications, length 70 ft, beam 17 ft, depth 6 ft, were practically the hull shape of a Norfolk Wherry.

As time passed, modifications were carried out to make them more suitable for river work. The best features of the Saxon 'coel' were incorporated and from these new craft sprang the Norfolk 'keel'.

For more than 500 years the square-sailed keel was the commercial carrier of the district. But a demand grew for quicker and more reliable means of transport which, through lack of an adequate road system, had to be satisfied by more efficient use of the river highways. The trouble with the keel was that she could not tack – the square-sail was only effective with the wind astern. The answer lay in the fore and aft sail which could drive a vessel against the wind. However, this revolutionary rig was unheard of on this side of the Narrow Seas.

Then, in 1568, several hundred Dutchmen fleeing from the religious oppression of the Spaniards came to Yarmouth in their flat-bottomed, fore and aft sprit-sailed vessels – craft which looked not unlike the Thames sailing barge of yesterday. Seeing these, local shipwrights conceived and built an entirely new vessel – the prototype wherry – capable of carrying 20 passengers and 5 tons of express goods, including mail.

In designing these experimental craft to earn quick money in the passenger trade, the Norfolk craftsmen kept to the well proven Viking hull shape. They borrowed only the details of masting and rigging, which they improved upon by discarding the sprit and hoisting the loose-footed (i.e. boomless) fore and aft sail on a gaff.

This subtle marriage of Viking hull and Dutch rig proved an immediate success. The term 'wherry' was borrowed from the Thames where rowing boats known as 'wherries' plied for hire like taxies. The ponderous keels continued to carry bulk cargoes but, before long, the speedier wherries began to cream-off the best of their trade.

This was the pattern until the latter half of the 18th century. Then, as a result of the Turnpike Acts, road improvements were made and the wherry owners found themselves faced with competition from horse-waggons. This challenge was met by the idea of a super-wherry, combining the wherry's speed and handling qualities with the cargo capacity of the keel. From this sprang the trading wherry we know

**Pleasure Boats, at Hickling, Norfolk, taken in 1899. Photo by Payne Jennings.*

**These three photographs are from the Library of Mr. L.A. Edwards, Hon Secretary, East Anglian Waterways Association Ltd.*

today. By 1800 they had grown to between 20 and 40 tons burden and had literally sailed the keels off the river.

The 19th century was the wherry's heyday. There were over 300 'black sailed traders' plying the Broadland waterways. Some made the sea-passage from Yarmouth round to Southwold and then up the Blyth Navigation to Halesworth in the heart of Suffolk. They carried cargoes of every imaginable kind – coal, timber, bricks, grain, maize, sugarbeet, beer, coffins – and provided the isolated villages and lonely marsh mills with the only all weather, all season link with the outside world.

Combining beauty with utility to perfection, like the deep-sea clipper ships, they became known as the 'clippers of the tideway' – an appropriate term in view of their superb sailing qualities. The advent of steam-power brought about their downfall and today *Albion* is the sole survivor still under sail.

However, the threat from the railways coupled with the 'discovery' of the Broads as a holiday playground in the 1860's led to what may be regarded as the wherry's final development – the pleasure wherry. The fashion for pleasuring by wherry became so popular that a number of specially constructed and luxuriously equipped wherries were built solely as pleasure craft.

In appearance and internal lay-out they differ from the traders. The sail is worn white instead of black, the woodwork is 'yacht finished' with varnish, the hold space is fitted out with cabins, saloon and galley, and the right-ups (i.e. coamings) replaced by dead lights (i.e. windows). The fact that pleasure wherries perpetuate the hull lines and rig of the class overrides the argument that they are not true wherries.

There are probably no more than a dozen Norfolk wherries afloat today. *Bramble* and *Hathor* at Martham, *Sun Dog* at Wroxham, *Solace* at Coltishall, *Olive* at Oulton Broad, *White Moth* at Neatishead, and *Reed Bird* at Thorpe are the known pleasure wherries. There is another one reported berthed at Horning Ferry, and I have just heard that *Olive May* is on the Thames near London, having been refitted at Geldeston and towed round after being sunk for

15 years at St. Olaves.

There may be one or two others hidden away privately and news of them may come to light as a result of this account. In addition to *Albion*, which is owned by the Norfolk Wherry Trust members and is unique because she is carvel-built whereas all other 'black sailed traders' were clinker-built, there is definitely one other trading wherry complete with mast and gear. She is the *Lord Roberts* and up to a year or so ago was owned by the Thains of Somerton, that famous family of wherrymen who have owned and skippered wherries for generations. She has since been acquired by the firm of May Gurney & Co., Ltd., who hope to extend her working life for as long as is possible.

There may still be one or two others — such as the *Fir* and *Go Forward* which I saw along the River Ant as recently as 1965 — stripped of their gear and motorized, scratching a humble living in the sugarbeet trade.

These few remaining Norfolk wherries are among the very last survivors from the bygone age of wind-power. When they eventually go to their final moorings the like of them will be seen no more. Their story may become a chapter in history or as forgotten as the art of wherry building.

Archway which was used for loading grain into wherries at Neatishead.

Sir Alfred Munnings at his Dedham Studio about 1935. *photograph by D. West*

Painter of Horses

The 100th anniversary of the birth of Alfred Munnings falls on 8th October this year and it gives us the greatest pleasure to publish this centenary article by R.A.N. Dixon, the founder of the *EAM* and its editor until he retired in 1957.

THE LITTLE BOY called Alfred, who remembered sleeping with his grandmother in her huge four-poster bed, whose bare bottom was spanked with a frying pan by two young aunts when he was naughty and who was to bring more renown to the name of Munnings even than his 16th century ancestor who fought and died at the battle of Vernoille, was born in the little Suffolk village of Mendham 100 years ago this October.

It was there at Mendham that his love of trees and skies – and especially of the horses that were to become the symbols of his genius – was born also. As a child he used to sketch the great horses – a long, patient line of them after harvest – as they waited for the carts of wheat to be unloaded at his father's mill.

It was there that he set off at 14 for six years' apprenticeship in a Norwich printer's studio, at a cost of £40 to his father and for a wage of two shillings and sixpence a week for himself.

While at Norwich he received the news that two of his paintings had been accepted by the Royal Academy. 'There was I,' he recalled half a century later in his autobiography, 'a raw simple, provincial youth, knowing nothing of the great Royal Academy . . . receiving a thrill I have never since experienced or ever will. When I became an A.R.A. or even President I did not feel the same overwhelming joy that was mine that morning.'

He was 19. A month later, his apprenticeship over, he went home to Mendham, bidding farewell to his fellow artists but promising to return. In due course he fulfilled the promise, riding into the yard on horseback, throwing the reins to the printers' lad, swaggering up the stairs into the 'dear old room'.

It was a sobering visit. 'I felt a queer feeling inside that if I wasn't careful pride would meet a fall.' Remorse for his arrogance served as a lesson he was never to forget. When success came progressively, bringing familiarity with prime ministers and acquaintanceship with kings, he was ever watchful for a resurgence of the bumptiousness of his 20's.

Sir Alfred at home.

Thus he never lost the art and pleasure of friendship with publicans and farmers, horse traders and gipsies and even editors of modest magazines like me.

A few days before his 21st birthday came what should by all normal standards have been disaster. He lost the sight of his right eye. He was lifting a dog over a fence when a thorn flipped up. He felt the prick of it and as he opened his eye there was nothing but grey fog and soon not even that. It was the end, one would have thought, of a budding artist. But he found one good eye enough and seldom referred to the loss of the other. At first it affected his judgement of distance. Sometimes the brush failed to reach the canvas. At others it all but went right through. But incredibly it failed to affect the development of his genius or his progress to the very top of his profession. Would anyone ever have believed that a one-eyed artist could become President of the Royal Academy of Arts?

Sir Alfred Munnings was a simple man with simple pleasures. He was more at home in slacks and jerseys than in boiled shirts, which he hated, but had the gift of looking elegant and distinguished whatever he wore. He could listen as well as talk and there was usually a twinkle in his one remaining eye. Though no great churchgoer, he was a firm believer and often used to wonder whether long-departed friends still looked down to share his memories and nostalgia. He loved horses, not just to paint or ride but to own. He sold only four horses in his life and regretted the sale of every one. He once accumulated more than 20, thereby 'keeping my old friends who have kept me'.

He was a product of the times before the 20th century started, when entertainment meant recitations and ballads in the drawing room or boisterous sing-songs with neighbouring farmers in local taverns. He never lost his enthusiasm for reading poetry aloud – or for composing the poetry he read. And if in his later years you went to see him at his home, which was my privilege many times, you were likely to be seized as an audience for a recitation or a song. He would stand beside you so that he could dig you in the ribs with his elbow to emphasise a particularly saucy passage or to bring you in *fortissimo* for the chorus.

Once I remember him half reading, half singing to me from a typescript an outrageously bawdy literary work which, he told me, was in great demand among members of the Athenaeum and he was always running out of carbon copies. It was the story of a certain Benjamin Bolt who one day sat down for a snooze after dinner and slept in his chair, like a gorging old sinner *–ri-tol-the-rol-lol-the-rol-diddle-dum-dum*. It transpired that with his mouth open wide like a two-ended boat a jolly great spider went straight down his throat – *tol-the-rol-lol-the-rol-diddle-dum-dum*. The rest of the story told how, after placing her husband face downward on the bed, his resourceful wife with the aid of a fly coaxed out the spider right into her eye with the fortuitous coincidence of a bout of flatulence, singing – *tol-the-rol-lol-the-rol-diddle-dum-dum*.

'Take it my dear fellow,' Sir Alfred said. 'Publish it. That's real humour.'

Not to his very great surprise, I think, I felt obliged to tell him that the editor regretted.

On another occasion he read me some very clever verses about a modernistic maiden in a portrait, written by Brian Barden, then an under-graduate at Cambridge. 'Peterborough published some of them in the *Daily Telegraph,*' said Sir Alfred. 'He daren't print them all. But you're not the *Daily Telegraph.* You're the good old *East Anglian Magazine.*'

'And if our readers complain, may I blame you?' I said.

'Blarst, yes!' he said.

So I published them and did.

For very many years – from 1918 until his death – Sir Alfred Munnings lived on the Suffolk-Essex border, right in the heart of the countryside immortalised 100 years before by Constable, himself, like Munnings, a miller's son. When you went to see him at Castle House, Dedham, the door would be opened by Violet, his dear wife, his staunch companion, his cook and treasurer who protected him from bills, taxes, tithes and wages from the day he married her.

She was short, dumpy, very ordinary but tremendously kind. It was difficult to reconcile her with the elegant figure of her younger days portrayed side-saddle on one of her horses. Followed by her Pekinese, Black Knight – the only dog ever to become a freeman of the city of London and the only dog (presumably) to be smuggled into a royal garden party in a muff – following at her heels, she would open the back door and yell:

'Al-fr-e-d!'

In due course Sir Alfred would appear, slightly out of breath.

'Mr. Dixon to see you, dear.'

'Good God,' he'd say. 'I thought the b - - - - - - house was on fire.'

My copy of Sir Alfred's autobiography is autographed in his typically extravagant, leg-pulling style: 'I inscribe this copy for and to the most intelligent, intellectual, brilliant, amazing editor in the world — R.A.N. Dixon who run the famous magazine, the East Anglian Mag. Alfred Munnings, Oct, 6th, 1952.'

That 'run' is, of course, pure Suffolk. It would betray a Suffolker's origin to a fellow Suffolker 10,000 miles from home. Munnings never ceased to use it and never lost the spoken accent either, because he didn't want to and therefore didn't try. It was present for all to hear when he made that famous speech of his at the 1949 Royal Academy dinner, a speech that brought him more fame than any horse he ever painted. The Duke of Gloucester was present and Winston Churchill. So were Montgomery and the Archbishop of Canterbury.

Those who heard the speech will never forget it. Its theme was 'all this — excuse me, my Lord Archbishop — damned nonsense called modern art', coupled with the clever critics who always knew more about pictures than the men who painted them and coupled also with some fellow members of the Academy who — 'their profound minds working' — were beginning to say there must be something in it. 'If you paint a tree,' shouted Sir Alfred, 'for God's sake try and make it look like a tree, and if you paint a sky, make it look like a sky.' There was this thing so praised by *The Times'* critic, this monstrous statue of the Madonna and Child in a Northampton church. 'I am speaking plainly. My horses may be wrong — we may all be wrong — but I'm damned sure that isn't right.' Even the surveyor of the King's pictures — 'Is he here tonight?' — once stood by his side in that very room and said that Sir Joshua Reynolds was not as good as Picasso. 'What an extraordinary thing for a man to say!' And in the room next door, where guests had that evening taken sherry, was a woman carved out of wood. 'God help us if all the race of women looked like that!' He knew he was right. He had the lord mayor and all the city aldermen and all the city companies on his side — and the newly-elected extraordinary member of the Academy, Winston Churchill, too. Perhaps he shouldn't mention names. But he didn't care. He'd had enough and was resigning. He wouldn't be there next year, thank God.

Not all those present enjoyed the entertainment. But the whole of Britain, jerked open-mouthed and unbelieving out of its seat beside the radio, certainly did. In every home that night it was the only topic of conversation and in every office, factory, shop and street next morning. People didn't have to agree with what he said — though undoubtedly most of them did — but they stood up and cheered the courageous, forthright, down-to-earth, no-nonsense way he said it. He was speaking their language and from that moment they loved him.

Nevertheless 40 people complained to the BBC about his four damns. On the other hand a parson wrote to Munnings saying that as a theologian he warmly approved the adjective in relation to modern art. Sackfuls of letters flooded in for weeks. Half a dozen were scathing — he was vulgar and disgusting, he was a disgrace to his profession, he had been drunk and ought to sign the pledge. (He later admitted to having had a little difficulty with the word innumerable.) But the rest of the letters were well and truly for him.

It was the first time Sir Alfred Munnings had ever broadcast and many people had not even heard of him. We in Suffolk were more privileged, for he had been a local character long before he became a national one. He was always a great campaigner, sometimes for good causes, sometimes for outlandish ones. But there was never any milk-and-water meekness about his opinions. 'Mr. A.J. Munnings, the well-known painter,' the *East Anglian Daily Times* used to tell us in the years before his presidency and his knighthood, 'says Ipswich has the most abominable modern buildings he's ever seen.' Or: 'Once-peaceful Essex coast now a jamboree of the damnedest huts,' says Mr. A.J. Munnings, the well-known painter.

But his great anathema was Picasso, his burning abomination dismembered bodies, eyes and ears floating in space and feet sticking out from the back of the neck. Alas, the voice and genius of Munnings, potent as they both were, failed to halt the popular movement towards modern art, which was to become a bigger avalanche still after he died. Had he lived to be 100 — had he lived till now — Mr. A.J. Munnings, the well-known painter, would not have liked the look of things at all.

'My wife, my horse and myself' by Sir Alfred Munnings.

The Colman Collection of Silver Mustard Pots

The earliest example in the collection: a pear-shaped 'blind' mustard with simple pull-off cover. Edward Gibbon, London, 1724.

The most recent addition to the Colman Collection, a hexagonal mustard pot with six ivory-capped turrets and tripartite gilt interior for three different varieties of mustard. Jocelyn Burton, London,1977.

by Honor Godfrey, the Collection's Curator

ON 3rd MARCH 1979, the Colman Collection of Silver Mustard Pots goes on public exhibition for the first time at the Castle Museum, Norwich. This unique collection of over 150 mustard pots made by British silversmiths ranges in date from 1724 to the present day; and mirrors – in miniature – changing styles and fashions in domestic plate. The collection, acquired by Colman Foods early in 1974, has never been viewed as a static one and, indeed has grown since then through acquisitions from auctions and dealers, and by means of gifts and commissions.

Following the launch in Norwich (the home of Colman's Mustard), the collection will be shown in major locations at home and abroad in a purpose-built travelling exhibition. A fully-illustrated catalogue will be available giving a brief history of mustard and a description of each pot.

Mustard was well known to the Romans and was deemed a necessity of life by the great medieval households. Seeds were steeped in vinegar and later made up into sauces, or crushed and sprinkled over food. During the 17th century, sieving the crushed seed began to be recommended and the resulting dry mustard might then be dispensed over food from a silver caster.

Colmans have been makers of powder mustard since 1814 when Jeremiah Colman took over a flour and mustard milling business at Stoke Holy Cross near Norwich. The commercial manufacture of mustard, however, pre-dates Colmans by nearly a century: c. 1720 a Mrs. Clements of Durham produced a finer mustard flour which could be made up into a mustard for the table by the addition of a liquid. This was served with a spoon either from

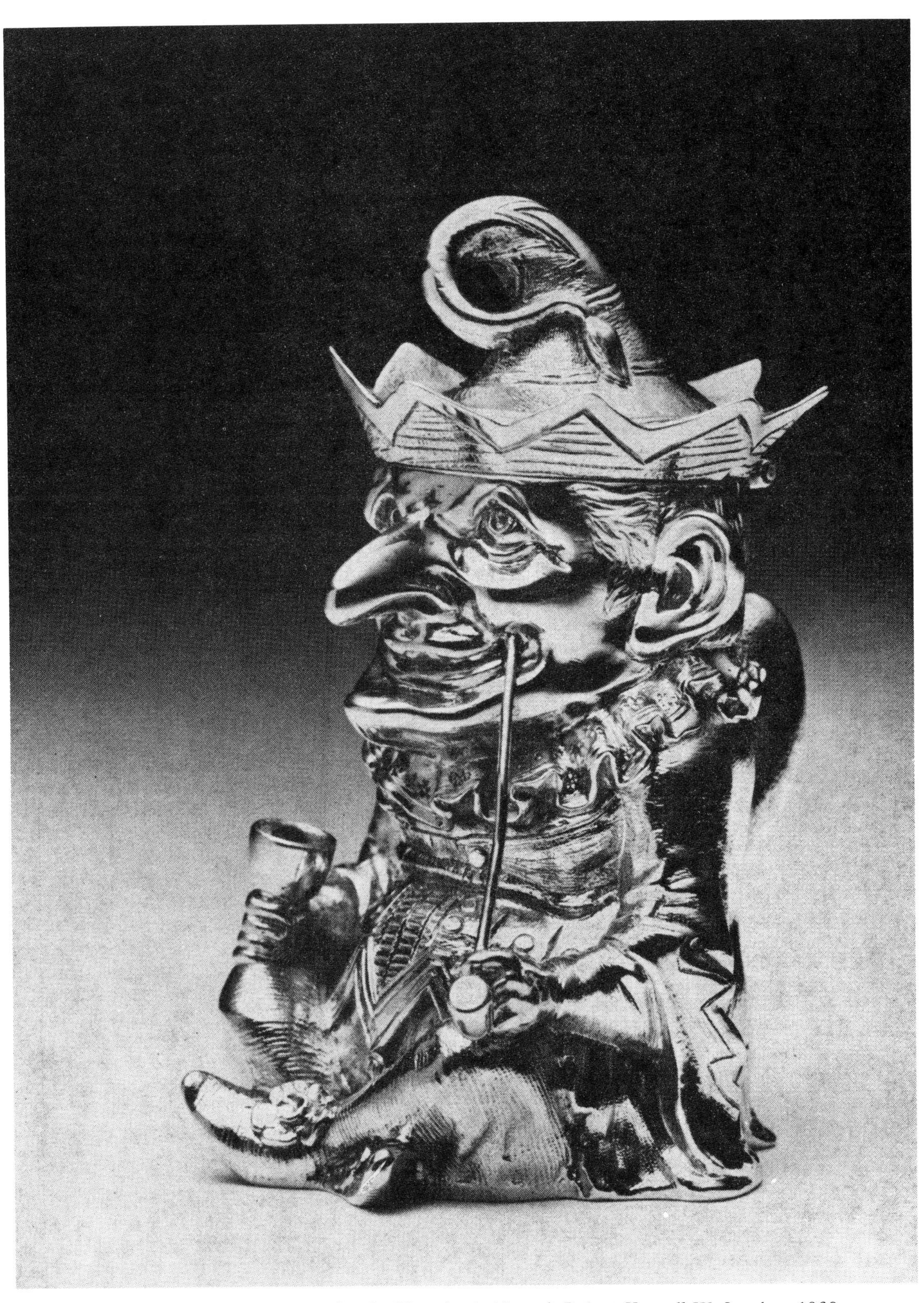

Mr. Punch – a delightful example of a Victorian 'tabletoy'. Robert Hennell IV, London, 1868.

A round mustard on a spreading foot with hammermark finish. Omar Ramsden, London, 1935.

'blind' mustards (casters with their now superfluous holes blocked by the insertion of a sleeve) or from little squat mustard pots (with which we are familiar today) which then started to make their appearance.

The earliest mustards in the Colman Collection are of lidded cylindrical form with bodies made of solid plate seamed beneath the handle. The solid bottoms found on these pots are modified to openwork circular bases on later examples so that the glass liners, which actually held the mustard, could be more easily removed by pushing up from beneath. During the 1760's, the artistic benefits of piercing began to be felt and cylindrical mustards were pierced with fine all-over repeating designs.

The influence of Neo-classicism is well seen in mustards of the 1780's. Vase-shaped pots on pedestal feet were pierced and engraved with geometric designs and classical motifs, their domed lids surmounted by cast or turned finials. At the same time, simple cylindrical pots were being pierced with a variety of attractive designs, all achieved with the minimum of tools.

Oval mustard pots with straight sides appeared in the 1790's. Their capacity was equal to that of the cylindrical pot, though they were shorter. Some had uprising ends, with a domed lid curved to the shape of the body, while others were flat-lidded. Convex sides with moulded bands became fashionable in the early years of the 19th century.

Other new shapes evolved c. 1800 — the rectangular mustard supported on ball feet and perhaps topped with a ball button; and the barrel, its body encircled with numerous incised rings.

The 1820's witnessed a revival of the rococo — that exuberant style of asymmetrical form and fantasy first seen nearly a hundred years before. Compressed circular mustards were embossed and chased with flowers and foliage, shells and sea monsters, birds and animals. The awakening Victorian interest in detailed naturalism manifested itself initially in floral engraving on cylindrical, hexagonal and octagonal mustards, and realistically cast flower and bud finials.

An oval mustard with moulded band and applied upper everted ovolo border.
John Emes, London, 1807.

By the mid-19th century, domestic silver was controlled and restrained, diverging more and more from the artistry of the ceremonial pieces — the flamboyant race cups and trophies — with which the Victorians honoured their great. Cylindrical mustards — bigger and heavier in keeping with the Victorian family — were becoming stereotyped. Other pots exhibited the eclecticism so beloved by the Victorians who honestly believed that excellence of the parts would lead to excellence of the whole.

Some of the most delightful mustards in the Colman Collection are the whimsical 'tabletoys' and novelties of the 1860's and 1870's. Scent bottles and inkwells, as well as salts, peppers and mustards, came in the shape of Punch and Judy, pigs and monkeys, cats and dogs, babies' heads and clowns.

In the next decade, shapes were being simplified for ease of production and surfaces were mechanically smoothed and brilliantly polished. Revivalist plate was becoming traditional and mustards were pierced in the style of the 1770's and 1780's.

In the Colman Collection, the 20th century is represented by a wide range of shapes and decorative styles — a bulbous mustard with scrolling strapwork and tendrils in the Arts & Crafts manner, pots with characteristic hammerwork finish by Omar Ramsden, a large mustard with contrasting textured surfaces by Stuart Devlin, and a silver and ivory pot of unusual form by Jocelyn Burton.

Early mustard spoons take the form of miniature ladles or teaspoons. Few have survived in the collection and those which have are unlikely to bear the same hallmarks as the pot they accompany, unless conceived as an integral part of the design. Pots are either gilded inside or fitted with a glass liner, often of intricate form and specially made.

The Colman Collection, novel for the layman and intriguing for the specialist, not only revives the image of gracious dining but also demonstrates the long-term achievements of English mustard.

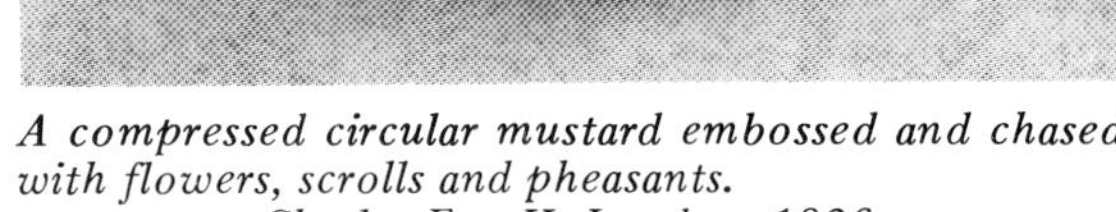

A compressed circular mustard embossed and chased with flowers, scrolls and pheasants.
Charles Fox II, London, 1826.

A Neo-classical vase-shaped mustard pot, pierced and bright-cut with Vitruvian scroll, lamps, floral festoons and ribbon swags.
Robert Hennell I, London, 1782.

A cast boar mustard pot, with realistically textured body and spoon with twiddly tail terminal.
James Barclay Hennell, London, 1880.

Joseph and his Brethren

by E.A. GOODWYN

Harold Freeman, August 1940.

LAST YEAR marked the 50th anniversary of the publication of a book considered by many people the best East Anglian novel – Harold Freeman's *Joseph and his Brethren.* It was an immediate success in 1928, and not only in England, for it was chosen as a 'Book of the Month' in the United States. When the sixth impression appeared the following year, R.H. Mottram in his preface claimed 'it does for the life of East Suffolk what Hardy is said to have done for that of Wessex'. Now that local history studies flourish in our region as never before, it is astonishing that our East Anglian literature is so neglected. *Joseph and his Brethren* has been out of print for many years.

After gaining a First in Classics at Oxford, Freeman might have had a distinguished academic career. He preferred a financially precarious freedom. For several years, between temporary teaching jobs, he travelled Europe on foot and on bicycle; and this wanderlust has never left him. Even now, when close on 80, he and his wife enjoy an annual journey to Italy and Greece. The action in several of his novels alternates between Italy and Suffolk. He wrote *Jospeh and his Brethren* in a Florence lodging-house.

Joseph and his Brethren is the story of a family and a farm: a thoroughly East Anglian theme. Freeman's treatment of the theme is in the tradition of our East Anglian literature with its emphasis upon the realities or ordinary work and endeavour. In the opening chapter, Emily Gaifer, wife of farmer Benjamin, has left her kitchen – 'now that she was old she still made the butter and cooked and cleaned and mended and washed for the husband and her five boys' – to join in the monotonous and gruelling task of cleaning twitch from the heavy soil by hand. She had never known a day's illness; but this proves at last too much. She collapses in the field. The doctor arriving an hour later, curtly announces to the stunned family that she has died from heart failure.

'He hurried out.

'The boys began to cry. Ben, too old for tears looked at his father with bewildered eyes, waiting for a lead. Benjamin was still dazed at the doctor's pronouncement. It had seemed so natural that she should go on for ever. At last, however, the truth seemed to penetrate his understanding.

' "Well, well," he said slowly. 'Wore up. I'd never have believed it. But I say, Ben, it's lucky young Harry's old enough to do without her to look after him." '

Freeman's Suffolk farmers, even the more prosperous ones, are peasant-like in their stoical accepttance of death and in their sense of necessary continuity; the work of the farm must go on without an interval for the indulgence of grief. But *Joseph and his Brethren* has a lighter side. Young Nancy Hambling who comes to Crackenhill as a housekeeper determines to bring some colour and comfort into the bleak living-room. Facing the hostility of old Ben and the indifference of the sons, she attacks them in their one vulnerable place — the stomach. She refuses them succulent dishes they had come to expect from her excellent cooking. Their resistance proves as feeble as their appetites are strong.

There are changes of fortune for both farm and family. At one period, after the death of old Gaifer, the brothers have to leave the farm, which reverts to its neglected state before the Gaifers worked it. But the end sees the family restored to Crackenhill with the promising young Jospeh Gaifer suitably married.

This brief account cannot do justice to the sterling qualities of *Joseph and his Brethren*, its strong and lasting appeal. It is a classic of rural life.

Freeman has published nine novels. The most ambitious is *Hester and her Family*. This contains some memorable scenes but, in my judgement, suffers from the absence of that farm setting in which he seems most at home — perhaps this is an East Anglian prejudice. The novel which rivals *Joseph and his Brethren* is *Chaffinch's*. It was unlucky to be published in 1941 and has never received the attention it deserves. Joss Elvin, its principal character, is Freeman's finest study of the sturdy, stubborn peasant-farmer. We first meet Joss as a small boy at school — the year is 1884 — hungry and unable to resist the temptations to pinch the sandwiches of a well-provided farmer's son. His own father is a labourer. Later that day, he goes down to the village pub, where his father is trying to earn a shilling with a song. Joss looks in through the window and sees a policeman addressing his father — ' "Matthew Elvin," he was saying, "I arrest you in the name of the law, for stealing a swede, the property of Martin Wright, of the Rookery Farm, Brettsleigh. You'd better come without any fuss." He took out a pair of handcuffs.

'Joss held his breath, wondering what his father would do. He had once seen him fight a man in the inn yard, a far better man than himself, and knock him senseless. There was nobody like his father. But after a moment's silence Matthew just laughed.

' "All right, bor," he said, "let me finish my beer." He emptied his mug and held out his hands. "How long shall I get, bor?"

' " Oh, three months, I should reckon," said the policeman, as he slipped on the handcuffs. "You know, mate," he added in a lower voice, "I can't help myself. Owd Wright's on the bench."

' "Yes, I know," said Matthew bitterly, addressing the whole room. "They on't give us work, they 'on't give us housen, they 'on't let us eat. Why don't they strangle us at birth?"

' "Come on, my man, that's enow," said the constable, seizing his elbow.

' "All right, constable," said Matthew, and started to follow him across the room, but after a couple of steps he stopped and stared at the door. "Why, blast," he cried, "if that aint my boy Joss! Come you here, my boy."

'Hanging his head with shyness of the public gaze, Joss obeyed.

'Matthew bent down and clumsily placed his fettered hands on the boy's shoulder.

' "Listen here, my boy," he said. "I want you to do an errand for me. Do you go home to your mother and tell her I've gone to prison for a swede, a swede as I took to fill your belly. But that warn't no good, my boy, and there ain't only one thing I can tell you. You 'on't never fill him till you grow your own."

' "Come on now," said the policeman, tugging impatiently at his arm, "we can't stay here all night."

There are many pub scenes in Freeman's novels, but none more effective than this.

I hope that this article will at least direct more readers to the work of a novelist of whom Suffolk should be proud. How gratifying it would be to see *Joseph and his Brethren* and *Chaffinch's* in print again, as they surely ought to be. After these two classics of East Anglian literature, I would choose from Freeman's novels the admirable *Fathers of their People* and its sequel, *Pond Hall's Progress*.

THE GRAVEDIGGER: AMOS LEGGE

by MICHAEL WATKINS

'I'VE BEEN a devil in my time,' Amos Legge announces proudly. He rubs his grizzled head, looking baffled but not at all contrite. 'God's a marvellous man . . . I uphold His views in every way. But all the rest are b- - - - - s. Snobbish too. Everyone's a snob today. They won't talk to you unless they're after something. They're all newcomers too – don't belong here. All the old ones have gone, moved away or died. I should know . . . buried most of 'em myself. I've buried thousands, *thousands.*'

Deersthorpe is 20 miles from King's Lynn, pressed in by the weight of surrounding agriculture in a way that a collector's wildflower is squashed between the pages of a book. The sap has been squeezed out of Deersthorpe, replaced by thinner stuff, etiolated city blood retired to modernised cottages called Sycamore View and Dunroamin. Television aerials take root among the thatch; net curtains, like gauze bandages, give the place an antiseptic look. Men polish Rover 2000's, and invite the golf club secretary home for gin and tonic.

When Amos emerges from his cottage, which is rare enough these days unless he has a job on, he hates what he sees. His hatred is savage; it is as if he is scheming his own gunpowder plot on Dunroamin.

Amos Legge's cottage faces on to the lane, partly screened by an untrimmed, unruly hedge. One wall is white, the next pink, as if the decorator simply used up whatever paint was handy, unconcerned by Ideal Home hints for colour schemes. Sheets of corrugated metal lie in the garden, together with oil drums, netting, a collection of weather vanes. There is a cold tap – the only source of water – and a couple of huts, one of which contains the lavatory.

The front room, which few people have been privileged to see, is said to contain huge quantities of bird seed. Upstairs is Amos' bedroom. There is no bathroom. Amos spends most of his waking hours in a downstairs room, once the kitchen, about nine feet long by five across. A crucifix is suspended above a bird cage containing four budgies: 'That's George, and that one answers to Blue Boy. The others don't have names. They all used to talk from morning 'til night, then one little fellow died. Lay there he did with his little feet in the air, and they all stopped talking to this day. I think they were grieving with me. They twitter all the time, 'specially when someone comes, it's just that they don't talk sensibly as they used to. Whatever that bird died of was contagious. I went into hospital next day for seven

weeks . . . prostate gland.'

Amos has always loved animals. As a child his hobby was making tiny coffins for pet guinea pigs, rabbits, cats. Then he would give them a decent Christian burial. He remembers dressing up once as a parson so that he could conduct a funeral service. He had no other interest. He didn't play football with the other village boys. Just made sure that dead animals were treated with proper respect.

In 1917, when he was 13 years old, he became a full-time gravedigger. Apart from five years' army service in the Second World War, this has been his life's work. He has been digging graves in 38 neighbouring parishes for 61 years, earning from 7s. 6d. to £4 or £5 for a grave. One undertaker pays him £12. He is a short man, only 5ft. 4ins., but with immensely broad shoulders. Shaking hands with him is a hazard; his grip could dislocate bones.

'I've got a back today. I wear a steel corset and a truss. There's a lot wrong with me these days – but I forget it all when I'm digging. Digging makes me better. My graves are neat, they fit well. It's my pride, my vocation. Rich or poor, I give them the same job. Graves are my life.

'Six foot six for a single, seven foot six a double, and nine foot for a treble grave. That's the measurements. Not that I like these family graves much . . . a woman wants to be put next to her husband when she dies a few years later, you see. Well, I have to open a grave . . . coffin's collapsed, very likely. Cremation's cleaner. It's against my own trade to say so, but I'll be cremated. Not that I'll have much say in the matter. They do what they want with you these days. No respect today . . . it's a modern world.

'When I dug my first grave, you could be buried for next to nothing. Good Lord, it costs £200 or so to be buried by the Co-op today, and that don't include the party afterwards. That's all people come for, the food and drink . . . and to see what they've been left. Families used to mourn, really mourn. They'd put the body in the parlour for 12 days so that friends could pay their respects . . . They used to wear black mourning bands for months. Today people attend the funeral in all colours of the rainbow. And when it comes to "earth to earth, ashes to ashes, dust to dust", they don't want to know. I throw some earth down on the coffin, but they don't – they can't wait to get away to their tea and ham sandwiches.

'Reminds me, there was this old fellow dying and he hadn't been allowed to eat for days. Then the doctor told his wife that the patient didn't have much time left, so she could feed him anything he fancied. After the doctor had gone the woman called up the stairs to let the dying man know he could eat what he liked. "I'd like some o' that there ham yow a'got cooken down there," replied the husband. "Yow can't hev thet," said his wife. "Thet's for the funeral."

'I've kept records of everyone I've buried since 1917, all by name. I know where they are and how I dug the grave. I miss some of 'em, but they're happier where they are. Takes me the whole day to dig a grave in clay, but I can do three in a day in good ground. You put 'em in so that their feet are to the east – all except the parson. You put him in the other way round so that when he's resurrected he'll blow his trumpet facing his flock. I asked the Bishop about this once: "What happens, my lord," I said, "When they bury the parson in the middle of the graveyard?" He didn't seem to make much of that.

'There was another old fellow whose wife lay dying and she threatened that if he married again she'd "scrab" her way out of her grave to haunt him. But this old fellow did marry again, and the new parson who had heard of the curse asked the man if he wasn't frightened. "Doan't yew know," the man told the parson, "I buried owd Bessie face down, so the harder she scrab the fudder down she keep a-goin'."

'You've got to be careful burying the dead . . . they might come back, as a dog or something. There's a lot worse things you could come back as than a dog. Yes, I like working for the dead – they're the best sort. Not that the ones walking about aren't half dead. This lady said to me, didn't I worry about working in a graveyard at dusk with all the dead, and I said no, it was them as was walking around that worried me.

"I've buried them from stillborns to well over 100 years old – buried a lady of 105 last month, fit as a fiddle she was, still living alone and looking after herself. I told you. I've buried thousands, and never had a single complaint . . .

'But still I'll be cremated if I get the chance. As I say, it's cleaner. Used to like the idea of being scattered on the wind, but I don't know if they allow it any more. Probably someone from the environment . . . he'll tell it's mucky having dead people's ash blowing all over the place. They'll have to put my ashes in a jar and bury me. Like to see how the parson works out where my head and feet are for the resurrection.'

Locally, Amos Legge is known as an irascible old man, the sort who sees good in nothing; and mostly he is given a wide berth. Perhaps too he is a little feared. When he sets off on his new Japanese motor cycle, gleaming fork and spade strapped to the carrier , it is known that he is on an errand of death. Each journey is a reminder that everyone will need his services once.

This social isolation distresses him. He admits to loneliness, particularly when he is not well. He keeps his courage up by ranting at the world in general, his face becoming suffuse as he considers the inustice of it all. But when he has huffed and puffed his fill, he suddenly subsides, looking desperately about his possessions as if they will give him substance. There are brass shell cases, a pile of O.H.M.S. buff envelopes, pipe rack (seldom is there a pipe or hand-rolled cigarette out of his mouth), faded newspaper cuttings, empty orange squash bottles. There is a photograph of him, smart in a suit and cloth cap, taken up against a headstone. Where else?

A clothes line stretches above his head, upon which hang the shirt and underpants he has washed. He eats chips and boiled potatoes, and Meals on Wheels give him three hot dinners a week; but he says he does not need much food. Usually he is in bed by eight, and there he stays until midday or so; unless there is a grave to dig. Nothing, even double-pneumonia, would keep him from his ordained duty of preparing the ground for the dead.

'Oh, I used to have another interest. I was verger and sexton at St. Peter's. Fifty-five years I never missed a service. Not one. I loved that church. Kept it tidy and clean, grass was always trimmed. Rang the bell, I did, and took the plate round. Then this new vicar came. Told me I needed help, that I was too old to do it all alone. He was really telling me I wasn't wanted. I knew how to do it. That church was spotless and I didn't need help. They just didn't want me. So I left and I've never set foot inside the church since that day.

'They aren't *real* parsons any more. They're ex-policemen or generals who've come to it and don't believe half they're paid to preach. You can't trust them. . . like women. I was married 25 years and my wife died when we moved here from the other end of the village. I dug her grave. Lived alone for three years, but couldn't stand that after a good woman, so I married again. I wanted a housekeeper, she wanted a position. We didn't love each other. She left me after a year and 10 months – hated my guts.'

Amos Legge is aggrieved. He has been done wrong; he has grown old and been rejected. He has few material comforts in life; and yet it is whispered about the village that he has saved a fortune, never spending a penny. So why won't he install a bathroom, an inside lavatory, buy an electric blanket?

'What do I want with a 'lectric blanket? I've never had one. It'd kill me. They give you shocks. Bathroom? That'd mean a grant and I'm not having them people about the place. They'd put up the rates. Once you get into their clutches . . . .' He becomes secretive, sly, yet obviously enjoying himself. 'Oh, yes, I've got a nest egg, something for a rainy day. You'd be surprised. If I die? (He appears surprised, as if he had not thought that one day someone might have to dig his grave.) 'Well . . . I'd leave it to someone, wouldn't I?'

He is silent for a while, the only sound coming from the chirping George, Blue Boy, and two nameless budgies. He looks defiant; then his eyes cloud over and he twists his calloused hands: 'I suppose I think of dying sometimes. It's no life alone, when the only callers are undertakers. No one wants you. Then I start thinking about the funeral service . . . "Man that is born of woman hath but a short time to live, and is full of misery. He cometh up, and is cut down, like a flower; he fleeth as it were a shadow, and never continueth in one stay." A bit morbid, isn't it? I'd rather have the one from Revelations, that's what I think about – "And I saw a new heaven and a new earth . . .".'

His expression changes back to defiance. He is better at being defiant. It is his anger that keeps him out of the grave: 'I've got no horror of funerals. I delight in them. I wish there was more dying. I'd rather go to a funeral than a wedding. When I go to a funeral I think to myself, it's all over, they're at peace; but when I go to a wedding I think, poor b - - - - - s, their troubles are just beginning.'